DATE DUE

GAYLORD PRINTED IN U.S.A.

IFLA

International Federation of Library Associations and Institutions
Fédération Internationale des Associations de Bibliothécaires et des Bibliothèques
Internationaler Verband der bibliothekarischen Vereine und Institutionen
Международная Федерация Библиотечных Ассоциаций и Учреждений
Federación Internacional de Asociaciones de Bibliotecarios y Bibliotecas

About IFLA **www.ifla.org**

IFLA (The International Federation of Library Associations and Institutions) is the leading international body representing the interests of library and information services and their users. It is the global voice of the library and information profession.

IFLA provides information specialists throughout the world with a forum for exchanging ideas and promoting international cooperation, research, and development in all fields of library activity and information service. IFLA is one of the means through which libraries, information centres, and information professionals worldwide can formulate their goals, exert their influence as a group, protect their interests, and find solutions to global problems.

IFLA's aims, objectives, and professional programme can only be fulfilled with the co-operation and active involvement of its members and affiliates. Currently, over 1,700 associations, institutions and individuals, from widely divergent cultural backgrounds, are working together to further the goals of the Federation and to promote librarianship on a global level. Through its formal membership, IFLA directly or indirectly represents some 500,000 library and information professionals worldwide.

IFLA pursues its aims through a variety of channels, including the publication of a major journal, as well as guidelines, reports and monographs on a wide range of topics. IFLA organizes workshops and seminars around the world to enhance professional practice and increase awareness of the growing importance of libraries in the digital age. All this is done in collaboration with a number of other non-governmental organizations, funding bodies and international agencies such as UNESCO and WIPO. IFLANET, the Federation's website, is a prime source of information about IFLA, its policies and activities: www.ifla.org

Library and information professionals gather annually at the IFLA World Library and Information Congress, held in August each year in cities around the world.

IFLA was founded in Edinburgh, Scotland, in 1927 at an international conference of national library directors. IFLA was registered in the Netherlands in 1971. The Koninklijke Bibliotheek (Royal Library), the national library of the Netherlands, in The Hague, generously provides the facilities for our headquarters. Regional offices are located in Rio de Janeiro, Brazil; Dakar, Senegal; and Singapore.

IFLA Publications 122

Newspapers of the World Online: U.S. and International Perspectives

Proceedings of Conferences in Salt Lake City and Seoul, 2006

Edited by
Hartmut Walravens

K · G · Saur München 2006

IFLA Publications
edited by Sjoerd Koopman

Recommended catalogue entry:
Newspapers of the World Online: U.S. and International Perspectives. Proceedings of Conferences in Salt Lake City and Seoul, 2006 / edited by Hartmut Walravens ; [International Federation of Library Associations and Institutions]. – München : K.G. Saur, 2006. – 195 p. : ill. ; 21 cm.
– (IFLA Publications ; 122).

ISBN 3-598-21849-4

Bibliographic information published by the Deutsche Nationalibliothek
The Deutsche Nationalbibliothek lists this publication in the Deutsche Nationalbibliografie; detailed bibliographic data is available in the Internet at http://dnb.d-nb.de.

∞

Printed on permanent paper
The paper used in this publication meets the minimum requirements of
American National Standard – Permanence of Paper
for Publications and Documents in Libraries and Archives
ANSI/NISO Z39.48-1992 (R1997)

Cover illustrations: pixelquelle.de (server) / aboutpixel.de (newspaper)

Printed in the Federal Republic of Germany by Strauss GmbH, Mörlenbach

ISBN 13: 978-3-598-21849-1
ISBN 10: 3-598-21849-4
ISSN 0344-6891 (IFLA Publications)

CONTENTS

Seoul, August 2006

Preface

Digitisation has been a hot topic in newspaper librarianship for some years now. And this for good reasons: Newspapers have long been the cinderella of libaries and archives – bulky and space-consuming, laborious to collate and to catalogue, a challenge for preservation officers and a difficult issue for circulation and access. Historical holdings are often too brittle to be provided to readers in the original, and so microfilm has been a popular surrogate – not so popular with readers who spent hours in front of the screen and complained about bad quality, changing formats and incomplete sets. Most newspapers do not have indices, and there are few, and usually not exhaustive bibliographies available.

Under these circumstances the progress of digitisation technology came as a godsend – the Scandinavian TIDEN project proved that hundreds of thousands of pages could be digitised satisfactorily and in a cost-efficient way from preservation microfilm and mounted in searchable format on the internet. Newspapers had always been a favourite with readers who find many details - family, local history – in the papers which are usually the only source material available. Contents management companies were quick to recognize the market value of newspaper digitisation and entered the market. Some large newspapers made their archives available in electronic form. The progress of software development – especially in OCR and text management – allowed to process papers printed in Gothic script and pull articles together that were printed in different columns. Automatic indexing by analysing headlines also rapidly developed.

Newspaper digitisation received additional momentum by the fact that the use of microfilm decreased dramatically owing to the soar of digital photogarphy. The supply of specialised microfilm for preservation purposes is becoming sometimes difficult – at any rate it turned into a niche market dominated by monopolists.

With this background it is hardly surprising that a few newspaper experts – so far very few – have changed their minds and consider digitisation also a means of long term archiving and preservation. Most specialists, however, still recommend microfilming as the only reliable preservation method.

Some libraries – especially in the Scandinavian countries – have working electronic mass storage devices of high capacity at their disposal, and they are faced with long term archiving of born digital material – newspapers, and internet publications. There is hardly any other option than eelctronic mass storage. So why follow a different and more costly way with regard to digitised material? The discussion is still going on. There is no doubt, however, that electronic storage is more sensitive to outside influence and destruction, e.g. natural desasters, terrorist activity, vandalism, etc. We do not have enough experience yet with maintaining file structures, software applications, etc. So there are many challenges.

The IFLA Newspapers Section has been active in the field of newspaper digitisation for years and monitored carefully the digitisation projectsworldwide – most of them were run by members of the Section. When both in Britain and the United States major national digitisation projects were initiated a conference seemed a good way of exchanging information and bringing the library community up-to-date. The University of Utah with its long experience in the field acted as host, and had the cooperation of the Library of Congress and the IFLA Newspapers Section. Considering the rapid development of both digitisation technology and applications it was planned to collect all contributions before the beginning of the conference and publish the proceedings immediately afterwards. Both IFLA Headquarters and IFLA's publisher, K. G. Saur in Munich, agreed but it turned out a difficult task to get full papers from the speakers. All of them provided their Powerpoint presentations but some of them were reluctant to fill the gaps to make their contributions better readable.

The editor therefore decided to print those powerpoint presentations which are just a very condensed form of papers while some which required a good technological background for proper understanding were left out – with regret.

As the Digitisation Conference took place in May, 2006, and the World Library and Information Congress followed suit in August, 2006, it seemed convenient to add the papers read at the Seoul Congress to the book and thus make it more comprehensive.

I would like to thank my colleagues who helped enormously, partly with the conference organisation, partly with the provision of papers: John Herbert (University of Utah Library), Georgia Higley (Library of Congress), Sandra Burrows (Library and Archives Canada), and Edmund King (The British Library Newspaper Library). My colleague Dr. Ulrich Wegner prepared the page layout in record time.

Last not least attention may be drawn to the recent (October 2006) newspaper conference organised by Poznan University Library, the Poznan School of Sopcial Sciences (Poznan University) and the IFLA Newspaper Section – electronic newspapers, digitisation, and digital libraries were strong on the agenda. This instance shows that more and more countries consider newspaper digitisation a must, and we will see a widespread and rapid application of the latest technologies worldwide!

Hartmut Walravens (Berlin)

NOTES ON INTERNATIONAL NEWSPAPER LIBRARIANSHIP AND DIGITISATION

Hartmut Walravens

Staatsbibliothek zu Berlin Preußischer Kulturbesitz

I would like to report on some activities of the IFLA Newspapers Section (see also www.ifla.org, section 39) and the situation of newspaper digitisation in some countries that are not represented by separate country reports.

The IFLA Newspapers Section started as small group of newspapers enthusiasts within IFLA, the International Federation of Library Associations, and liked its previous name «Round Table of Newspapers» which characterised it very well. The Section continues its successful activities as to events (open sessions at the World Library and Information Congress, conferences), projects, and publications.

Among the publications are the Section's Newsletter and several volumes in the IFLA Publication Series:

- International Newspaper Librarianship
  Edited by Hartmut Walravens
  München: Saur, 2006, 298 p.
  (IFLA Publications; 118)
  ISBN 13 : 978-3-598-21846-0
  ISBN 10 : 3-598-21846-0

- Newspapers in Central and Eastern Europe
  Zeitungen in Mittel- und Osteuropa
  Edited by by Hartmut Walravens in cooperation with Marieluise Schillig
  München: Saur, 2005, 251 p., ISBN 3-598-21841-9

- Newspapers in International Librarianship
  Papers presented by the Newspapers Section at IFLA General Conferences
  Edited by Hartmut Walravens and Edmund King. 2003, 260 p.

Particularly important in today's context is

- Microfilming for Digitisaton and Optical Character Recognition
  (Supplement to Guidelines for Newspaper Preservation Microfilming) /

- Microfilmage en vue de la numérisation et de la reconnaissance optique de caractères

- 用于數字化處理及 OCR 的縮微處理
  Chinese translation of: Microfilming for Digitisaton and Optical Character Recognition /
  Recomendaciones: Microfilmación de Conservación de Periódicos para Digitalización

It is based to a large extent on the practical experience of Microfilming and Digitisation Centre of the Finnish National Library.

Among the projects I only want to mention the current effort to support African libraries: «Survey on Holdings of African Newspapers Kept in National Archives, National or University Libraries in Africa» (2004). This survey resulted in a desiderata list of major African libraries that would like to have some of their own major papers, preferably in microform, and we now try to find ways to have those papers microfilmed (if not yet available in microform) and have a user copy donated to the respective instititutions.

Besides offering papers and presentations at WLIC – this summer in Seoul, on the subject of Newspapers of East Asia – we combined our midwinter business meeting with international conferences to increase our outreach and get in contact and cooperation with colleagues from all over the world. Considering the large number of newspapers and newspaper collections there are relatively few newspaper experts in the library and archival sectors, and much work remains to be done. Newsplan and the US Newspaper Project have been comprehensive and successful projects to improve the situation.

The Section organised conferences during the last years in Cape Town (2003), in Shanghai (2004), and Canberra (2005). For 2007 preparations are under way to hold a newspaper conference in Santiago de Chile.

Before I leave the international context to focus on the digitisation of newspapers in several countries, let me point out that the Section would be pleased to win more members, both personal and institutional, to exchange information and experience and to establish cooperation with newspaper people worldwide.

Germany

While Germany lost large holdings of newspapers owing to WW II, there is still a considerable amount of material left. The German Union Catalogue of Serials (Zeitschriftendatenbank/ZDB, URL: www.zdb-opac.de) comprises about 80,000 titles of newspapers and similar publications like magazines, gazettes, etc. This may one third of what is still extant, according to rough estimates. The institutions participating in ZDB which is also a shared cataloguing network are advised to enter their newspaper holdings but owing to the tight staff and budget situation newspapers do not have a high priority. In addition, the major portion of newspapers is held by archives which again have different priorities. Only Bavaria received funding for checking and cataloguing its newspaper holdings, both in libraries and in archives.

At present, there is nothing to report on major new newspaper digitisation projects. Two small completed projects may be mentioned nevertheless.

- Exilpresse digital. Deutsche Exilzeitschriften 1933–1945 (URL: www.ddb.de)

The situation of Hitler refugees was not conducive to founding newspapers nevertheless there are a few titles among the selected 30 serials have newspaper characteristics, like *Pariser Tageblatt*, and *Pariser Tageszeitung*. The whole project comprises 100,000 pages which are offered as images. Search is possible by title and date, by article and author/illustrator, as well as full text.

This is a list of the digitised titles:

Aufbau (New York)
Acht-Uhr-Abendblatt (Shanghai)
Das Andere Deutschland/+ La Otra Alemania (Buenos Aires/Montevideo)
Das blaue Heft (Paris)
Der deutsche Schriftsteller (Paris)
Der deutsche Weg (Oldenzaal)
Europäische Hefte (Pragl)
Freie deutsche Kultur (London)
Freie Kunst und Literatur (Paris)
Gelbe Post (Shanghai)
Gemeindeblatt der Jüdischen Gemeinde Berlin (Berlin)
Gemeindeblatt der Jüdischen Gemeinde Shanghai (Shanghai)
Internationale Literatur (Moskau)
The Jewish Voice of the far East (Shanghai)

8 UHR ABENDBLATT

10 cts

DER SHANGHAI WOCHE

19 Avenue Edward VII — Telefon 84084

Chefredakteur: WOLFGANG FISCHER

Jahrgang 2. Sonntag, 7. Januar 1940 No. 6

Leningrad im Alarmzustand

Moskau, 7. Jan. (United Press) Die Misserfolge der Roten Armee haben, wie erwartet, bereits ihre Auswirkung im Innern gezeitigt. Die G.P.U. hat alle Haende voll zu tun. In allen Fabriken werden Sabotageakte festgestellt. Die Folge sind Massenverhaftungen in den Arbeiterkreisen.

In Leningrad selbst herrscht infolge des Vorrueckens der finnischen Truppen ausserordentliche Erregung unter der Bevoelkerung. Man haelt einen direkten Angriff der Finnen durchaus fuer moeglich und trifft daher in aller Eile militaerische Vorbereitungen. Die Stadt gleicht einem Heerlager. Militaerpatrouillen durchziehen die Strassen, alle wichtigen Gebaeude haben Sonderschutz erhalten.

Kronstadt evakuiert

Helsingfors, 6. Jan. (Havas) Die wichtigste russische Festung Kronstadt wurde im Hinblick auf das stete Vorruecken der Finnen in Kriegsbereitschaft gesetzt. Die gesamte Bevoelkerung wird evakuiert. Man schickt die Zivilisten teilweise nach Leningrad, teilweise ins Innere Russlands.

Rumaenien zur Verteidigung entschlossen

Bukarest, 7. Jan. (Reuter) Anlaesslich der traditionellen Epiphani Tags-Feier in Chisianu an der russisch-rumaenischen Grenze fand in Anwesenheit Koenig Carols eine eindrucksvolle Kundgebung statt.

Der Gouverneur des Landes drueckte dem Koenig die Bereitschaft der gesamten Bevoelkerung aus, das Land bis zum Aeussersten gegen jeden Angriff zu verteidigen. Koenig Carol antwortete in einer laengeren Ansprache u.a.:

"Wenn ich den Fuss auf den Boden Bessarabiens setze, so fuehle ich nicht, dass ich mich in einem Lande befinde, das Rumaenien nur angeheftet ist, sondern in einem Land, das immer rumaenisches Territorium bleiben wird. Das ganze Land garantiert, dass diese Grenzen niemals verletzt werden duerfen, und die Worte, die heute an mich gerichtet wurden, bewiesen die unerschuetterliche Einheit der Nation, die niemals zugeben wird, dass ein Feind seinen Fuss auf den heiligen Boden Bessarabiens setzt."

Der kaelteste Tag des finnischen Winters

Helsingfors, 7. Januar (Reuter) Die Temperaturen zeigten gestern 54 Grad unter Null. Es war der kaelteste Tag dieses Winters.

In Helsingfors, das von Fliegerangriffen in den letzten Tagen verschont blieb, kehrt allmaehlich wieder normales Leben ein. Sogar die Kinos wurden wieder geoeffnet.

Geschaeftssperren in Deutschland

Amsterdam, 6. Jan. (Reuter) Am. Februar muessen 15 der groessten Bekleidungsgeschaefte Deutschlands ihre Pforten wegen Warenmangel schliessen. Gerade diese grossen Betriebe sind bei den Belieferungen immer noch bevorzugt worden.

Hollaendische Korrespondenten melden, dass fast alle kleinen Textil- und Lebensmittelgeschaefte gezwungen waren, ihre Betriebe zu schliessen, da Waren nicht mehr zu erhalten sind. Die Kaelte hat neue Versorgungsschwierigkeiten gebracht: Kartoffel, Gemuese und Kohle koennen kaum mehr herangeschafft werden.

Die aus den Betrieben entlassenen weiblichen Angestellten werden in Munitionsfabriken untergebracht.

Arbeiter der Siegfriedlinie zurueckgerufen

London, 7. Jan. (Reuter) Durch eine Sonderverlautbarung des deutschen Rundfunkes sind alle Arbeiter, die an der Siegfriedlinie beschaeftigt sind, von ihrem Urlaub unverzueglich zurueckgerufen worden.

Das Hochwasser hat schwere Schaeden an der Linie angerichtet, die schleunigst ausgebessert werden muessen, da die deutsche Heeresleitung andernfalls einen Durchbruch der Franzosen befuerchtet.

Freiwillige fuer Finnland

Stockholm, 6. Jan. (Reuter) Eine neue Abteilung schwedischer Freiwilliger hat sich nach Finnland begeben. Unter ihnen befunden sich auch die ersten daenischen Freiwilligen. Denselben Zug wird auch ein Kontingent norwegischer Freiwilliger benutzen.

Italienisch-ungarische Verhandlungen

Rom, 7. Jan. (Reuter) Die Besprechungen, die in Venedig zwischen dem Grafen Ciano und dem ungarischen Aussenminister Graf Csasky stattfand und an denen entgegen anfaenglich behaupteten Meldungen *Deutschland nicht teilnahm*, waren folgender Problemen gewidmet:

Die Folgen fuer Ungarn als Grenznachbar Sowjetrussland's. Die Beziehungen zwischen Ungarn und Rumaenien, die im Hinblick auf den gemeinsamen russischen Gegner unbedingt verbessert werden sollen. Die Beziehungen Ungarns zu Yugoslavien. Die Stellung Italiens und Ungarns zum gegenwaertigen Krieg.

Ein offizielles Kommuniquee wurde nicht ausgegeben. Graf *Ciano* erklaerte, dass er ausserordentlich *befriedigt* ueber die Aussprache ist. In politischem Kreisen nimmt man an, dass zwischen den beiden Staatsmaennern gewisse Abwehrmassnahmen und Verkehrungen gegen eine russische Invasion auf dem Balkan besprochen worden sind.

Vor allem wuenscht Italien, dass Ungarn alle kleinen Balkanstaaten zu einem festen Block zusammenfuegt und Sonderinteressen zuruecktreten laesst.

Graf Ciano wird noch heute per Flugzeug nach Rom zurueckkehren, um Mussolini Bericht zu erstatten.

Polen von neutralem Schiff geholt

Berlin, 6. Jan. (Reuter) An Bord des schwedischen Dampfers "Konung Oskar" befanden sich 42 Polen, die im militaerpflichtigen Alter stehen. Das Schiff wurde in der Ostsee von einem deutschen Schiff aufgehalten, das die Polen herunterholte. Die verhafteten Polen, die sich auf dem Wege nach England befanden, wurden in einen deutschen Hafen gebracht, desgleichen der schwedische Dampfer, der sich dort einer Kontrolle unterziehen soll.

Heutige Abendkurse

	Kauf:	Verkauf:
amer. $	12.85	12.80
engl. £	46.50	46.00

Ill. 1

Ill. 2

Jüdische Revue (Mukacevo u.a.)
Kunst und Wissen (London)
Neuer Vorwärts (Karlsbad; Paris)
Ordo (Paris)
Pariser Tageblatt (Paris)
Pariser Tageszeitung (Paris)
PEM's Privatberichte (Wien; London)
Das Reich (Saarbrücken)
Shanghai Jewish Chronicle (Shanghai)
Shanghai Echo (Shanghai)
Sozialistische Warte (Paris)
Die Tribüne (Shanghai)
Über die Grenzen (Affoltern a.A.)
Zeitschrift für freie deutsche Forschung (Paris)
Die Zeitung (London)

Full text search does not feature highlighting of the search term.

The second project to be mentioned is

- Compact Memory. Internet Archiv jüdischer Periodika (www.compactmemory.de)

Among the numerous serial titles there are a few which might qualify as newspapers:

Allgemeine Zeitung des Judentums
Altneuland
Bar Kochba
Bayerische Israelitische Gemeindezeitung
Ben Chananja

Berichte für die Lehranstalt für die Wissenschaft des Judentums
Berliner Vereinsbote
Blau-Weiß-Blätter [Alte Folge]
Blau-Weiß-Blätter [Führerzeitung]
Blau-Weiß-Blätter [Neue Folge]
Central-Anzeiger für Jüdische Litteratur
CV-Zeitung
CV-Zeitung [Monatsausgabe]
Das Zelt
Deborah
Der Anfang [Alte Folge]
Der Anfang [Neue Folge]
Der Israelit
Der Israelit des neunzehnten Jahrhunderts
Der israelitische Volkslehrer
Der Jude [1768-1772]
Der Jude [1832-1835]
Der Jude [1916-1928]
Der jüdische Arbeiter
Der jüdische Student [Alte Folge]
Der jüdische Student [Neue Folge]
Der jüdische Wille [Alte Folge]
Der jüdische Wille [Neue Folge]
Der junge Jude
Der Morgen
Der neue Anfang
Der Orient
Der treue Zions-Wächter
Dibre Emeth oder Stimmen der Wahrheit an Israeliten und Freunde Israels
Die Freistatt
Die Kreatur
Die neue Welt
Die Stimme [Alte Folge]
Die Stimme [Neue Folge]
Die Wahrheit
Die Welt
Dr. Bloch's Österreichische Wochenschrift
Esra
Frankfurter Israelitisches Familienblatt
Freie Tribüne
Freie Zionistische Blätter
Gemeindeblatt der Israelitischen Gemeinde Frankfurt am Main
Illustrirte Monatshefte für die gesammten Interessen des Judenthums
Im deutschen Reich
Israelitische Annalen
Israelitische Religionsgesellschaft Frankfurt a. M. [Einladungschriften / Jahresberichte]
Israelitische Rundschau
Jahrbuch der Gesellschaft für Geschichte der Juden in der Cechoslovakischen Republik
Jahrbuch der Jüdisch-Literarischen Gesellschaft
Jahrbuch für die Geschichte der Juden und des Judenthums
Jahrbuch für jüdische Geschichte und Literatur
Jahrbücher für jüdische Geschichte und Literatur
Jahresberichte der Jacobson-Schule
Jahresberichte der Landes-Rabbinerschule in Budapest
Jahresberichte des jüdisch-theologischen Seminars Fraenckelscher Stiftung
Jeschurun [Alte Folge]
Jeschurun [Neue Folge]
Judaica
Jüdische Arbeits- und Wanderfürsorge
Jüdische Korrespondenz
Jüdische Presse

Jüdische Rundschau
Jüdische Schulzeitung
Jüdische Volksstimme
Jüdische Welt-Rundschau
Jüdische Zeitschrift für Wissenschaft und Leben
Jüdische Zeitung
Jüdisches Jahrbuch für die Schweiz
Jüdisches Jahrbuch für Sachsen
Jüdisches Volksblatt
Jüdisch-liberale Zeitung/Jüdisch allgemeine Zeitung
Kalender und Jahrbuch für Israeliten [I. Folge]
Kalender und Jahrbuch für Israeliten [II. Folge]
Kalender und Jahrbuch für Israeliten [III. Folge]
Kartell-Convent-Blätter
Kartell-Convent-Mitteilungen
Korrespondenzblatt des Vereins zur Gründung und Erhaltung einer Akademie für die Wissenschaft des Judentums
Liberales Judentum
Magazin für die Wissenschaft des Judenthums
Menorah
Mitteilungen aus dem Verband der Vereine für jüdische Geschichte und Literatur in Deutschland
Mitteilungen der Arbeitsgemeinschaft jüdisch-liberaler Jugendvereine Deutschlands
Mitteilungen der Gesellschaft für Jüdische Volkskunde [Alte Folge]
Mitteilungen der Gesellschaft für Jüdische Volkskunde [Neue Folge]
Mitteilungen des Gesamtarchivs der deutschen Juden
Monatsschrift für Geschichte und Wissenschaft des Judentums
Nachalath Zewi
Nachrichtendienst der Zentral-Wohlfahrtsstelle der deutschen Juden
Nationalzeitung
Neue jüdische Monatshefte
Neue Nationalzeitung
Neue Zeitung
Ost und West
Österreichisch-ungarische Cantoren-Zeitung
Palästina
Palästina Nachrichten
Philanthropin [Einladungsschriften / Jahresberichte / Programme]
Populär-wissenschaftliche Monatsblätter zur Belehrung über das Judenthum für Gebildete aller Confessionen
Selbst-Emancipation
Stenographische Protokolle der Verhandlungen der Zionisten-Kongresse
Sulamith
Unsere Tribüne
Volk und Land
Wiener Morgenzeitung
Wissenschaftliche Zeitschrift für jüdische Theologie
Zeitschrift für Demographie und Statistik der Juden [Alte Folge]
Zeitschrift für Demographie und Statistik der Juden [Neue Folge]
Zeitschrift für die Geschichte der Juden in der Tschechoslowakei
Zeitschrift für die Geschichte der Juden in Deutschland
Zeitschrift für die religiösen Interessen des Judenthums
Zeitschrift für die Wissenschaft des Judenthums
Zion

Full text search has been established so far for a small amount of the serials. A search leads to the metadata of the respective articles, and by clicking on them these articles appear on the screen, again without highlighting so that the user may have to read through the article.

The Bavarian State Library so far offers two newspapers in digitised form, the *Coburger Zeitung* (1854–1935) and the *Augspurgische Ordinari Postzeitung* (1770–1806). Search is

Mittwoch, den 2. Januar 1935 74. Jahrgang • Nummer 1

Coburger Zeitung

Aelteste nationale Tageszeitung Coburgs

Beiblätter: „Zum Wochenende" — „Unterhaltungs-Beilage" — „Coburger Scholle"

Erscheint mit Ausnahme der Sonn- und Feiertage täglich mittags. — Bezugspreis für den Monat 1.90 ℳ, Zustellungsgebühr 25 Pfg. Ausgabestellen: Ottomar Müller (W. Thomas), Hintere Kreuzgasse 4, Max Opitz, Mohrendrogerie, Mohrenstraße 31, Max Richter, Sattlermeister, Ketschengasse 45.

Verlag, Schriftleitung und Geschäftsstelle: Steingasse 24
Tel. 2068 Postscheckkonto Nürnberg 24756 Tel.-Adr.: Zeitung
Im Falle von höherer Gewalt hat der Bezieher keinen Anspruch auf Lieferung der Zeitung oder Rückzahlung des Bezugspreises.

Anzeigenpreis: Die 6gespaltene 46 mm breite Millimeterzeile oder deren Raum 8 Pfg.; kleine Anzeigen, Vereinsanzeigen usw. siehe Tarif. Reklameanzeigenpreis: Die 4gespaltene 72 mm breite Millimeterzeile 25 Pfg. Bei Wiederholungen Rabatt. — Platzvorschrift wird nur nach Möglichkeit eingehalten.

Neujahrsempfänge beim Führer

Berlin, 2. Jan. Die Neujahrsempfänge beim Führer und Reichskanzler fanden auch in diesem Jahre in der beim verewigten Reichspräsidenten Generalfeldmarschall von Hindenburg üblichen Weise statt.

Die Feierlichkeiten zum Jahreswechsel wurden eingeleitet durch das Beziehen der neuen Wachträume des Heeres in der Reichskanzlei. Hierzu marschierte kurz vor 10 Uhr vormittags mit klingendem Spiel eine Ehrenkompanie des Wachregiments vor dem Hause Wilhelmstraße 78 auf. Nachdem der Kommandant der Stadt Berlin, Generalmajor Schaumburg, Meldung erstattet hatte, schritt der Führer die Front der in Paradeaufstellung stehenden Ehrenkompanie ab und nahm ihren Vorbeimarsch ab.

Hieran schloß sich um 11 Uhr der Empfang der

Vertreter der Wehrmacht

im „Hause des Reichspräsidenten". Es waren erschienen der Reichswehrminister, der Chef der Heeresleitung und der Chef der Marineleitung. Außerdem nahm an diesem Empfang teil General der Infanterie Göring. Nachdem der Reichswehrminister in kurzer Ansprache dem Führer die Wünsche der Wehrmacht zum Ausdruck gebracht hatte, tauschte der Führer mit jedem der erschienenen Herren Neujahrsglückwünsche aus. Die Ehrenwache im „Hause des Reichspräsidenten" erwies bei der Anfahrt und Abfahrt der Vertreter der Wehrmacht die vorgeschriebenen militärischen Ehrenbezeugungen.

Um 11.15 Uhr empfing der Führer eine Abordnung der Halloren. Alsdann folgte der feierliche

Neujahrsempfang der Diplomaten

durch den deutschen Reichskanzler. Der Führer und Reichskanzler empfing in der traditionellen Weise sämtliche hier beglaubigten fremden Botschafter, Gesandten und Geschäftsträger. Dieser Staatsakt fand im großen Saale des „Hauses des Reichspräsidenten", Wilhelmstraße 73, statt. Um 11.30 Uhr begann die Auffahrt der ausländischen Missionschefs, denen die Ehrenwache des Heeres die vorgeschriebenen militärischen Ehrenbezeugungen erwies.

Der Führer und Reichskanzler, in dessen Begleitung sich der Reichsminister des Auswärtigen, Freiherr von Neurath, die Staatssekretäre Dr. Meißner, von Bülow und Dr. Lammers, der Chef des Protokolls, Graf von Bassewitz, befanden, betrat um 12 Uhr den großen Saal, in dem die Diplomaten bereits Aufstellung genommen hatten.

Der Doyen des Diplomatischen Corps

der Apostolische Nuntius Monsignore Cesare Orsenigo, richtete an den Führer eine Ansprache, in der er u. a. ausführte:

Unter den Gütern, die die Menschen heutzutage am meisten begehren, erhebt sich ohne Zweifel über alle anderen der Weltfriede mit all seinen Auswirkungen auf politischem, wirtschaftlichem und sozialem Gebiet. Das schmerzliche Erleben jeden Tages zeigt uns, daß ohne den Weltfrieden das Wirtschaftsleben abstirbt, die Arbeit fehlt und der menschliche Fortschritt zum Stillstand kommt.

Eure Exzellenz, wir verhehlen uns nicht, daß sehr ernste Hindernisse dem Weltfrieden noch im Wege stehen. Aber wir sind überzeugt, daß, so schwer sie auch sein mögen, sie sich nicht als unüberwindlich erweisen werden dank des Zusammenwirkens aller Menschen, die guten Willens sind und unter dem Zeichen der Gerechtigkeit und der Menschenliebe, dieser Tugenden, die für die Erreichung einer weltweiten Verständigung unerläßlich sind. Mit diesem Wunsche, den sicherlich jedermann teilen wird, geben wir der Hoffnung Ausdruck, daß das neue Jahr uns diese Annäherung der Geister bringen möge, die die beste Gewähr für den Frieden ist.

In diesem Wunsch, Exzellenz, sind zugleich die besten Wünsche für Ihr Land ausgedrückt, denn gerade durch wohlgefestigte brüderliche Beziehungen zwischen den Völkern wird man diese reiche Blütezeit wieder herbeiführen können, die einer der Hauptpunkte Ihres machtvollen Programms für den Wiederaufbau Deutschlands ist.

Der Führer und Reichskanzler

antwortete hierauf mit folgenden Worten:

Herr Nuntius!

Mit aufrichtigem Danke nehme ich die Glückwünsche entgegen, die Eure Exzellenz im Namen des Diplomatischen Corps und zugleich im Namen Ihrer Souveräne und Staatsoberhäupter zum Beginn des neuen Jahres dem deutschen Volke und mir dargebracht haben.

Sie haben, Herr Nuntius, von dem heißen Wunsche der Menschheit nach Erhaltung des Friedens gesprochen und mit Recht hervorgehoben, daß ohne die Gewißheit des Friedens auf keinem Gebiete menschlicher Tätigkeit ein gedeihlicher Fortschritt zu erhoffen ist. Sie können überzeugt sein, daß diese Worte der Auffassung des ganzen deutschen Volkes entsprechen. Kein Land kann das Bedürfnis nach Frieden tiefer empfinden als Deutschland, das nach schweren Jahren voller Not und Leid alle Kräfte für seinen inneren Wiederaufbau zusammengefaßt hat, das diesen Wiederaufbau in Ruhe vollziehen will und das für seine Lebensrechte von den anderen Ländern nur die gleiche Anerkennung und Achtung fordert, die es ihnen selbst entgegenbringt. Mit seiner Politik, die unverrückbar auf diesen Grundsätzen beruht, wird Deutschland stets ein sicherer Garant des Friedens sein.

Wenn Sie, Herr Nuntius, auf Schwierigkeiten und Sorgen hingedeutet haben, die sich aus der gegenwärtigen Lage ergäben, so bin ich mit Ihnen der Ansicht, daß sie sich bei allseitigem gutem Willen sehr wohl beseitigen lassen. Ich sehe in den Beziehungen der Völker kein Problem, das nicht bei verständnisvoller Behandlung einer gütlichen Lösung zugänglich wäre! Ich vermag auch nicht zu glauben, daß es heute irgend einer verantwortlichen Stelle des Auslandes an dem guten Willen fehlte. Das deutsche Volk und seine Regierung sind jedenfalls entschlossen, das ihrige zu einer Gestaltung der Völkerbeziehungen beizutragen, die ein ehrliches Zusammenwirken auf der Grundlage der Gleichberechtigung aller sicherstellt und dadurch allein das Wohl und den Fortschritt der Menschheit gewährleistet. Möge das neue Jahr uns diesem erhabenen Ziele näherbringen!

In dieser Hoffnung spreche ich Ihnen, Herr Nuntius, sowie Ihnen, meine Herren, zugleich für Ihre Staatsoberhäupter, Regierungen und Völker, im Namen des deutschen Volkes und in meinem eigenen Namen meine herzlichsten Neujahrswünsche aus!

Nach dem Austausch der Ansprachen begrüßten der Führer und Reichskanzler und nach ihm der Reichsminister des Auswärtigen die einzelnen Botschafter, Gesandten und Geschäftsträger und nahmen deren persönliche Glückwünsche entgegen. Nachdem der Führer mit seinem Gefolge sie verabschiedet hatte, verließen auch die fremden Missionschefs das „Haus des Reichspräsidenten", wobei die Ehrenwache erneut unter Gewehr trat und militärische Ehrenbezeugungen erwies.

In der Silvesternacht vor der Reichskanzlei

Begeisterte Kundgebungen für Adolf Hitler

Berlin, 2. Jan. Trotz des strömenden Regens hatten sich in der Silvesternacht Tausende von deutschen Männern, Frauen und Kindern vor dem Gebäude der Reichskanzlei in der Wilhelmstraße eingefunden, um den Beginn des Neuen Jahres im Angesicht ihres Führers zu begehen. Sie sangen das Deutschland- und das Horst-Wessel-Lied, riefen immer wieder: „Wir wollen unseren Führer sehen!" In ihre Rufe hallten um Mitternacht die feierlichen Glockenklänge der nahen Kirchen.

Endlich, um 12½ Uhr, erhellte sich plötzlich ein Fenster im ersten Stockwerk der Reichskanzlei. Unter brausenden Heilrufen der Menge trat der Führer an das Fenster und begrüßte seine Volksgenossen, die ihm wieder und wieder die Hände entgegenstreckten und ihrer Liebe und Treue in Jubelrufen Ausdruck gaben. Nur langsam lösten sich die Menschenmassen auf, immer noch zurückschauend nach dem Hause des Führers.

Das neue Jahr und die SA

Berlin. Im Lustgarten fand am Dienstag ein großer Neujahrsappell der Ehrenformationen der Berlin-Brandenburger SA statt. In einer Ansprache betonte Obergruppenführer v. Jagow, das Jahr 1935 werde die SA voranbringen. Das sei der Wille des Führers und so laute der Befehl des Chef des Stabes. Anschließend fand ein Vorbeimarsch vor dem Führer in der Wilhelmstraße statt.

Der Führer an die Partei

Der Führer hat zum Jahreswechsel folgenden Aufruf an die NSDAP erlassen:

Nationalsozialisten, Nationalsozialistinnen, Parteigenossen!

Ein für Deutschland ereignisreiches Jahr ist zu Ende gegangen. Zum zweitenmal feiern wir in unserem Staat den 1. Januar. Mit Stolz kann die Bewegung auf ihre Leistungen in den letzten 12 Monaten zurückblicken, denn die staatliche und moralische Regeneration sowohl wie die wirtschaftliche Wiederaufrichtung unseres Volkes sind ihr Werk. Wohin wäre Deutschland gekommen ohne sie?

Die Nachwelt wird dereinst die Größe dieser allgemeinen Umwälzung geschichtlich feststellen, die im zweiten Jahre des nationalsozialistischen Regimes fortgeführt und befestigt wurde. Noch vor 12 Monaten prophezeiten unsere Gegner für das Jahr 1934 den unausbleiblichen Zusammenbruch des neuen Reiches.

Deutschland und das deutsche Volk aber sind auf allen Gebieten ihrer nationalen Existenz und Selbstbehauptung stärker geworden.

Trotzdem uns in diesem Jahre die Vorsehung in dem Generalfeldmarschall den großherzigen Vermittler genommen hatte, ist die geistige Uebereinstimmung zwischen der Idee der nationalsozialistischen Bewegung, ihrem Wollen und dem deutschen Volk eine immer innigere geworden. Nach der im letzten Sommer vorgenommenen Säuberung der Partei von unwürdigen Elementen ist sie heute mehr denn je der tatsächliche politische Willensträger der Nation, und dies nicht etwa aus unberechtigter und damit überheblicher Anmaßung, sondern zu Recht, bestätigt durch die erneut festgestellte Willensmeinung der überwältigenden Mehrheit unseres Volkes.

Ich weiß, meine Parteigenossen, daß dies im kommenden Jahre nicht so bleibt, sondern sich noch verstärkt, denn die große reformatorische Arbeit an Volk und Reich wird weitergeführt. Der Kampf gegen die Arbeitslosigkeit und soziale Not wird fortgesetzt.

Den Feinden und Phantasten aber, die soeben wieder glauben, durch eine Flut von geschriebenen Lügen und Verdächtigungen das nationalsozialistische deutsche Volk und Deutsche Reich entzweien und das ihnen verhaßte Regiment stürzen zu können, wird die harte Wirklichkeit nach 12 Monaten die gleiche Widerlegung zuteil werden lassen, wie in dem Jahre, das hinter uns liegt.

An der Disziplin und Treue der Nationalsozialistischen Partei und ihrer Anhänger sowie am unerschütterlichen Willen und der Beharrlichkeit der Führung wird jeder Versuch, Deutschland zu schädigen, am Ende ergebnislos sein.

Nach dem Abschluß dieses Jahres danke ich all meinen Mitarbeitern und Führern der politischen Organisation der Nationalsozialistischen Partei, den Führern der SA., SS., des Arbeitsdienstes, der Hitlerjugend und des NSKK., den Führern unserer Bauern- und Arbeiterorganisationen sowie den Führerinnen der Frauenschaften und des BDM. für die unentwegte Treue und den blinden Gehorsam, die sie mir entgegenbrachten und in denen sie mir folgten.

Ich danke damit aber auch den Millionen der Parteigenossen und Anhänger, den zahllosen braven SA.- und SS.-Männern für die treue Anhänglichkeit an meine Person als ihren Führer, für die Hingabe an die Bewegung, für ihre Opfer und für ihre Arbeit im Dienste unseres Volkes und damit für ihren Glauben an Deutschland. Ich danke auch den Millionen Unbekannter und Namenloser, die die Erfüllung unseres Wollens durch ihre fleißige, sachliche Mitarbeit ermöglichen halfen.

Das Jahr 1935 soll uns alle erfüllt sehen von einem verstärkten Eifer des Kampfes und der Arbeit für unser Volk.

Diesem aber wollen wir nichts besseres wünschen als ein Leben in Ehre und Frieden. Denn dann wird es unserer Arbeit mit Gottes Hilfe gelingen, der Nation auch das tägliche Brot zu sichern.

Am heißesten aber wünschen wir für dieses Jahr 1935 die Rückkehr jenes deutschen Gebietes, das durch seine Stimme des Blutes am 13. Januar die unlösbare Gemeinschaft mit dem Deutschen Reiche vor aller Welt bekunden wird.

Es lebe die nationalsozialistische Bewegung!

Es lebe unser einiges deutsches Volk und Deutsches Reich!

München, den 1. Januar 1935.

gez. Adolf Hitler.

Ill. 3

only possible by date (www.bayerische-landesbibliothek-online.de/zeitungen/coburger-zeitung/).

Austria

AustriaN Newspapers Online is known through its acronym ANNO (http://anno.onb.ac). Its website gives a chronology of its activities since 2003, and already on February 20, 2004, it reported "1 million pages online!) This is from the list of papers (titles in italics are scheduled for digitisation):

12 Uhr Blatt
Der Abend
Acht Uhr Blatt
Die Arbeit
Allgemeine Bauzeitung (in Kooperation mit: Wien – Stadtentwicklung und Stadtplanung)
Belehrendes und Unterhaltendes
Die Bombe
Christlich-sociale Arbeiter-Zeitung
Die Debatte
Deutsche Zeitung (in Kooperation mit: Die P@rlamentsbibliothek)
Eideseis dia ta anatolika mere
Ephemeris (in Kooperation mit: Akademia Athenon und der Griechischen Botschaft Wien)
Der Floh
Forst-Zeitung (in Kooperation mit: Universitätsbibliothek der TU Wien)
Freies Blatt
Freies Wiener Montagblatt
Freiheit!
Gesundheits-Zeitung
Hellenikos telegraphos
Hermes ho logios

As there is not sufficient funding for an active continuation of the project, ANNO is constantly looking for partners to digitise individual papers in cooperation.

Scanning is done either directly from the (usually bound) volume, or the binding is removed and the single pages are scanned. OCR is not applied, and therefore there is no full text search. Nevertheless ANNO has been providing about 2 million pages on the net, and that is no mean accomplishment.

Luxemburg

The National Library of Luxemburg (http://luxemburgensia.bnl.lu) has increased the number of digitised papers to 10. Like ANNO the papers are offered as images, and they may be accessed by title and date.

A-Z : Luxemburger illustrierte Wochenschrift
1933 - 1934 - 1935 - 1936 - 1937 - 1938 - 1939 - 1940
Catalogue Bibnet.lu

Courrier du Grand-Duché de Luxembourg
1844 - 1846 - 1847 - 1848 - 1849 - 1850 - 1851 - 1852 - 1853 - 1854 - 1855 - 1856 - 1857 - 1858 - 1859 - 1860
Catalogue Bibnet.lu

Das Vaterland – Wochenblatt für luxemburgische National-Literatur
1869–1870
Catalogue Bibnet.lu

Floréal : revue libre d'art [et] de littérature
1907–1908
Catalogue Bibnet.lu

Jonghemecht - Zeitschrift für heimatliches Theater, Schrift und Volkstum

Nᴏ. 4 - JAHRGANG 1

14. JANUAR 1934

Herausgeber: FRANZ STOLTZ
Redaktion: LUXEMBURG,
6, KÖNIGINSTRASSE,
TELEPHON 34.19

A-Z

ABONNEMENTSPREIS:
EIN JAHR . . . . 70 fr.
SECHS MONATE . . 38 fr.
DREI MONATE . . . 20 fr.

LUXEMBURGER ILLUSTRIERTE WOCHENSCHRIFT

Ill. 4

1926 - 1927 - 1928 - 1929 - 1930 - 1931 - 1932 - 1933 - 1934 - 1935 - 1936 - 1937 - 1938 - 1939 - 1940
Catalogue Bibnet.lu

Journal de la ville et du Grand-Duché de Luxembourg
1827 - 1828 - 1829 - 1830 - 1831 - 1832 - 1833 - 1834 - 1835 - 1836 - 1837 - 1838 - 1839 - 1840 - 1841 - 1842 - 1843 - 1844
Catalogue Bibnet.lu

Luxemburger Illustrierte
1924 - 1925 - 1926 - 1927 - 1928 - 1929 - 1930 - 1931
Catalogue Bibnet.lu

Luxemburger Illustrierte - Edition spéciale: Tour de France
1925
Catalogue Bibnet.lu

Luxemburger Land (Das)
1882 - 1883 - 1884 - 1885 - 1886
Catalogue Bibnet.lu

Luxemburger Wochenblatt
1821 - 1822 - 1823 - 1824 - 1825 - 1826
Catalogue Bibnet.lu

The whole issue is displayed on the screen in reduced size and by clicking the desired page is blown up to screen size. The project information points out that there two main objectives, one, to provide easy access to the material, two, to protect the often rare and fragile originals. The option of possible tong term preservation is not mentioned.

Greece

Newspaper	Digital Pages	Pages with Content	Articles	Year	
				.. from	.. up to
Eleftheria	43.832	43.832	944.361	1944	1967
Empros	77.793	77.793	-	1896	1917
Rizospastis	54.203	54.203	33.851	1917	1983
Scrip	19.006	19.006	-	1893	1911
Tahidromos (of Egypt)	25.172	25.172	-	1958	1977

Tab. 1

The National Library of Greece now offers 5 newspapers on its website (http://www.nlg.gr):

Access is by title and date. No full text search is possible.

Latvia

The National Library of Latvia (http://www.lnb.lv) offers newspapers as part of their Digital Library. Besides papers in Latvian also serials in Russian and German are offered. Most projects focus on the years 1904–1905 but some are covered even up to 1949. Again search is by title and year. If the reader wants to print a page, he receives not just this page but the whole issue.

Mantojums – 1 : Latvijas periodisko izdevumu saglabāšana

Apskats. - Rīga, 1905–1906
Astoņpadsmitais Novembris. - Kuldīga, 1944

Atbalss. - Kuldīga, 1928
Auseklis. - Pēterburga, 1906–1907
Balss. - Rīga, 1905
Baltija. - Rīga, 1907
Baltijas Vēstnesis. - Rīga, 1905
Bitīte. - Ventspils, 1913–1915
Brīvā Venta. - Ventspils, 1940–1941, 1945–1949
Brīvā Venta : Pielikums Brīvā Venta ostā. - Ventspils, 1946
Cīņa. - Rīga, 1904–1905
Dienas Apskats. - Rīga, 1905–1906
Dienas Lapa. - Rīga, Petrograda, 1886–1905, 1918
Drywa. - Pēterburga, Rēzekne, 1908–1917
Drywa : Gorīgajs pīlykums. - Pēterburga, 1912–1913
Drywa : Pielikums Gorīga Maize. - Pēterburga, Rēzekne, 1914–1917
Drywa : Pielikums Orōjs. - Pēterburga, 1914–1915
Drywa : Ziniskajs pīlykums, 1912–1913
Dzimtene. - Rīga, 1905–1906
Gaisma. - Pēterburga, 1905–1906
Gaisma. - Ventspils, 1911–1912
Gaisma: Literāriskais pielikums. - Ventspils, 1912
Jaunā Avīze. - Ventspils, 1912–1915
Jaunā Avīze : Literāriskais un Satīriskais pielikums. - Ventspils, 1912–1915
Jaunā Dienas Lapa. - Rīga, Petrograda, 1905–1918
Jaunā Dzīve. - Ventspils, 1924–1931
Jaunais Kurzemnieks. - Kuldīga, 1932–1940
Jaunais Ventspils Apskats.–Ventspils, 1928–1931
Jaunākās Ziņas. - Rīga, 1911–1920
Jaunas Zinias. - Pēterburga, 1912–1914
Jaunō Drywa. - Rēzekne, 1918
Jaunō Letgola. - Pēterburga, 1918
Klints. - Kuldīga, 1922–1930, 1936
Kuldīgas Balss. - Kuldīga, 1932–1940
Kuldīgas Vēstnesis. - Kuldīga, 1909–1910, 1923–1932
Kuldīgas Vēstnesis : Ilustrētais pielikums. - Kuldīga, 1928
Kuldīgas Vēstnesis : Pielikums Pilsēta un Lauki. - Kuldīga, 1926–1927
Kuldīgas Ziņas. - Kuldīga, 1926–1928, 1933
Kurzeme. - Ventspils, 1914–1915
Kurzemes Vārds. - Liepāja, 1918–1944
Kurzemes Ziņas. - Kuldīga, 1933–1934
Kurzemnieks. - Kuldīga, 1910–1913, 1922–1923, 1929–1934, 1944–1945
Latgolas Words. - Rīga, Rēzekne, 1919–1940
Latvietis. - Liepāja, 1905
Latvijas Kareivis. - Rīga, 1920–1923
Latvijas Šaha Vēstnesis. - Ventspils, 1924–1925, 1932
Latvju Rakstnieku un urnālistu Arodbiedrības Provinces Preses Sekcijas izdevums. - Rīga, 1931
Liau u Bolss. - Petrograda, 1917
Mājas Viesis. - Rīga, 1905–1906
Mūsu Dzīve. - Rīga, 1907
Mūsu Laiki. - Rīga, 1906–1907
Padomju Kuldīga. - Kuldīga, 1945–1956
Pēterburgas Avīzes. - Pēterburga, 1905
Pēterburgas Latvietis. - Pēterburga, 1905–1906
Rīgas Apskats. - Rīga, 1907–1908
Rīgas Avīze. - Rīga, 1902–1906
Rīgas Pilsētas Policijas Avīze (Ведомости Рижской городской полиции = Zeitung der Rigaschen Stadtpolizei). - Rīga, 1904–1907
Sākla. - Pēterburga, 1906
Sēkla. - Liepāja, 1905–1906
Spēks. - Jelgava, 1905
Strādnieks. - Saldus, Kuldīga, 1940–1941
Tēvija. - Jelgava, 1905

Tēvija. - Rīga, Liepāja, 1941–1945
Uz priekšu! - Rīga, 1918–1919
Ventas Balss. - Ventspils, 1921–1945
Ventas Straume. - Ventspils, 1911–1914
Ventas Straume : Literāriskais pielikums. - Ventspils, 1911
Ventspils Apskats. - Ventspils, 1907–1914
Ventspils Apskats. - Ventspils, 1933–1934
Ventspils Apskats : Literāriskais pielikums. - Ventspils, 1909–1914
Ventspils Apskats : Svētdienas pielikums. - Ventspils, 1910–1914
Ventspils Atbalss. - Ventspils, 1923
Ventspils Avīze. - Ventspils, 1919, 1933–1934
Ventspils Izglītības, Audzināšanas un Saimniecības Vēstnesis. - Ventspils, 1910–1911
Ventspils Komunists. - Ventspils, 1919, 1929
Zemgales Balss. - Jelgava, 1924–1934
Zemgales Komunists. - Jelgava, 1944–1949
Лифляндские Губернские Ведомости. - Rīga, 1905
Рижский Вестник. - Rīga, 1905
Anzeiger für Goldingen und Windau. - Kuldīga, 1927–1929
Goldingenscher Anzeiger. - Kuldīga, 1911–1915, 1929–1930
Mitausche Zeitung. - Jelgava, 1905–1906
Windausche Zeitung. - Ventspils, 1901, 1903, 1907–1914, 1924–1925, 1927–1931

This is an example of the search by date, for *Mitausche Zeitung*:

1905. gads (Nr./datums)

1/1.01.	**2**/5.01.	**3**/8.01.	**4**/12.01.	**5**/19.01.
6/22.01.	**7**/26.01.	**8**/29.01.	**9**/2.02.	**10**/5.02.
11/9.02.	**12**/12.02.	**13**/16.02.	**14**/23.02.	**15**/26.02.
16/2.03.	**17**/5.03.	**18**/9.03.	**19**/12.03.	**20**/16.03.
21/19.03.	**22**/23.03.	**23**/26.03.	**24**/30.03.	**25**/2.04.
26/6.04.	**27**/9.04.	**28**/13.04.	**29**/16.04.	**30**/20.04.
31/23.04.	**32**/27.04.	**33**/30.04.	**34**/4.05.	**35**/7.05.
36/11.05.	**37**/14.05.	**38**/18.05.	**39**/21.05.	**40**/25.05.
41/28.05.	**42**/1.06.	**43**/4.06.	**44**/8.06.	**45**/11.06.
46/15.06.	**47**/18.06.	**48**/22.06.	**49**/25.06.	**50**/29.06.
51/2.07.	**52**/6.07.	**53**/9.07.	**54**/13.07.	**55**/16.07.
56/20.07.	**57**/23.07.	**58**/27.07.	**59**/30.07.	**60**/3.08.
61/6.08.	**62**/10.08.	**63**/13.08.	**64**/17.08.	**65**/20.08.
66/24.08.	**67**/27.08.	**68**/31.08.	**69**/3.09.	**70**/7.09.
71/10.09.	**72**/14.09.	**73**/17.09.	**74**/21.09.	**75**/24.09.
76/28.09.	**77**/1.10.	**78**/5.10.	**79**/8.10.	**80**/12.10.
81/15.10.	**82**/19.10.	**83**/26.10.	**84**/29.10.	**85**/2.11.
86/5.11.	**87**/9.11.	**88**/12.11.	**89**/16.11.	**90**/19.11.
91/23.11.	**92**/3.12.	**93**/7.12.	**94**/10.12.	**95**/14.12.
96/17.12.	**97**/21.12.	**98**/24.12.	**99**/28.12.	**100**/31.12.

Tab. 2

Hawaii

If Hawaii is included here than not because of a geographical misunderstanding but just because particularly rare material in a language other than English is presented. Hawaiian is experiencing a renaissance, and therefore publications in Hawaiian are much in demand. The website of the University of Hawaii (http://libweb.hawaii.edu) gives a title list:

Titles Currently Available

Ke Aloha Aina Oiaio - 1896–1897
Ke Au Hou - July 1910–January 1912
Ke Au Okoa - April 24, 1865–June 5, 1865 (1 of 4 reels)
Hawaii Holomua - 1912
Ka Hoku o ka Pakipika - September 23, 1861–May 14, 1863
Ke Kilohana o ka Malamalama - 1907–1919
Ka Lama Hawaii - February 14, 1834–December 26, 1834
Ka Lanakila - July 1, 1909–October 21, 1909
Ka Lei Momi - June 21, 1893–September 22, 1893
Ka Lei Momi e Mau Kou Olino Ana - August 5, 1893–December 25, 1893
Ka Leo o ka Lahui - 1889–1896
Ka Loea Kalaiaina - 1897–1900
Ka Makaainana - 1887–1899
Ka Manawa - November 7, 1870–December 12, 1870
Ka Na'i Aupuni - 1905–1908
Ka Nupepa Kuokoa - 1861–1927

The user interface is partly in Hawaiian, by the way. The poor quality of some of the early Hawaiian papers does not lend itself to OCR. So again, search is title and date.

All the institutions emphasized, in reply to questions, that they are planning on using OCR in the future to provide searchable full text. Some lacked the funding, some the staff to do so, others lacked experience in OCR and intended to wait until fast and efficient software was available. The general view was that newspapers are among the most popular and looked after library materials, and their presence on the net was a really good service. It was pointed out, however, that readers demanded more recent papers and had little understanding of the sometimes very intricate copyright situation.

While the services mentioned are free of charge to users, some newspaper publishers and some providers offer their services for a fee. The search options are usually very attractive, and not being forced to spend a couple of days in front of a microform reader is attractive, too.

The mentioned institutions, with the exception of ANNO, do not publicize their work procedure on their websites, e.g. whether they scan from film or from the originals. If high quality microfilm, prepared according to standards, is available it is certainly an excellent basis for digitisation. A survey of some major newspaper collections has shown, however, that a number of earlier films are not up to standard, and re-filming would not only be necessary for digitisation but also in the interest of long-term preservation.

In closing two news items may be of interest (Jan. 4, 2006):

Scanning and processing of one page costs now between 35 and 48 cents, depending on the work involved. Processing includes among others, spot removal. If so desired the articles will be prepared for full text search to make them easily available to editorial staff and internet users. But only *Die Zeit* offers some of the archival material online and free of restrictions.

The other one is related to a pilot project of the Belgian *De Tijd*: The (e-paper reader) Iliad display offers 16 grayscales and 150 dpi; this corresponds to the usual printed newspaper

KA LEI MOMI

BUKE I. — HONOLULU, OAHU, AUGATE 2, 1893. — HELU 36

NUPEPA PUKA [illegible]

KA LEI MOMI

W. H. KAPU,

Luna Nui a Lunahooponopono.

Ma Honolulu kona wahi noho.

UKU PAPA.

No ka Makahiki	$10 00
No ka Mahina	1 00
No ka Pule	25
o ke Kope Hookahi	10

Kumu Ka Nui.

E hoopuka mau ia ana Keia a me keia la, koe ka Sabati.

O na hooponopono dala a me na kanaka nupepa ana, aia wale no me ka Luna Nui.

Aia wale no me Ka Luna Nui a Lunahooponopono na kuka ana no na mea e pili ana i ka uku o na olelo hoolaha, na kenikau, na mele inoa, a pela aku. Aole loa e hoopukaia kekahi o keia mau mea ke hookaa mua ole ia mai ka uku.

O na poe a pau e makemake ana e lawe i ka Nupepa Ka Lei Momi e hookaa mua ia mai ka uku, ina ma ka Pule a ma ka Mahina paha. Aole hoaie.

E hoopukaia aku no na manao o na makamaka ma keia Nupepa i ku i ke ano hoonaauao mai a me na mea hou o keia a me keia ano, koe na hoopaapaa pilikino ano ole. E hoouna mai i na manao i ka Lunahooponopono.

Keena Hana: Ma kahi noho (no ka manawa), Alanui Kula.

MONE TIKERO

HOLOLIO I KA WA HOOILO

KA

UI MAALO I KE KUPULAU.

AOKE

KEIKIALII MARE MATENE

KIAHA OPAKA O NINEWA.

MOKUNA [illegible]

Ka huakai hele imi Kiaha Opakaopaka o Ninewa—Ka kupuaFuginidala iloko o na mauna o Uralo—Ka pahikaua a ka Mea i hanaia e ke kuhihewa—Ke kahuna Lapaau [illegible] a ka mea [illegible]

Me he mea la i kona hoomaopopo aku aia ke hoopii ae la iluna o ke kualono ana e Ku [illegible] iho la.

No ia mea i hoomau aku ai oia i ka pokiokio ana, a ke lohe ia no oia i ka palalu mai o ka ihu o kona lio, ma ke ala kahi ana i hele mai ai i kinohi ma luna pono o ua kualono la.

A i ka manawa pokole, ua hoea mai la na lio keokeo ia me Igebosoda iluna o kona kua, a i kona ike ana mai ia Mone Tikero, pane mai la oia me ka huaolelo a ka mea i ike i kona hewa maoli i hana ai:

"E ke kanaka opio, ua aie au ia oe no kau hana lokomaikai a ku i ke aloha."

"Heahaia ka'u uku [illegible] [illegible] ai ia oe no koe kokua a me kou ahonui ana mai ia'u i kou manawa [illegible] hou o Igebosoda e pane aku ai.

"He hookahi wale no uku makana, e hoao iho oe i ke aloha, a [illegible] o haule aku ka mea nana oe i hoopakele i keia po iloko o ka pilikia, alaila, e hoomanao iho oe he manawa kupono ia nou e haawi iho ai i ka uku o ka mea nana oe i hoopakele. E hoomanao iho oe he manawa kupono ia nou e hoike iho ai a e [illegible] mai ai hoi i kau mau kokua ana nou," wahi a Mone Tikero.

Iloko o ia manawa i lalau aku ai [illegible] me ka puhaka o Igebosoda [illegible] hooku ia ia ilalo, me ka hoouka aku ia ia maluna o ka lio eleele.

Kau ae la no hoi o Mone Tikero iluna o ka lio keokeo, a hoomaka aku la laua no ka hele ana me ka ukali aku o Igebosoda mahope.

I ka hala ana aku o laua ma o aku o ua pali [illegible] kamailio aku la na Igebosoda la ia Mone Tikero e moe laua ma ia wahi, aka ua hoole aku la ka opio puuwai aloha.

A no ia mea i pane aku ai ka hiona o luna o Hagara ia Mone Tikero penei:

"Kupanaha maoli oe e ka opio, ke hiamoe nei na holoholona o ke kula i keia wa,—a o kaua anei o na mea uhane e hele no i ka po, me ka haawi ole iho i manawa e hoolulu ai ko kaua mau wawae?"

I mai la ua kanaka opio la me ka akaaka pu ana iho:

"E hoomanawanui e kuu hoaloha, aole pono i na mea i hiula iloko o ka pilikia i like me kaua ke ano, ke moe iho ma keia wahi me ke o-pu malumalu ole nona e pale aku ma paka-ua; a he mea hoi naaa e hooi loa aku i ka pilikia o loaa ana ia oe a e pakele loa aku hoi ka luhi e loaa mai ana ia'u i ka mea nana e hoopakele nei ia oe."

Me keia mau huaolelo iwaena o laua na kaaahele hele kuahiwi, i hoomau aku ai no ka laua huakaihele me ka hoomaha ole, e naku hele ana ma o a maanei, e haluku ana na paka ua iluna o laua me ke kololio mai o na kulu kehau o ka po, o ini mai ana i na papalina o na mau kamahele la. A me ia ano laua i kaukaa aku ai a hiki i ka hoea ana mai o ka malamalama o ka la o kekahi la ae.

Kukuna olinolino o ka la a hoolei pu mai la hoi i kona nani nui maluna o ka aina, na mauna kiekie a me na awawa laiki aku no hoi o waiho hamama mai ana, a o ka manawa hoi ia i ikaika iki mai ai ka wela o na kukuna o ka la.

Ua lele iho la laua ilalo, mai luna iho o ko laua mau lio pakahi, a malalo o ka malumalu o kekahi Kumulaau i paina iho ai laua i ko laua aina kakahiaka, a e moani mai ana hoi ka alahuihui o na lau hauliuli o ua uka waokele la, a he onaona hoi ke ea i ko laua mau ihu ke hanu hooman mai.

Mahope iho o ka pau ana o ka laua paina kakahiaka ana, ua hoomakaukau iho la laua i ko laua mau lio no ka alo hou ana aku iloko o na hiiipoa oloko o ua mau kuahiwi la i noho ia e ke anoano.

Kau ae la laua ma na lio a haalele iho la i kahi a laua i noho ai e paina i na minute mamua iho.

(Aole i pau.)

Ill. 5

text resolution. The screen keeps the information even without power supply until new information is selected. The screen is compensate for daylight effects and manages without background illumination. The power demand is just one hundredth of a flat screen. The reader manages pdf, html and normal text so that it may be used also for other material. The display is writing sensitive; documents may therefore be edited with a writing utensil and stored (condensed translation from log.netbib.de/archives/2006/01/04/digitale-und digital-isierte-zeitungen/).

THE PRESS IN BRITAIN: PRINTED AND DIGITAL DEVELOPMENTS

Edmund King

Head of Newspaper Collections
British Library Newspapers

Abstract

This paper is in two parts. The first gives a brief introduction to some recent developments and events relating to the Press in Britain. The picture is one of significant ongoing activity, of businesses continuing to seek to increase profit from printed newspapers, as well as seeking opportunities to expand their activities via databases available on the Internet. The second part describes digitization developments for runs of older newspapers, with the activities of the British Library as an example.

Part I. Introduction

This is an appropriate time to take a snapshot of the Press in Britain. The year 2006 has the characteristics of a crossroads. Newspapers printed on paper continue to be a successful and profitable medium, for national titles and regional ones alike. Yet there are concerns about the future of print. The Internet, buttressed by the global availability of cheap mass computer storage and sophisticated software, has flourished in recent years. All involved in publishing newspapers (and journals too) have needed to consider the new audiences that the Internet offers, and to see how business models can be developed to reach far greater numbers, using rapidly developing new computer related devices. We are living through a revolution, and, exciting though this is, it does bring uncertainties, not only for publishers but also for libraries.

It is also a certainty that there are so many printed newspapers published in the UK at present that it is practically impossible to describe all the characteristics of their publication. Suffice to say that the layout and format of very many conforms to well established patterns, established in the last hundred years. The mix is specifically designed to capture readers' attention. There are more features and magazine content, and this is conspicuous in both national and regional titles (e.g. property, motoring, arts, business sections). The same can be said for the large number of newspapers now published online in the UK.

Current Newspapers in Printed Form

The regional press continues to innovate, to push for the extension of local brands. There are some 1,299 local, daily and weekly titles, together with 400 "stand alone" magazines. As the UK Newspaper Society website says:

> The latest release of regional newspaper ABC/VFD figures (Jan–Jun 2005) … also demonstrates that the regional press is the one print sector to have successfully tackled the issue of bulk sales and discounted copies, with 99.4% of the sector's total ABC circulation now actively purchased up from 99.2% a year ago. A massive 84.4% of the industry's titles are now 100% actively purchased. Full rate sales have grown from 96.9% to 97.8% in the past year.[1]

---

1 From the UK Newspaper Society Website: http://www.newspapersoc.org.uk/Default.aspx?page=776#circulation (visited March 2006).

With regard to Readership, the same source declares:

> British people are among the most avid newspaper readers in the world. 83.6% of all British adults (40 million people) read a regional newspaper, compared with 69.6% who read a national newspaper. Regional press has a high solus readership; 33.3% (15.8 million adults) of those who read a regional newspaper do not read a national daily and 23.9% (11.3 million adults) do not read a national daily or Sunday. Readership of weekly paid-for titles alone have grown by 15.0% since 1994. Over 14 million adults read a regional newspaper but do not use the internet.

The claims of the publishers are real. At this time, regional and local newspapers have a strong presence. The amount of news and editorial varies from paper to paper; the number of special sections (e.g. motoring, property) has grown greatly in the last 20 years, and, as a result, in strict page count terms, news can be a minority of the paper produced. The results of this recent publisher survey are laid out in Tables 1 and 2. In Table 1, we see that the average circulation of the top 20 UK paid regional weekly titles is between 33,014 for the Westmorland Gazette and 55,109 for the Kent Messenger Series. For the top 20 UK Free Regional Weeklies, circulation ranges from 96,518 for the Herald & Post – Luton & Dunstable to 309,516 for the Manchester Metro News Series. In Table 2, for Paid Regional morning newspapers, published Monday-Saturday, we see circulation of 10,017 for the Daily Ireland up to 84,612 for the Aberdeen – Press & Journal. As for the Free Regional Morning papers, the publications of Associated Press predominate, with Metro London having a distribution of 490,423 copies each day.

The publishers of the regional press are certainly not standing still. A sign of the nervousness about the future was shown in the decision by the Northcliffe Group (owned by the Daily Mail General Trust, DGMT) to sell all its newspaper titles.[2] This was announced in December 2005 and it was known widely that the Northcliffe Group yields profits to Associated Press. The proposed sale was not taken further by March 2006, as it was reputed that DGMT had not received sufficiently high offers. The episode highlights the possible uncertainty about the future viability of regional newspapers. The profit margins of printed regional papers are unlikely to compare with those profits being earned by the Associated Press for other online businesses that it owns, such as Jobsite. Jobsite is reported to be earning a margin in excess of 40%.[3]

National Newspapers

The Newspaper Publishers Association (NPA) is the association for British national newspapers and its role is to represent, protect and promote the national newspaper industry. It was founded in 1906 and its current members comprise Associated Newspapers, Express Newspapers, Financial Times, Guardian Newspapers, Independent Newspapers (UK), MGN (Trinity Mirror national titles), News International and Telegraph Group.

UK National newspapers continue to be a phenomenon. The drive to secure increases in circulation continues for daily and weekly newspapers. Slightly falling circulations is occurring for daily newspapers, as a recent article by Jon Slattery shows.[4] The Guardian, The Times and Financial Times were the only national daily newspapers to show year-on-year rises in December 2005, according to recently published ABC figures. The Guardian circu-

---

2 Roger Nicholson. Northcliffe sale: a sign of the regional times? *Press Gazette*, 9.12.2005, p. 10.

3 Ian Burrell. Meet the Mail's Online Revolutionary [Andy Hart]. *Independent Media Weekly*, 27.3.2006, p.8.

4 December ABCs: cheer for the Times, Guardian and FT. Published: Friday, January 13, 2006. By Jon Slattery. From the *Press Gazette* Website: http://www.pressgazette.co.uk/article/130106/ abc_cheer_for_times_guardian_and_ft

lation was up by 5.78 per cent on December 2004, the Financial Times by 2.75 per cent and The Times by 1.37 per cent. Sales of the Daily Telegraph in December (2005) dipped below the 900,000 mark to 897,385. The circulation results are less good for the daily "red-tops", with all titles losing sales. The Sun was down 1.9 per cent, The Mirror down 1.29 per cent and the Star down 3.79 per cent. In the mid-market the Daily Express has fallen 10.94 per cent, compared to a drop of only 0.34 per cent in circulation for the Daily Mail.

As for Sunday newspapers, year-on-year, the Daily Star Sunday circulation was down 26.76 per cent, the People down 4.91 per cent and the News of the World down by 4.75 per cent. The Sunday Mirror fared best with a fall in circulation of just 1.54 per cent. There was better news for the quality Sundays, with circulation rises of 7.18 per cent for the Independent on Sunday, 8.8 per cent for the Sunday Herald and 0.64 for the Sunday Times. The Observer in its new Berliner format, launched last week, is believed to have sold more than 500,000 copies when first issued. The results are presented in more detail in Table 3. The combination of greater automation of existing production, and the advance of the audience for newspaper readership via the Internet offer a background proposed changes to the number of staff employed by newspapers. An example of this is the recent decision by the Daily Mirror to reduce its editorial staff.[5]

Online Newspapers: National

We have witnessed the rapid rise recently of online versions of UK newspapers. Examples of the UK national daily newspapers are easily accessible:

- *Guardian Unlimited*: http://www.guardian.co.uk/
- *The Times*: http://www.timesonline.co.uk/uk/
- *The Telegraph*: http://www.telegraph.co.uk/portal/main.jhtml;jsessionid=ERMXVXP-WJORZ3QFIQMFCFFOAVCBQYIV0?view=HOME&grid=P13&menuId =-1&menuItemId=-1&_requestid=176076
- *The Daily Mirror*: http://www.mirror.co.uk/

Many of these online sites have the "look and feel" of printed newspapers, in so far as the layout of screen information is not so very removed from printed newspapers layout. The Daily Mirror website offers news in brief and a look of "file tabs", to enable users to go quickly to a chosen story, and view it in more detail.

Regional Newspapers

The Joint Industry Committee for Regional Press Research (JICREG) has a great deal of data relating to demographic profiles and readerships of newspapers. The JICREG site offers immediate statistics.[6] Searches (without paying a subscription) may be carried out by location, by newspaper, by local authority area, etc. The results can be down loaded. A copy of the search for newspapers for any UK area can be found by loading the data from their website. If one accepts the validity of the sampling methodology, it is clear that printed newspapers, both national and local are read by substantial proportions of the UK population. Additionally, JICREG 'historic topline readership' data can be accessed (see Table 4).[7]

There are certainly hundreds of regional newspapers now available on the Internet via dot UK (".uk") URLs. Newspapers Publishers have grasped the opportunity in reaching out to

5 Dominic Ponsford. Staff Axed at Trinity Mirror Flagship National Titles. Press Gazette 8.12.2005.
6 See: http://www.jicreg.co.uk/ visited 3.4.2006)
7 See: http://jiab.jicreg.co.uk/JIAB.cfm?NoHeader=1 (visited 3.4.2006)

new audiences via the Internet, people who would not necessarily buy a printed newspaper. The first and the last pages of the tables of the February 2006 sample are shown in Table 5, as examples of the depth of data that can be gained. The table provides data on whether the newspaper is Free or Paid For. Across all titles, the balance appears roughly even between and paid for printed newspaper titles. The table provides details of the number of adults reading an average issue of each paper; the percentage of coverage of all adults in the newspaper marketing area; the average number of adults reading each copy of the newspaper. This allows trends to be ascertained and business planning to take place.

Very many regional newspapers, at least hundreds of titles, have online versions. A passing view of the titles of some of the larger publishing groups, such as Johnstone Press[8], DGMT: Northcliffe Group[9]; Newsquest Media Group[10]; Trinity Mirror[11] – all show just how much investment has been made in presenting current news online via the Internet.

"New" News Providers

BBC News: A national institution in the UK, the BBC News website has attracted large amounts of use since its inception. Typical recent use figures are presented at Table 5 – some 1.5 million hits in a day on Headline stories alone. With this level of use, it is interesting to speculate how many users are looking at websites such as BBC News and purchasing paper copies of newspapers.[12]

Web Logs – "BLOGS"

The spread of these has been rapid. There seems to be no end to people's desire to pace their writings on the Web. This desire is more than matched by the curiosity of those who want to read what is written. As many examples are unedited (which remains a valuable, not so say crucial) function of printed newspapers, their value may be limited as measured sources of information. Their advantage is that debate is vigorous, fresh, and often uninhibited. An article in the *Press Gazette* speculates on the current and possible future role of "bloggers" and of journalists in relation to the "blogging community".[13] The role of journalists in providing intermediary editing of information needs to be re-assessed, with links being developed between mainstream news and the ability of users to provide comment on news items. Another recent example which relates to the debate about newspapers' online readership states that online newspapers are not as mature as may be thought.[14] It is by no means true that online sites are as well designed as they might be, and their publishers have to do more to attract and retain users to read their contents. The article notes that the *New York Times* has been considering a service which places some of the texts of its most popular colum-

---

8 Johnston Press plc. See: http://www.johnstonpress.co.uk/Websites.aspx (visited 5.4.2006)

9 DMGT: Northcliffe Newspaper Group Ltd. Regional Sites. See: http://www.dmgt.co.uk/corporatestructure/northcliffenewspapersgroup/nngwebsites/ (visited 5.4.2006)

10 Newsquest Media Group. See: http://www.newsquest.co.uk/portfolio_digital_media.html and follow the link to Audited (visited 5.4.2006)

11 Trinity Mirror plc. Regionals. See: http://www.trinitymirror.com/brands/regionals/ (visited 5.4.2006)

12 BBC News usage: See: http://news.bbc.co.uk/1/shared/spl/hi/newswatch/online_stats/html/17.stm. Visited 27.03.2006)

13 See: Mike Ward. Finding a role in the realm of the bloggers. Press Gazette 23.03.2006. http://www.pressgazette.co.uk/?t=article&l=finding_a_role_in_the_realm_of_the_blogger (visited 3.4.2006.)

14 Editors Weblog-Analysis. Thursday, November 3, 2005. Newspapers' online readership does not make up for declining print circulations... yet. Source: http://www.editorsweblog.org/analysis/2005/11/implications_of_moving_newspapers_online.php (visited March 2006)

nists behind a "paid wall". However, the *Los Angeles Times* and *El Pais* have taken away payments for access, as they may wish to increase use, and increased use attracts more advertising.

Older Runs of Newspapers

There is increasing interest being shown by national newspapers in digitizing their back runs of published newspapers. The Times of London has been a recent notable example.[15] The Scotsman, published in Edinburgh, has also converted its run from its start in 1817.[16] Access to the texts is by subscription. Other projects seem bound to follow soon – competition drives developments. Publishers, at least for UK national newspaper titles, have begun to realize that there may be commercial advantages in offering their archives to a wider public via the Internet. This will act as a counterpoint to the perception in many newspaper groups that "old" newspapers are those published only a year ago.

The Debate about the Future of Newspapers

This topic generates a large quantity of reviews, and comment. In the UK in March 2006, Rupert Murdoch gave a speech in London, in which he gave prominence to the future role of newspapers within the rapidly developing technologies.[17] Murdoch asks the question about what will happen to print journalism when consumers are being offered so many outlets to choose from for their information. His answer is "…that great journalism will always attract readers. The words, pictures, graphics that are the stuff of journalism have to be brilliantly packed; the must feed the mind and the heart. And, crucially, newspapers must give readers a choice of accessing their journalism in the pages of the paper or on websites such as Times online or – and this is important – on any platform that appeals to them, mobile phones, hand-held devices, iPods, whatever." As a sign of his commitment to the future, News International has purchased a company called www.MySpace.com, a networking site which enables people to talk online to each other about whatever interests them. The numbers of users clearly is a great attraction to News International, possibly with regard to future advertising opportunities.

In the same issue of *Independent Media Weekly*, an interview with Bill Gates is published.[18] Gates believes in a future for printed newspapers, and believes that markets still exist for them, for example, in India, where newspaper readership is growing. Gates believes that as regards implementing digital technologies "The Businesses have done very well adopting the digital technologies; UK companies are very international and very competitive markets." Perhaps his most interesting comments are made about the future form of accessing digital information (he believes and has invested much in "the tablet"); and also about the future use of pictures in relation to text – which is why he has invested in developing the Corbis picture agency.

As for digitizing older runs of newspapers, the work has begun, but will take many years of sustained investment to incorporate even the majority of older newspapers into the digital

15 The Times Digital Archive. See: http://www.gale.com/Times/ (visited 5.4.3006)

16 The Scotsman Digital Archive. Every issue of The Scotsman from 1817 – 1950. See: http://archive.scotsman.com/ (visited 5.4.2006)

17 Dynamic Content is Everything. The Independent Media Weekly, 20.3.2006, pp. 8–9 prints an edited version of Rupert Murdoch's speech to the Worshipful Company of Stationers and Newspaper Makers.

18 Where do we go from Here? Ibid. pp.5–7.

environment, to allow us to view online the vast and varied production of thousands of newspapers produced over the last three centuries.

What this all gives to us is the impression of an industry in flux. The one thing we all need to do, is to be active in looking at developments. The position of libraries and archives will be greatly altered by the huge technical developments taking place. In a world where information is frequently seen to be absorbed in short, often staccato spasms of interest, libraries have a real role to offer, in promoting themselves as places where sustained thinking and linking of information, and of its presentation to others, may take place in a neutral environment, to the benefit of all.

Part II. Digitization of Newspapers in the Public Sector: British Library Example

Seen in the context of recent publisher activity to move texts online, the work by the British Library to digitize portions of its older collections is also a first step. There is growing public sector interest in digitizing newspapers. The British Library conducted a pilot project early in 2001. The aim was to see whether older newspapers could be successfully scanned, have their articles zoned, and have OCR applied to articles. A number of issues of four nineteenth and early twentieth century newspapers (two daily, two weekly in publication) were selected for the years 1851, 1886, 1900 and 1918. The work is described in more detail in a recent article.[19] Conversion work was carried out by OCLC and Olivesoftware, and the results are still available today online as an example of what can be achieved.[20]

The British Library, as part of its Collect Britain Project, to include a complete sequential run of one newspaper.[21] The newspaper selected was the *Penny Illustrated Paper*, for the years 1860–1918. This run is an estimated 50,000 pages. The paper of the printed original was in poor condition, so microfilming it provided a surrogate, and digitizing the microfilm enabled the content to be presented to a wider audience.[22] The Collect Britain website was launched in the spring of 2003.

For both these projects, the use of Olivesoftware had the additional advantage of the user being able to benefit from fuzzy logic search features, which, as users key search words, enhances the unedited OCR to improve the likelihood of search words being found. The work on these two projects enabled the Library to plan for a scaling up of activity to digitize more of its historic newspaper collections.

Early, in 2004, The British Library secured funds from the Joint Information Systems Committee (JISC)[23] in the UK to develop further the concept of mass digitization for older newspapers. The British Newspapers Project 1800–1900 Project aims to digitize up to 2 million pages of UK nineteenth century newspapers.[24]

There has been a long gestation period for this project. A description of project progress was given by Jane Shaw at the IFLA General Conference held in Oslo in 2005.[25] Project

---

19 The work and methods used are detailed in: The Digitzation of Historic Newspapers. The British Library Pilot; In: Digital Resources for the Humanities, 2001-2002. Editied by Jean Anderson, et al., pp. 71-87

20 See: http://www.uk.olivesoftware.com/archive/skins/bl/navigator.asp (visited 27.3.2006)

21 For details of Collect Britain, see: http://www.collectbritain.co.uk/ (visited 27.3.2006)

22 To search this newspaper, see: http://www.collectbritain.co.uk/system/paper/ (visited 27.3.2006.)

23 JISC homepage is: http://www.jisc.ac.uk/ (visited 30.3.2006)

24 For details of this Project see: http://www.bl.uk/collections/britishnewspapers1800to1900.html (visited 27.03.2006) and : http://www.jisc.ac.uk/index.cfm?name=digitisation_bln (visited 27.03.2006)

25 World Library and Information Congress: 71st IFLA General Conference and Council. Session 97. Jane

Learning has been valuable and summarized for this paper. Table 6 details some recent experiences and learning in the British Library, and these are offered as a guide to others who are thinking about or planning a newspapers digitization project.

Full production of the digitization work is under way at the time of writing, with the texts planned to be available for users by the end of 2006. Work had to be undertaken simultaneously to:

- Prepare bound volumes for microfilming in the British Library
- Create metadata for transfer at scanning stage onto fuller records in XML attached to page and article level images
- To engage in a procurement of a supplier to undertake all the steps of production after microfilming
- The procurement process had to be conducted via an European Union contract process; this took up to 8 months to realize, with the contract being signed in March 2005.
- Planning for a set of web pages which would act as the platform for users to initially view the collection and to conduct searches of the texts.

In 2005, it became possible to start planning to realize the final portions of the Burney Collection of Newspapers digitization project.[26] The Burney Collection comprises up to 1 million pages of British eighteenth century newspapers. Work has taken place in a number of stages over a number of years. A project is now in hand to ensure the steps necessary to have the pages available via the Internet.

All of this is work in progress. In the world of the Internet that we now find ourselves within, we shall all need to be responsive to technical developments, and also alert to react to changes requested by users, wherever they may be.

May 2006

Shaw. 10 Billion Words: The British Library British Newspapers 1800-1900 Project: Some guidelines for large-scale newspaper digitisation See: http://www.ifla.org/IV/ifla71/Programme.htm (visited 5.4.206)

26 Burney Collection of Newspapers. See: http://www.bl.uk/collections/burney.html and http://www.ala.org/ala/acrl/acrlpubs/crljournal/backissues1999b/september99/carpenterbook.htm; and http://www.rlg.org/legacy/preserv/diginews/v6-n3-faq.html; and http://www.cbsr.ucr.edu/Burney_newspaper_digitization_project.html (visited 5.4.2006)

UK Paid Regional Weeklies

	Newspaper Title	Circ	% change	Actively purchased	Full rate sale
1	Kent Messenger Series	55,109	-4.1%	100.0%	100.0%
2	Mansfield Chad Series	48,467	-1.2%	100.0%	100.0%
3	West Briton Series	48,357	-4.6%	99.9%	100.0%
4	Barnsley Chronicle	44,544	-0.3%	100.0%	100.0%
5	Derbyshire Times Series	42,290	-3.2%	100.0%	100.0%
6	Hereford Times Series	41,799	-2.3%	100.0%	100.0%
7	Essex Chronicle Series	41,376	-5.3%	98.6%	96.1%
8	Isle of Wight County Press	40,415	-1.5%	100.0%	100.0%
9	Western Gazette Series	39,849	-4.4%	99.2%	99.3%
10	Cornish Guardian Series	39,815	-2.9%	100.0%	95.7%
11	Cumberland News Series	37,361	-3.6%	100.0%	100.0%
12	Chichester Observer Series	36,940	-2.8%	100.0%	100.0%
13	Kent and Sussex Courier Series	36,088	-4.5%	98.0%	92.5%
14	Doncaster Free Press	36,079	-4.4%	100.0%	100.0%
15	Warrington Guardian	35,766	-2.8%	100.0%	99.8%
16	Rotherham & South Yorkshire Advertiser	34,252	0.9%	100.0%	100.0%
17	Surrey Advertiser Series	33,548	-6.0%	100.0%	100.0%
18	North Devon Journal Series	33,458	-3.8%	100.0%	99.3%
19	Wakefield Express Series	33,149	-3.3%	100.0%	100.0%
20	Westmorland Gazette	33,014	-1.9%	100.0%	100.0%

Tab. 1. Paid Regional Weeklies and Free Regional Weeklies.
Top 20 titles by circulation
Source: http://www.newspapersoc.org.uk/Default.aspx?page=1548

UK Free Regional Weeklies

	Newspaper Title	Distribution	Average pagination	Ave % advertising
1	Manchester Metro News Series	309,516	80	73
2	Nottingham & Long Eaton Topper	210,023	53	83
3	Nottingham Recorder	149,675	55	81
4	Southampton Advertiser (Jul 25 - Jan 1)	138,711	32	76
5	Herald & Post Edinburgh (Aug 8 - Jan 1)	138,348	57	85
6	Wirral Globe Series	134,430	84	71
7	The Glaswegian Series	129,646	52	57
8	Coventry Observer	120,713	59	74
9	Derby Express Series	120,192	56	74
10	Coventry Citizen	119,889	55	78
11	The Press Series	113,464	93	77
12	Sheffield Weekly Gazette Series	108,231	28	71
13	Sutton Guardian Series	107,565	81	62
14	Croydon Guardian	104,867	70	58
15	North Staffs Advertiser Series	104,470	53	77
16	KM Extra (Bromley)	100,795	96	48
17	Milton Keynes Citizen	100,459	308	79
18	Croydon Borough Post	99,301	140	88
19	Bromley News Shopper	99,062	93	67
20	Herald & Post - Luton & Dunstable (Oct 24 - Jan 1)	96,518	144	81

Tab. 1 (cont.). Paid Regional Weeklies and Free Regional Weeklies.
Top 20 titles by circulation
Source: http://www.newspapersoc.org.uk/Default.aspx?page=1548

UK Paid Regional Mornings (Mon-Sat)

	Newspaper Title	Circ	% change	Actively purchased	Full rate sale
1	Daily Record - Scotland*	456,237	-4.8%	n/a	97.3%
2	Aberdeen - Press & Journal	84,612	-3.7%	99.0%	97.4%
3	Dundee Courier & Advertiser	78,010	-3.7%	99.8%	99.9%
4	Glasgow Herald*	75,794	-3.8%	n/a	99.1%
5	Norwich - Eastern Daily Press	69,355	-2.4%	100.0%	99.7%
6	Scotsman	66,462	-2.8%	n/a	90.1%
7	Leeds - Yorkshire Post	54,730	-5.6%	100.0%	98.5%
8	Darlington - The Northern Echo	53,481	-3.9%	100.0%	99.0%
9	Irish News	48,323	-3.4%	99.9%	99.9%
10	Bristol - Western Daily Press	47,306	-1.6%	98.2%	97.4%
11	Plymouth - Western Morning News	44,767	-3.1%	98.0%	97.7%
12	Wales - The Western Mail	42,956	-0.7%	100.0%	99.0%
13	Newcastle-Upon-Tyne Journal	40,945	-1.7%	95.0%	93.5%
14	Daily Post (Wales)	39,595	-3.0%	100.0%	100.0%
15	Ipswich - East Anglian Daily Times	37,338	-5.0%	100.0%	98.7%
16	Ulster - News Letter	28,616	0.7%	97.6%	95.6%
17	Liverpool Daily Post	18,741	-7.2%	100.0%	100.0%
18	Birmingham Post	13,002	1.5%	81.2%	80.4%
19	Paisley Daily Express	10,683	-3.7%	100.0%	100.0%
20	Daily Ireland	10,017	n/a	87.2%	86.5%

Note: Mon-Fri figures are used for titles not published on Saturday
* Reported as a national by ABC

UK Free Regional Mornings

	Newspaper Title	Distr	% change
1	Metro London	490,423	0.00%
2	Metro Scotland	117,891	-0.02%
3	Metro North West	109,356	0.50%
4	Metro Midlands	86,588	1.04%
5	Metro Yorkshire	75,681	-0.13%
6	City AM *	69,035	n/a
7	Herald AM *	63,077	n/a
8	Metro North East	53,653	-0.55%
9	Metro East Midlands	43,217	4.49%
10	Metro South West	28,265	9.56%
	* Dec 2005	1,137,186	n/a

* Reported as a national by ABC

Tab. 2. Paid and free Morning Regional Papers. Top 20 titles by circulation
Source: Average Net Circulation, July – December 2005

UK Paid Regional Mornings (Mon-Fri)

	Newspaper Title	Circ	% change	Actively purchased	Full rate sale
1	Daily Record - Scotland*	456,237	-4.8%	n/a	97.3%
2	Aberdeen - Press & Journal	84,908	-3.6%	98.9%	97.4%
3	Dundee Courier & Advertiser	77,511	-3.7%	99.8%	99.9%
4	Glasgow Herald*	75,794	-3.8%	n/a	99.1%
5	Norwich - Eastern Daily Press	67,441	-2.3%	100.0%	99.8%
6	Scotsman	66,462	-2.8%	n/a	90.1%
7	Darlington - The Northern Echo	53,988	-4.0%	100.0%	99.0%
8	Irish News	48,554	-3.4%	99.9%	100.0%
9	Leeds - Yorkshire Post	48,345	-6.7%	100.0%	98.2%
10	Bristol - Western Daily Press	44,128	-1.9%	98.0%	97.3%
11	Plymouth - Western Morning News	41,733	-3.5%	97.8%	97.5%
12	Wales - The Western Mail	40,188	-0.5%	100.0%	98.9%
13	Daily Post (Wales)	38,648	-3.1%	100.0%	100.0%
14	Newcastle-Upon-Tyne Journal	37,798	-0.9%	94.0%	92.4%
15	Ipswich - East Anglian Daily Times	36,773	-5.1%	100.0%	98.8%
16	Ulster - News Letter	25,957	0.7%	97.4%	95.2%
17	Liverpool Daily Post	18,838	-6.9%	100.0%	100.0%
18	Birmingham Post	13,366	3.3%	79.7%	79.0%
19	Paisley Daily Express	10,856	-3.8%	100.0%	100.0%
20	Daily Ireland	10,046	n/a	87.2%	86.5%

Note: Mon-Sat figures are used for titles reported as nationals by ABC

- Reported as a national by ABC

Tab. 2 (cont.). Paid and free Morning Regional Papers. Top 20 titles by circulation
Source: Average Net Circulation, July – December 2005

UK national newspapers circulation for December 2005					
	Current month Dec 05	Last Month Nov 05	mth/mth +/- %	Last Year Dec 04	Yr/Yr +/- %
National morning popular					
Daily Mirror	1,678,997	1,671,950	0.42	1,700,902	-1.29
Daily Record	438,652	442,546	-0.88	452,357	-3.03
Daily Star	779,556	795,308	-1.98	810,238	-3.79
The Sun	3,119,757	3,192,976	-2.29	3,180,141	-1.90
Total of average daily net circulation	6,016,962	6,102,780	-1.41	6,143,638	-2.06
National morning mid market					
Daily Express	800,403	796,592	0.48	898,697	-10.94
The Daily Mail	2,311,023	2,341,437	-1.30	2,318,824	-0.34
Total of average daily net circulation	3,111,426	3,138,029	-0.85	3,217,521	-3.30
National morning quality					
The Daily Telegraph	897,385	903,405	-0.67	904,647	-0.80
Financial Times	439,563	431,806	1.80	427,808	2.75
The Herald	74,328	76,159	-2.40	77,336	-3.89
The Guardian	380,693	401,029	-5.07	359,891	5.78
The Independent	250,195	263,449	-5.03	252,552	-0.93
The Scotsman	63,263	65,392	-3.26	64,986	-2.65
The Times	661,400	691,283	-4.32	652,442	1.37
Total of average daily net circulation	2,766,827	2,832,523	-2.32	2,739,662	0.99
Overall total of average daily net circulation	11,895,215	12,073,332	-1.48	12,100,821	-1.70
National morning sporting					
Racing Post	72,994	74,570	-2.11	75,223	-2.96
London evening					
Evening Standard	321,227	346,489	-7.29	347,523	-7.57
National morning group					
The Daily Mirror / Daily Record	2,117,649	2,114,496	0.15	2,153,259	-1.65

Tab. 3. National Newspaper Circulation, December 2005.
Source: Press Gazette Website at
http://www.pressgazette.co.uk/article/130106/abc_cheer_for_times_guardian_and_ft

	Current month Dec 05	Last Month Nov 05	mth/mth +/- %	Last Year Dec 04	Yr/Yr +/- %
National sunday popular					
Daily Star Sunday	382,231	395,708	-3.41	521,869	-26.76
News of the World	3,509,189	3,733,025	-6.00	3,684,161	-4.75
Sunday Mail	530,996	538,971	-1.48	563,732	-5.81
Sunday Mirror	1,513,323	1,421,348	6.47	1,537,006	-1.54
The People	886,235	870,389	1.82	932,015	-4.91
Sunday Sport	139,489	147,241	-5.26	149,753	-6.85
Total of average Sunday net circulation	6,961,463	7,106,682	-2.04	7,388,536	-5.78
National sunday mid market					
Sunday Express	809,041	871,312	-7.15	928,839	-12.90
The Mail on Sunday	2,215,765	2,337,740	-5.22	2,335,266	-5.12
Total of average Sunday net circulation	3,024,806	3,209,052	-5.74	3,264,105	-7.33
National sunday quality					
Independent on Sunday	219,040	225,629	-2.92	204,358	7.18
The Business	178,984	171,983	4.07	213,440	-16.14
The Observer	430,403	436,882	-1.48	433,934	-0.81
Scotland on Sunday	71,691	83,449	-14.09	73,711	-2.74
Sunday Herald	60,465	61,452	-1.61	55,567	8.81
The Sunday Telegraph	642,256	714,992	-10.17	687,435	-6.57
The Sunday Times	1,313,258	1,395,046	-5.86	1,304,919	0.64
Total of average Sunday net circulation	2,916,097	3,089,433	-5.61	2,973,364	-1.93
Overall total of average Sunday net circulation	12,902,366	13,405,167	-3.75	13,626,005	-5.31

Tab. 3 (cont.). National Newspaper Circulation, December 2005

Newspaper	Type	Freq	Format	Pages	Ad%	A/M	TSR	Adult AIR	AIR%	RPC
Aberdeen & District Independent	F	W	T	62	73	M		114335	54.9	1.4
ABERDEEN CITIZEN	F	W	T	42	81	A	16	81114	52	1.1
ABERDEEN EVENING EXPRESS	P	E	T			A	34	121406	29.7	2.1
Abergavenny Chronicle	P	W	B	56	65	M		23341	32.5	2.5
ACCRINGTON OBSERVER	P	W	T			A	34	34172	37.5	2.3
ADNEWS - WILLENHALL, WEDNESBURY,DARLSTON	F	W	T	24	55	A	20	24495	45.6	1.3
ADVERTISER - BARROW	F	W	T	38	93	A	13	60790	77.2	1.5
AIRDRIE & COATBRIDGE ADVERTISER	P	W	T			A	28	51356	35.7	2.6
ALDERSHOT MAIL SERIES	P	W	B	44	35	A	16	38412	11.6	3.0
ALDERSHOT NEWS SERIES	P	W	B	88	67	A	18	74948	22.7	3.7
Alfreton & Ripley Echo	F	W	T	17	63	M		19782	39.5	1.5
ALFRETON CHAD	F	W	T	54	79	A	19	26837	60.9	1.5
Alloa & Hillfoots Advertiser Journal	P	W	T			M		22748	33.9	2.5
ALLOA & HILLFOOTS WEE COUNTY NEWS	P	W	T	40	45	A	22	27262	67.8	3.8
Alton Gazette & Alresford Advertiser	P	W	T	16	72	M		11004	23.4	2.7
Andover Advertiser	P	W	T			M		45924	43.9	2.7
Andover Advertiser Midweek	F	W	T	27	80	M		36075	47.4	1.5
Annandale Group	P	W	T			M		28707	95	2.6
Arbroath Herald	P	W	T	32	35	M		25497	38.2	2.5
Ardrossan & Saltcoats Herald	P	W	T			M		42677	67.7	2.3
Ashbourne News Telegraph	P	W	B	43	29	M		15537	29	2.5
Ashby Coalville & Swadlincote Times	P	W	T	40		M		27865	30.6	2.6
ASHFORD & TENTERDEN ADSCENE - KRN	F	W	T	59	70	A	13	53323	53.9	1.7
ASHFORD KM EXTRA	F	W	T	49	78	A	15	55345	73.9	1.7
Ayr Advertiser	P	W	T			M		13295	13.3	2.5
Ayrshire Extra Group	F	W	T	44	84	M		95684	44.8	1.4
AYRSHIRE POST SERIES	P	W	T			A	37	82189	67.3	2.8
Ayrshire World Group	F	W	T			M		33870	26.1	1.4
Banbury Cake	F	W	T	47	79	M		52968	58.7	1.5
BANBURY GUARDIAN	P	W	B	64	68	A	35	50003	42	2.5
BANBURY REVIEW	F	W	T	36	60	A	13	45458	48.1	1.3
Banffshire Journal	P	W	T			M		12115	34.6	2.5
Bangor Mail (Ch Series)	F	W	T	106	64	M		17828	56.9	1.6
BARKING & DAGENHAM POST	P	W	T	96	62	A		65952	17.5	4.5
Barking & Dagenham Yellow Advertiser	F	W	T	27	73	M		27489	37.4	1.5
Barnet Hendon Press	F	W	T	100	78	M		176099	57.6	1.5
BARNSLEY CHRONICLE	P	W	B	120	67	A	42	134985	13.6	3.0
BARNSLEY INDEPENDENT	F	W	T	36	90	A	22	100271	62.5	1.5
BARROW - NORTH WEST EVENING MAIL	P	E	T			A	25	55904	51.7	2.8
Barry & District News	P	W	T		35	M		16223	28	2.5
BARRY POST	F	W	T	28	81	A	13	31661	61.6	1.4
BASILDON & SOUTHEND ECHO	P	E	T			A	23	129313	25.1	3.4
Basildon Recorder	F	W	T	72	88	M		78915	72.8	1.4
BASILDON YELLOW ADVERTISER	F	W	T	116	84	A	17	90182	64.5	1.6
Basingstoke Extra	F	W	T	78	59	M		69605	59.3	1.5
Basingstoke Monday Gazette	P	W	T			M		26501	21.7	2.6
Basingstoke Thursday Weekend Gazette	P	W	T			M		63601	52	2.6
BATH CHRONICLE	P	E	T			A	27	37400	12.5	2.7
Bath Times	F	W	T	46	71	M		47426	43.9	1.5
Bearsden Milngavie & Glasgow Extra	F	W	T	34	79	M		42110	59.7	1.4
BECCLES & BUNGAY JOURNAL	P	W	T	56	55	A	30	16833	27	2.4
Bedford Times & Citizen Group	F	W	T	196	80	M		121964	65.8	1.5
Bedfordshire On Sunday	F	S	T			M		161039	69.6	1.5
BEDWORTH ECHO	P	W	T			A	20	10625	4.63	3.2
Belper News	P	W	T	33	43	M		11453	8.45	2.6
Berrow's Worcester Journal	F	W	T	49	78	M		71162	39	1.5

Tab. 4. Joint Industry Committee for Regional Press Research. Top line readership data for all JICREG subscribers based on February 2006 data release

Newspaper	Type	Freq	Format	Pages	Ad%	A/M	TSR	Adult AIR	AIR%	RPC
WEST WILTSHIRE ADVERTISER	F	W	T	78	77	A	15	70658	49.1	1.5
WESTERN DAILY PRESS	P	M	T			A	39	93252	3.58	1.9
WESTERN GAZETTE	P	W	T			A	41	121005	20.8	2.9
WESTERN MORNING NEWS	P	M	T			A	36	113517	5.53	2.5
Western Telegraph	P	W	T			M		64361	54.6	2.4
Westmorland Gazette	P	W	B			M		85305	71.9	2.6
WESTON & SOMERSET MERCURY	P	W	T	124	63	A	31	43329	22.6	2.7
WESTON & WORLE NEWS	F	W	T	106	77	A	28	60558	76.4	1.6
WESTON SUPER MARE ADMAG	F	W	T	53	97	A	18	64338	70.3	1.4
Weymouth & Dorchester Advertiser	F	W	T	22	72	M		52898	61	1.5
Wharfe Valley Times	F	W	T	57	75	M		67191	68.4	1.5
Wharfedale & Airedale Observer	P	W	B			M		14521	29	2.7
Whitby Gazette – Friday	P	W	T	48	58	M		32077	51	2.7
Whitby Gazette - Tuesday	P	W	T	48	58	M		16076	35.9	2.7
Whitchurch Herald	P	W	T			M		13569	64.9	2.7
WHITEHAVEN NEWS	P	W	B			A	33	38568	68.7	2.2
WIGAN OBSERVER	P	W	T	64	42	A	25	76597	37.2	4.2
WIGAN REPORTER	F	W	T	104	78	A	25	101631	58	1.6
WILMSLOW EXPRESS FREE	F	W	T	79	81	A	24	22838	65.7	1.5
Wilmslow Express Paid	P	W	T	74	80	M		5568	16.9	2.7
Wilts & Gloucestershire Standard Series	P	W	B			M		40612	39.7	2.4
Wiltshire Gazette & Herald	P	W	B			M		72833	18	2.6
Wiltshire Star	F	W	T	75	89	M		72398	38.4	1.5
Wiltshire Times	P	W	T			M		50435	15.2	2.6
Wimbledon Guardian Series	F	W	T	45	65	M		76265	36.6	1.4
Wirral Globe	F	W	T	90	71	M		194933	74.2	1.4
WIRRAL NEWS GROUP	F	W	T			A	22	247196	94.1	1.6
WISHAW PRESS	P	W	T			A	30	34528	30.6	3.1
Witney Gazette	P	W	T			M		19620	24.3	2.6
Woking Informer	F	W	T	36	80	M		55585	58.1	1.5
WOKING NEWS & MAIL SERIES	P	W	B	144	52	A	18	39366	23.7	3.8
WOKING REVIEW SERIES	F	W	T	100	77	A	15	82935	70.2	1.8
WOKINGHAM TIMES	P	W	B	120	66	A	24	24482	10.7	2.7
WOLVERHAMPTON AD NEWS	F	W	T	45	66	A	21	96475	50.9	1.4
WOLVERHAMPTON CHRONICLE	F	W	T	74	81	A	18	112774	61.4	1.6
Worcester News	P	E	T			M		50246	19.8	2.6
Worcester Standard	F	W	T	60	71	M		74005	68	1.5
WORKSOP GUARDIAN SERIES	P	W	T	80	60	A	31	45950	31.1	2.7
WORKSOP TRADER	F	W	T	50	80	A	17	54949	79.7	1.6
Worthing & District Advertiser	F	W	T			M		103793	54.3	1.4
Worthing Herald Group	P	W	T	112	44	M		80999	40.7	2.5
WREXHAM LEADER	F	W	B	38	73	A	24	84264	76.9	1.8
Wrexham Mail	F	W	T	51	63	M		56180	48.1	1.5
WYMONDHAM & ATTLEBOROUGH MERCURY	F	W	T	65	65	A	19	24971	48	1.5
Yeovil Express	F	W	T	40	58	M		49333	52.6	1.5
YEOVIL TIMES	F	W	T	51	84	A	18	64223	52.2	1.4
York Star	F	W	T	39	85	M		80980	51.3	1.5
Yorkshire Gazette & Herald	P	W	B			M		31988	7.8	2.4
YORKSHIRE POST	P	M	B	89	22	A		152724	3.72	3.0
Your Leek Paper	P	W	T			M		11869	3.84	2.6

Tab. 4 (cont.). Joint Industry Committee for Regional Press Research. Top line readership data for all JICREG subscribers based on February 2006 data release

Type	Paid, free or combined (part paid/part free)
Frequency	Morning, evening, Sunday or weekly
Format	Tabloid or broadsheet
Pages	Average tabloid pagination per issue
Ad %	Average advertising percentage per issue
TSR	Time spent reading in minutes per issue. This data is only available for titles that have conducted research.
A/M	Whether the readership data is Actual, based on a survey conducted to JICREG standards by the paper, or the JICREG models. Titles with actual data are also shown in capitals.
Adult AIR	The number of adults reading an average issue of the newspaper.
% cover	The percentage coverage of all adults within the newspaper marketing area.
RPC	The average number of adults reading each copy of the newspaper.

MOST POPULAR STORIES - UK EDITION	
Headline	**Page views**
Scientist defends clinical trials	294,000
Pitt and Jolie 'to wed in Italy'	270,000
Tories planning party cash reform	251,000
Four guilty of Mary-Ann's murder	199,000
Final farewell for Celtic legend	162,000
FTSE breaks through 6,000 barrier	135,000
Body Shop agrees L'Oreal takeover	126,000
Jackson shuts down Neverland home	125,000
Hackers get Mac running Windows	121,000
US launches 'major Iraq assault'	121,000
Partial journals win for prince	117,000
MOST POPULAR STORIES - WORLD EDITION	
Headline	**Page views**
Pitt and Jolie 'to wed in Italy'	109,000
US launches 'major Iraq assault'	106,000
Jackson shuts down Neverland home	97,000
Weekly world news quiz	73,000
US evangelicals warn Republicans	71,000
How US assault grabbed global attention	58,000
Mandela the teenage pig stealer	56,000
'No sign' of Milosevic poisoning	54,000
Hackers get Mac running Windows	50,000
Low carb diet health risk fears	49,000
Doubt cast on Venus catastrophe	45,000
TOP E-MAILED STORIES	
Headline	**E-mails sent**
Hackers get Mac running Windows	2,519
Low carb diet health risk fears	1,749
Body Shop agrees L'Oreal takeover	1,035
Hospital probed over baby release	970
Pitt and Jolie 'to wed in Italy'	883
US evangelicals warn Republicans	748
In pictures: Crazy cycle lanes	712
Film to celebrate maths genius	704
Scientist defends clinical trials	620
Mandela the teenage pig stealer	606
Disabled users to test websites	574

Tab. 5. The most popular stories requested from the BBC News website on Friday 17 March 2006.
Source: http://news.bbc.co.uk/1/shared/spl/hi/newswatch/online_stats/html/17.stm

Original newspapers

- Preparation is the key: in depth survey and assessment of the physical characteristics of source material to set a benchmark for later QA.
- Page counting and weeding out of duplicate issues and variant editions (as decided for each title) necessary to produce our work packages and monitor progress against our overall total.
- Consider concept of 'Set Asides' – titles too fragile to film as benchmarks for the future. Tolerate and accept gaps in full runs and do not seek to fill these until later on.
- The format of a long run will often change during a century, so page counting is vital to understand the structure of a long run.
- The BL's collection of nineteenth century newspapers is in better shape than predicted, with less than 2% unfit to film. However, due to the mechanical processes of scanning (too slow and too harsh for vulnerable fragile source material) it was decided to digitize from microfilm.
- Define criteria for selection early on to guide User Panel deliberations.
- An early decision was made to re-film as many newspapers as possible – to secure the greatest possible quality for all the other production steps.

Intellectual Property Rights

- Intellectual Property Rights – address issues early, take a robust and consistent approach and maintain an ongoing dialogue with the newspaper industry.
- the amount of preparation work is real: establishing which titles are deceased or incorporated; writing letters to publishers

Community and Consultation

- Conduct an online consultation with user communities during the funding process. A large potential list of titles meant we could not focus.
- Place a User Panel, at the core of the project, to act as ambassadors and take ownership.
- User Panel pre-selected our potential 2 million pages, followed by an online consultation that did not suggest completely new and untried titles (apart from Eire ones)
- Manage future expectations through online endorsement of titles lists by user communities.
- User Panel participates in the website design

Microfilm

- Consider the quality of your microfilm [re-filming a proportion of your content will add value in the longer term] in order to adapt many of the risks around heterogeneous originals and variable quality microfilm which should in turn aid image capture.
- Filming for digitization is highly desirable to optimise the quality of the scan and of the OCR. This means one page per frame; improved resolution levels.
- Aspirational production targets do not work. Sustainable targets based on real work done should be regularly reviewed and re-profiled as necessary to forecast trends.

Tab. 6. Recent experience and learning from the British Newspapers 1800–1900 Digitization Project, 2004–2006.

- Use "Doubles" or intentional second microfilm exposures of a page as a quality assurance technique, after weighing this up in relation to efficient workflows.

Procurement

- A framework contract for the digitization of newspapers was created via an EU tendering process – this was time consuming, but once done, no new contract will be needed for further call off orders

- The Framework contract also ensures consistency of documentation, of templates, and of methods, for later projects.
- Supplier is responsible for QA on scans once re-filming is done

Metadata

- Keep metadata simple to enhance prospects for interoperability in future
- In-house QA team creates benchmarks for engaging with the original printed structures (pagination, format, condition of paper)
- creating subject categories for newspaper article mark-up is new for a publicly funded project

Staffing

- The posts of Selection Co-Ordinator, Project Analyst (to provide management information) and Quality Specialist have proved most necessary to success to date, and these functions will need to be continued.
- The Project Manager is essential to success of managing the whole process and to deliver the product

Newspaper Selection

- There have been three criteria aimed for and applied in the British Newspapers 1800-1900 Project
- All of the UK is to be covered
- All of the century is to be covered
- The complete run of a newspaper is digitized, once selected

Key Lesson

This is the need, once scans are made, to ensure the best mark up (zoning) of newspaper articles within each page before OCR. At this time, completely automated allocation of mark up (zoning) of newspaper articles is not possible. It is preferable for teams of people to do markup manually, to achieve greater levels of accuracy to a BL specification.

Tab. 6 (cont.). Recent experience and learning from the British Newspapers 1800–1900 Digitization Project, 2004–2006

THE PRESENT PAST – THE HISTORY OF NEWSPAPER DIGITISATION IN FINLAND

Majlis Bremer-Laamanen

National Library of Finland

Our digitised historical newspaper collections and the born digital ones are connecting the users to places, questions, nations and human life over centuries. Incidents from the past are suddenly easily accessible. The past is living in the present.

I will give you a short glimpse into the past and present of the very early Historical Nordic Newspaper Project – one of the pioneers in digitising historical newspapers – which began in 1998 - the same year when Google was born. I will also shortly discuss the popularity of Newspapers in the Nordic countries and the feedback that we have got from our users of the Finnish Historical Newspaper Library http://digi.lib.helsinki.fi.

The Nordic Historical Newspaper Library – TIDEN was launched in 2001 and it celebrates its fifth anniversary this year. The website is http://tiden.kb.se.

The participating countries have altogether a population of 23 million inhabitants of which 5 million live in Finland.

Newspapers

Newspapers are perhaps astonishingly, still the most important media in Finland. The Norwegian national library tells us that Norway is the country with the largest newspaper reading population. We can say that newspapers have a very high status in all the Nordic countries.

Way of Life in Finland

The average use of newspapers in Finland is almost an hour per person per day and it has not diminished.[1] The daily paper is a way of life. It is delivered to your front door in the morning, to be enjoyed with a cup of coffee or tea. It gives the reader a moment of peace and comfort together with the national and local news before the day starts. Free newspapers are delivered on the subways and trains on your way to work.

Media Channels

The look and feel of many newspapers have changed in appearance to a modern outlook, tabloid format, actively reaching out to its customers and the youth at schools, delivering information, science, leisure and advertisements. Surprisingly perhaps, the heavy users of computers are heavy newspaper readers. Over ninety per cent of young Finns read a newspaper each week.[2]

---

1 www.sanomalehdet.fi/en/tietoa/index.html, page 2.
2 www.sanomalehdet.fi/en/tietoa/index.html page 3.

Newspapers are the media channel that daily is best reaching the Finns. Hence, over half of all money spent on advertising is in the newspaper business. It is for example the major channel for information on stock exchange today.[3]

Newspapers are the most important research media in Finland. They are the prime source of investigation in more than half of the research projects in Finland and almost in half in Sweden. They are used as source material for research in the fields of media, history, political science, sociology, pedagogy, art, business, natural sciences and technology.[4]

As such the interest in our historical newspapers is high. Newspapers are the most used individual group of the Finnish national library collection.

The Role of Online Newspapers

Online newspapers are produced all over the world, also in the Nordic Countries. These papers are usually available via the National Libraries. We have about one hundred newspaper titles on the web among the 900 periodicals in Finland.

Surprisingly the role of the Finnish online paper is to support the paper version. Thus their monetary importance is still quite low. These papers are improving and the overall development in knowledge society will influence their use. Also paper look-alike editions of newspapers are available on the web in Finland since 2002.[5]

The Nordic Historical Newspaper Project

The newspaper holdings have been considered a nightmare for digitisation. There are reasons for this belief. The size of newspapers grew in the late 1900th century to four times the size of a tabloid of today. The poor print, the poor quality of paper and the use of Gothic Fraktur and Roman text in the Nordic countries made it a challenge for digitisation. Even more of a challenge was the Optical Character Recognition needed to make the text searchable from the image of the paper.

Digital newspaper projects are a hot topic in Europe and around the world today as we can see at this congress.

The libraries participating in the Nordic TIDEN project, the pioneer in this field, were the Royal Library of Stockholm, the National Library of Norway and the State and University Library of Århus. The coordinator for the project was Helsinki University Library, the Centre for Microfilming and Conservation.

The aim of the TIDEN-project was:

- to test criteria for microfilm as a platform for digitisation and full text search;
- to build production lines for the digitisation of newspapers;
- to integrate the digitisation to the libraries ordinary functions;
- to give a continuous widening access to newspapers out of copyright.

Today the amount of online pages has risen from 400,000 at launch to 1.6 million. In Finland, Sweden and Norway full text search is available.

---

3 Hufvudstadsbladet, 2005, April; www.sanomalehdet/en/tietoa/ index.fi, page 3.

4 www.sanomalehdet.fi/suomenlehdistö/fi.

5 www.sanomalehdet/en/tietoa/index.shtml, page 4.

Some Important Factors

The User

The user is even more important today than when the project began. We did look at two aspects relating to the user: the demand of the material and user-friendly solutions. In Finland we made a survey to the libraries about the most needed material and the demand for digitised newspapers was outstanding.

User friendly solutions again relates to good readability, to the interface as it should be easy to use and to the content which should be easy to find. There are of course many decisions behind these and other user friendly solutions. In Finland we are dealing with image quality, good searchability tools:

- high quality preparation and microfilming;
- greyscale digitisation of newspapers;
- full text search and article search;
- TIFF and PDF format;
- Highlighting of words;
- Easy use: Google-like.

Long term preservation all along the process

Metadata should be gathered all along the process. Technical metadata from the scanning, metadata of the document structure like articles and if chosen also sub-articles, writers, text coordinates for the words in the text after OCR-recognition and so on.

The establishment of the metadata structure is quite time consuming. But it is essential that it is gathered and delivered in a standard format like TIFF or mets-xml for preservation purposes.

The past processing procedures include the importation of the material into the database and the search options available, like fuzzy search because of the old language or article search possibilities.

Economy

Financially it is a wonder that we have come this far. The first year of the TIDEN project was funded by Nordic Council for Scientific Information with altogether 10.000 €, growing to 40.000 € for the next years. The Finnish Newspaper Library was also funded from the Ministry of Education, which made it possible for us to extend the project.

The economical situation forced us to think very cost-effectively and carefully about our processes. The most cost-effective way is to process large amounts of material with the highest possible quality. In the long run it is the obtained user satisfactory that gives credit to the site.

Automation

When dealing with large collections like newspapers the production has to be as fully automated as possible. This was one of the aims when TIDEN started. The possibilities to do so are far better today than five years ago. Today we are changing our half automated processes to a faster automated process. We are now using the DocWorks by CCS and we are looking forward to see the results on the handling of 1 million pages by the end of this year. We are licensing the software and handling the metadata structure inhouse.

The Process

The first step in the production line is the digitisation of newspapers, from microfilm or from the original. Newspapers have been a main target for the reformatting programmes in Finland, Sweden, Norway and Denmark since 1950. This makes it possible for us to use microfilm as intermediary for digitisation if the film quality is high enough.

The process of digitising newspapers includes

- Microfilming: refilming the newspapers if the quality of the present microfilms is not good enough;
- Digitisation: scanning of the microfilms; in black and white or grey scale
- OCR: conversion of the images to text files; requires many adjustments and training of the software;
- Identification: of the title, issue, date, pages and attachments requires some human treatment
- Database import: by a separate software

IFLA Guidance

When using microfilm as intermediary the quality of the original newspaper and the microfilm is the key to success. Some advice is given in «Guidance on the best practice for microfilming of newspapers in preparation for possible future digitisation», 2003. English, French, Spanish and Chinese versions are available on the IFLA-net.

The Guidance was based on the information gathered within the TIDEN project. Information is also available on the TIDEN web-page at http://tiden.se.

Goals today ?

Our goals in Finland are to require:

- an industrial production environment
- an automated optical character recognition (OCR) of both Fraktur and Roman text even within a page
- highest possible quality
- highlighting of search words on the newspaper page
- cost effectiveness
- speed of the process
- xml-METS-standard (Library of Congress)

The results of the OCR conversion in Finland and Sweden have shown that there are several factors influencing the quality of the conversion, the most important of them being the text font, language and reduction rate. From the very start of the TIDEN-project it was obvious that a hundred per cent OCR conversion is impossible. Due to the old language and the great mass of text proofreading was not our way to enhanced search. It was thus decided that the ASCII versions of the text would be used for searching purposes only. The basic tool for the users was the digital facsimile of the original pages. A retrieval ware with fuzzy search possibilities was chosen in Sweden and Finland to identify the search words even if one to three letters would differ from the word sought for. The search tool processes the words as bit-strings and uses pattern recognition to find matches.

he speed and automation of the production environment is essential when comparing the process 5-8 years ago to the possibilities today. The automated processes offer the coordinates to each word in the paper. Thus users get better service as the words are highlighted. Other improvements are available. Images are of a better quality as the microfilm scanners and the OCR-software are able to handle greyscale images automatically. Previously, Roman text had to be especially trained for the OCR-software. Now we are looking at a breakthrough where the text is interpreted automatically.

Today OCR is still done with the Finereader program that we used from the start. It is now included in the DocWorks by CCS mentioned earlier. The process is still not fully automated but is much faster than the half automated system we used before. The former separate parts like OCR and metadata input are now included in the DocWorks.

The Site

You can find the Finnish Historical Newspaper Library via Google or directly via the portals mentioned. You can browse by choosing a paper, year, month and day.

It is more convenient to search via full text search by choosing for instance Salt Lake City and you will find for example Dagens Nyheter from 9 August, 1877 page 2 describing the important news from Utah at this time in history. You will also find descriptions of the beautiful city with cows walking freely around in the streets and drinking water from the ditches.

An article index in Finnish is included in the Newspaper Library. It originally consisted of approximately 110 typewritten volumes. The index had classified Finnish newspaper articles by persons, subjects and places from 1771 to 1890 and covers thus the whole period of the Library. By using the index you can go directly to the newspaper including the article in question.

Feedback

Ms. Tiina Hölttä from the National Library made a study on the feedback gathered during four years from the Finnish Historical Newspaper Library. The Library is experienced as a great cultural deed. The users have been extremely happy about it. People have also greeted our personnel in the street and asked if we do understand the impact that it has for citizens in Finland. It is an important search service for research in history and genealogy and it was immediately referred to in the newspapers and at the Agricola site for researchers.

The site is seen as:

- systematic, organised, easy to use, free of charge;
- experienced by the users as a great cultural service

Growth of Use

In 2005, 1.9 million page requests and 160,000 visits have been registered.

Topics

- wars of Napoleon;
- indings of hedgehogs;
- forest economy;
- harbour industry;
- religious movements.

Global

- feedback from 14 countries: Argentina, the Netherlands, Iran, Great Britain, Canada, China, Poland, Sweden, Germany, Singapore, Turkey, New Zeeland, Russia, the US;
- a need for automatic translation of the text into English was expressed.

There is a need for more newspapers in the Digital Library – also copyright based – and for personal service relating to the Digital Newspaper Library.

The Present

In digital futures the digital collection management will be an exiting challenge. It is not enough to digitise our collections and put them on the web with enhanced search possibilities. The infrastructure around our collections is changing fast as well as the expectations of our users. We have to improve access in various ways, including automatic translation to our old holdings, including meeting places for users.

Today the Historical Newspaper Library in Finland has found its place. It has been and will remain the cornerstone of development for the digitisation of critical masses in Finland. As a result the Microfilming and Conservation Centre of the Helsinki University Library – the National Library of Finland will in the near future become the National Digitisation Centre for the archives, libraries and museums in Finland.

The Finnish journalist Magnus Londén wrote in August, 2004 in the newspaper *Hufvudstadsbladet HBL* that he would give the highest award of Society for the Finnish Historical Newspaper Library. The tax payers have paid for it and they have certainly got value for their money. The past is living in the present.

NEWSPAPER DIGITISATION IN FRANCE: PRESENT DEVELOPMENTS

Else Delaunay

National Library of France

1. Introduction

My colleague who is in charge of the Newsprint Office at the Bibliothèque Nationale de France, the French National Library, was not able to come to Salt Lake City to give a presentation on newspaper digitisation at the BNF. Therefore I was asked recently to introduce you briefly to present developments in Newspaper digitisation at the BNF so I shall try to sum up the digitisation programme and some other projects such as they have been announced and commented in French newspapers and on radio and television. I give of course this talk in my own name.

1.1 The Newspaper Collection in the Bibliothèque Nationale de France

The BNF has a vast and valuable Newspaper Collection of French and foreign newspapers dating back to the first paper published in France in 1631, *La Gazette*. Today the Collection includes some 60,000 retrospective and current titles of which the main provider is, of course, the Legal Deposit.

1.2 The Newspaper Microfilm Collection

The Newspaper Microfilm Collection includes some 2300 titles representing round 100,000 reels. It comprises the great national retrospective and current titles (ex. all the dailies from the 19th and 20th centuries) and a large choice of past and running regional newspapers and overseas papers from the former French colonies and territories. The yearly increase is ca. 5500 reels including microfilming of several national and regional dailies as well as of retrospective holdings.

2. Reasons for Digitising French Newspapers

BNF's Digitisation Programme is, of course, considering only French newspapers. Since mid-19th century the highly circulated newspapers have attracted not only journalists' articles but also contributions from politicians, writers, artists and researchers. All of them got hold of this new media whose vast circulating was unknown until then, in order to publish essays, reviews, debates and novels. The newspapers became an unrivalled supply to the study of the political, social, scientific, literary and artistic life.

The digitization of newspapers and magazines therefore is contributing to exploit such information collections in a still unequalled way.

2.1 The 2005–2009 Digitisation Programme of Retrospective Daily Newspapers

This programme was defined and launched in 2004 but started finally in February 2005 and is running regularly now.

2.1.1 Selection of Titles

Twenty-seven main newspapers from the first issue up to 1944 were selected for digitisation. Since then some more titles have been added such as *Les Echos*, 1928–1944, Le Canard enchaine, 1915–1939 and, quite recently, *Le Monde diplomatique*, 1954–1978, the period 1979–2005 being available on a commercial CD-ROM. Most of these newspapers have very long runnings, sometimes more than a hundred years. Some of the dailies stopped before 1944, others were not published during the Second World War and some are still running as *La Croix*, *Le Figaro*, *L'Humanite* …

The choice of the 1944 limit has allowed the BNF to make agreements rather quickly with the administrations of running newspapers which rightfully could aim at digitising and putting online commercially their proper holdings of the last 60 years. It also was agreed that the 1944 limit should form a mobile barrier which may go up a year each year. This means that the BNF gradually will be able to give access online to following years of a given paper.

2.1.2 Methods and Formats

It was decided to use image digitising for two reasons: image mode is well controlled today and less expensive than text mode; research workers using retrospective newspaper holdings should be able to overview articles in their original aspect, the page-setting and the reference to illustrations, etc.

In many cases pages are digitised from the original copy in paper format, sometimes from the microfilm if it is good enough for scanning, and preserved in non compressed TIFF format which seems to be the most reliable for long-term preservation. But circulation will be in JPEG format on BNF's website in its digital library Gallica.

2.1.3 Digitisation Providers

Digitisation is carried out by three workshops: two are within the library – BNF's Centre in Sable (300 km West of Paris) and its Centre in Bussy-Saint-Georges (30 km East of Paris). The digitised newspaper collection will be accessible through the BN-OPALE Plus Catalogue (BNF's database) which clearly points out the items available in an electronic version, or the user may search directly in the Gallica database that is supposed to be linked gradually to the European Digital Library.

So as to make available other access methods needed by the users, the second stage of BNF's programme will be the preparing of the conversion of the original product in image mode to a digital collection accessible in text mode after OCR treatment which should ensure 95 % character recognition. Actually the following functions have been selected:

- search by date,
- access through a calendar (year, month, day) or a «kiosk» function (ex. all newspapers of a given day),
- full text search with possible segmentation (search of a given article on a full text page)

within the same issue:

- logical consulting of the layout to know about the structure of an issue;
- advertising of pagination so as to find one's way in this structure;
- zooming of an abstract for reading facilities,
- possibility of navigating from one issue to another within the same title.

2.1.4 Funding

The estimated amount of the digitisation costs in image mode of twenty-seven newspaper holdings is 3.5 million euros including salaries and national insurance contributions to BNF's Staff members in charge of the work, costs of data storage, and providings committed to the sub-contracting off site (workshop 3). The amount of 3.5 million euros is entirely supported by BNF's proper budget, supplied with grants from the Ministry of Culture during the first two years.

For the further development by OCR treatment the Senate has allocated a three-years grant of 150,000 EUR per year form 2005 to 2007. This is, of course, to be considered as a start funding. Public and private sponsorship will be necessary.

2.1.5 Future Possibilities of Developing and Enlarging of the Programme

It should be a closer co-operation with other French libraries and archives, or with the newspapers themselves as far as running titles are concerned.

2.1.6 Completing of Possible Gaps in the Holdings

Completing is a heavy but indispensable task so as to make available complete holdings of a title. Co-operation with libraries and archives in France is necessary. It may even be useful to contact the newspaper administrations which, in some cases, have a complete holding of the paper.

2.1.7 Developing by Including Regional Dailies

The programme may also be developed by including regional dailies. Some projects in co-operation are in progress. For instance, digitisation of the regional dailies *L'Union*, *L'Est-Éclair*, *L'Ardennais* in co-operation with the three main libraries in the region and the BNF.

Another example is the largest circulated French newspaper *Ouest France* whose first title *Ouest Éclair* with its three local editions will be digitised by the BNF and *Ouest France*, that means round 300,000 pages.

The agreement between *Ouest France* and the BNF was signed on 7th September 2005. It also includes a new principle which is an experiment at the moment: the legal deposit online of the 42 local editions of *Ouest France*. Until now these editions were regularly acquired on microfilm. This new system may result in agreements with many other regional papers publishing local editions.

The Legal Deposit Office at the BNF has also started another experiment, the regional daily *Le Populaire du Centre* is making the deposit of its digitised files. Today it is suggested that this experiment should be extended to other newspapers such as *Ouest France* (all editions), that means some 240,000 pages per year.

3.3 National Co-Operation

Co-operative projects with other libraries for special collections of rare items are being launched: BDIC (the Library for International Contemporary Documentation) and BNF have decided to carry out a shared digitisation programme on trench newspapers, papers written and printed by soldiers in the trenches in Eastern France during the First World War.

A similar programme could be set up on Clandestine papers from World War II but the physical condition of these papers printed on low quality paper with low quality ink is very poor and therefore a real problem. The microfilms too are not good enough for scanning.

3.4 New Tools to Facilitate Researches

Some new tools may facilitate searching. The digitisation of indexes, newspaper yearbooks and tables, in order to link them to the digitised newspaper collection, could improve search possibilities.

In this field it could be a capital tool for French newspaper history to digitise the *Bibliography of French Local Political and General Information Newspapers* published department by department (French administrative districts). Fifty-eight volumes have been published so far.

3.4.4 International Co-operation

It is also clear that the Digitisation Programme matches very well with international co-operation :

- the French dimension (that is la Francophonie), especially with regard to the connecting of BNF's programme and the initiative of the National Library of Quebec concerning digitisation of newspapers from both countries;
- the European dimension with the creation of the European Digital Library (EDL) supported by the European Commission and several member countries. Here newspapers should occupy an essential position.

4. The European Digital Library

If Google with the Google Book Project will make available the largest amount of books and authors to the largest amount of users, the idea of the European Digital Library is to preserve and make available the extraordinary rich collections of various European countries, respecting copyright and authors' and publishers' ownership, and with a co-operation between public and private initiatives. The EDL also garantees high quality digitisation and long-term electronic storage.

How far is the EDL today? The EDL has become a highlight of the global strategy of the European Commission to stimulate digitisation economy. Large digitisation programmes are developed in various European countries. In France the next four years will be crucial. In March 2006, the co-operation in digitisation between six national libraries from French speaking countries was announced (Belgium, Canada, France, Luxemburg, Quebec and Switzerland). The same month the European Commission organized the first meeting of the Group of twenty experts highly qualified in digitisation requirements for digital libraries.

At present, the debate is dealing with formats. Should they be open or closed? If the interoperability between systems and users has to be a reality, formats should be open standards.

At the end of 2006, a co-operation project between the national libraries of the European Union should be ready. The Commission will introduce its strategy for developing digital libraries devoted to scientific and university contents. At the same date, the Commission on online contents will make a communication on important questions such as managing of copyright in a digitising era.

In 2008, two million books, films, photos, manuscripts and other cultural works will be accessible through the EDL. In 2010, at least six million items should be available. Each library, archive or museum in Europe will be able potentially to link its digitised collections to the EDL.

To meet these objectives Europe will need a real political engagement in the EDL. France, and especially the BNF whose president took the initiative to the EDL is, of course, very much involved in all steps of the project. Gallica's 80,000 digitised items in image mode must be converted gradually into a combined text-image mode with standardized formats for the internet user.

BNF's digitisation programme will be extended. The near future will be very busy for the BNF as well as for other French libraries participating in the EDL, if deadlines are to be met. One of the main points of the next months and years will be further funding of the programme so BNF is looking for sponsorship.

CANADIAN NEWSPAPERS AND DIGITIZATION: PROVINCIAL PROJECTS AND THE NATIONAL SCENE

Sandra Burrows,

Newspaper Specialist, Library and Archives Canada

Abstract

Many of the provincial projects for digitization of newspapers have been thematic projects where newspapers provide the text and photographs to support an historic subject. Library and Archives Canada has also concentrated on thematic projects mainly because of the restrictions imposed by funding agencies.

However, some excellent full-text projects are underway and this presentation will focus on a sampling of them. As well, two projects are being proposed at Library and Archives Canada, one that will be done with in-house resources and the other seeking outside funding and sponsorship. I will conclude with some finding aids developed to locate digital projects underway in Canada as well as brief mention of the web archiving initiatives.

As of this month, I had linked to 180 Canadian web sites that provided content from Canadian newspapers. Although these links include large-scale listings of obituaries and other genealogical information extracted from newspapers with common owners and a few large-scale commercial projects such as Paper of Record, the majority of these sites are free of charge and provide the user with the ability to search full-text newspapers by keyword. These websites may be found on one of two Internet links on Library and Archives Canada's webpage:

http://www.collectionscanada.ca/8/16/r16-211-e.html

http://www.collectionscanada.ca/8/16/r16-211-f.html

for Canadian and Canadiana-related web sites including general sites, indexes, provincial/territorial sites, aboriginal, ethnic and student sites and alternative newspapers.

and

http://www.collectionscanada.ca/8/16/r16-214-e.html

http://www.collectionscanada.ca/8/16/r16-214-f.html

for links to International Newspapers as well as by specific countries.

Newspapers have not been digitized extensively outside of the Paper of Record project mainly because of copyright and storage considerations. Canadian libraries tend to provide access to newspapers through site-licensing agreements with companies such as Canadian Newsstand and CED-ROM Eureka where online products reproduce articles going back to the 1980's.

Non-Commercial Web Sites

Last year I mentioned in my paper, a Bibliothèque et Archives nationale du Québec project to add three million pages of Quebec newspapers to a database. This project has recently been discussed in connection with a Francophone database of holdings of six national libraries: la Bibliothèque nationale de France, la Bibliothèque royale de Belgique, Bibliothèque et Archives Canada, la Bibliothèque nationale du Luxembourg et la Bibliothèque nationale de Suisse. In the communiqué, BaNQ mentions two-million pages of newspaper and periodical collections to be scanned.

I also mentioned the Manitobia project which became a reality in late 2005. This was an OCLC Canada and Manitoba Library Consortium (University of Manitoba, University of Winnipeg, Archives of Manitoba and Legislative Library of Manitoba) joint project to digitize more than 122,000 pages of historically-important newspapers as well as an atlas, books and historic maps as part of *Manitobia: Life and Times*. This CCOP-funded project worked from 30 newspapers on 133 microfilm reels for 1859 to 1919 from a custom-created service centre and also provided a mobile service to handle fragile items that needed to remain on the premis of the housing institution.

OCLC Canada's post-scanning processes included cropping, deskewing, padding and noise reduction to prepare files for distillation through Olive Inc.'s PipeX. As a result of this process, the content of the newspapers was delivered as an XML repository to allow for future manipulation by the Manitoba Library Consortium. As well, the distillation process needed to proceed carefully to extract the French and English vocabulary in context.

Library and Archives Canada Web Sites with Canadian Newspapers

In addition to my main finding aid to newspaper collections at Library and Archives Canada, at

http://www.collectionscanada.ca/8/16/index-e.html, and
http://www.collectionscanada.ca/8/16/index-f.html,

we hope to undertake two digital projects in the near future.

Library and Archives Canada presently receives funding for digitization projects from Canadian Heritage the governing body to which Library and Archives Canada reports. We also have a small program to digitize material in the public domain for accessibility. All of the Canadian Culture Online Program proposals must also involve partnerships with outside organizations and the project must produce a bilingual (English/French) interface and be free of charge to all users. There are other criteria for eligibility in the CCOP yearly funding including presentation, thematic interest, consultation of experts, importance of the content in the context of Canada's cultural heritage and educational value.

The first project will be recommended for the 2007–2008 fiscal year as the planning process this year became as two-year process and other projects had already received approval. We hope to scan a representative number of multicultural newspapers from across Canada. We have holdings in both print and microfilm and we are looking at newspapers that are outside of copyright restriction or, published generally prior to 1950 and not currently publishing. We realize that this will restrict us to older settlement groups and exclude some of our newer cultural communities but we hope that if we are able to scan a sampling of multicultural newspapers, we will attract other current publishers to either give permission for us to scan their papers or to partner with us. This project is at a very early scoping stage. In fact, to date, I have just identified those papers which fit the outside-copyright criteria.

One complication in this process is something I have mentioned at previous meetings. Library and Archives Canada does not microfilm newspapers. We rely on commercial microfilming as well as purchase from provincial/territorial archives and libraries any microfilm that they have completed. In order to scan from the microfilm edition, which, in many cases, is the only edition that exists for some of the papers, we need to determine what copyright arrangements need to be made with the microfilming companies. Other considerations of which we are well aware are the differing quality of the microfilming and whether or not it will be possible to have access to a filming master for scanning.

Another possible problem is the move of collections to an interim storage facility in 2008. At present, our print material for which a microfilm edition exists, is housed in two large offsite storage facilities. Plans, if the budget remains in place for the move, include a large reboxing and stabilization element and this may mean that the publications will not be accessible for this period of time. As well, the Printed Heritage unit intends to include the large number of print runs of multicultural newspapers possibly involving unique issues for which microfilm is not available. We are expecting to still have access to this material as our project will include a microfilm component if the print issues are unique but we are not able to guarantee that the storage project and the mutlicultural newspaper scanning project will not happen at the same time.

A second smaller project is more feasible and part of the work has been completed; i.e. the scanning of the pages. This year, I received a request to scan first issues of Canadian newspapers from each province and territory for reproduction at a small museum near Niagara Falls this summer. We have just scanned all of the pages (the front pages will be reproduced as posters in the museum) and I hope to add a bilingual interface as well as some basic information on each newspaper to a new web page in connection with a previous project called Engine of Immortality: Canadian newspapers from 1752 until today at

http://www.collectionscanada.ca/halifaxgazette/index-e.html, and

http://www.collectionscanada.ca/halifaxgazette/index-f.html.

Some front pages from historic events in Canada have been scanned in part of this website under Historic Milestones at

http://www.collectionscanada.ca/halifaxgazette/h28-6000-e.html, and

http://www.collectionscanada.ca/halifaxgazette/h28-6000-f.html.

Within the Canadian National Context

In January 2007, the Legal Deposit Regulations will likely apply to online publications, including newspapers. As the legislation update is still in front of Canadian Heritage, I am not able to discuss any details but this will raise concerns related to storage of electronic content, which «edition» is deposited and what constitutes an electronic edition and access to this material. At present, Library and Archives Canada is collecting some born-digital newspapers on a voluntary basis as a prelude to the legislation. This is part of a web-harvesting effort which will allow LAC to preserve selective web sites such including newspaper sites for born-digital papers such as *The Dominion* from Halifax, Nova Scotia. Similarly, Library and Archives Information Technology Branch has harvested 1,489 Government of Canada domains comprising 40.7 million digital objects between December 2005 and March 2006 and Library and Archives Canada's Digital Collection Catalytic Iniative staff will be analysing the results of this harvest in order to develop a web management methodology including a combination of metadata and keyword indexing of the web sites.

More information on Library and Archives Canada's Digital Initiatives is available at:

http://www.collectionscanada.ca/cdis/012033-700-e.html, and
http://www.collectionscanada.ca/scin/012033-700-f.html.

Other Issues and Concerns

In her paper called *Following the Trail of the Disappearing Data*, Victoria McCarger points out that technology which provides the genetic framework of newspaper design can be its own worst enemy in ensuring longevity. In addition to the short life of many text, photo and multimedia types of software, other inherent problems crop up in platform and operating systems, storage structure, technical metadata, content description, copyright and institutional discipline. I appreciate the mention of the latter as it relates to policy. Victoria McCarger mentions it in relation to responsibility for long-term storage and the bottom dollar line at newspapers but the same problem can be seen in any library or archives. If the role of traditional archival and librarian describers moves to the more expedient IT department or to the off-shore cheaper indexing services, the content-based indexing coming from the more traditional metadata providers will be gone. This deprivation is something more than just a disappearance of policies and standards – it is the loss of the collective memory of the long-time journalist and the newspaper librarian in the case of news libraries and the appreciation of the information professional in the case of other libraries and archives. Our greatest danger in the loss of information may not be in the inability to migrate technologies or safeguard metadata but in the inability of the increasingly non-professional administration to recognize the value of the professionals they employ.

A cautious approach to digital archives does not mean no approach at all nor should it frighten institutions and newspapers that have preserved their archives through traditional means. What it does require of the policy makers is to recognize that IT must work with content specialists to put the context in metadata and that a vision will be required to appreciate the longterm use of newspaper archives. Historical archives, once the venue of academics, will be opened to the public and the general educational sectors in a way in which they have never been previously available. We have to be careful, to use an old phrase, not to throw out the baby with the bathwater. We need to keep a professional eye on the ever-changing newspaper industry in order to ensure that we are the champions for proven archival means of preservation at the same time that we are not left out of encouraging the use of newspapers in accessible formats.

Again, I think that, as information professionals working on newspaper preservation, we need to emphasize two factors related to electronic publishing. Electronic archives should not be seen to replace print (when available) or microform archives. Secondly, the means by which we archive the news will continue to be a combination of traditional and new methods and it will not be cheaper. If we see electronic archiving as applied to newspaper preservation as a replacement technology, we will only gain short-term accessibility at the loss of a large amount of newspaper records.

COUNTRY REPORT – NEW ZEALAND

David Adams

Coordinator, Copying and Digital Services
National Library of New Zealand.

Last year I attended the previous IFLA PAC newspaper conference in Canberra. There I co-presented a paper on the National Library of NZ digital newspaper collection Papers Past with the Library's curator, Clark Stiles. Today I wanted to give an update on what has happened since then, and the progress the Library is now making toward a more functional digital newspaper collection for our users.

Let's set the scene for the country update from New Zealand – here we are in the Pacific ocean.... New Zealand is a country with 39 million sheep, 4 million people, and 1 million pages of early New Zealand newspaper online.

This is a reasonable achievement for our national online collection of early newspapers. If we compare this population wise, this is equivalent to Australia having 5 million pages, the United Kingdom having 15 million pages, or the United States having 74 million pages online.

Our current online collection «Papers Past» (http://paperspast.natlib.govt.nz/) has been achieved by additional Library funding specifically for digitisation. That budget allocation has been close to US$ 70,000 per year. The digitisation of microfilmed newspapers has been a sustainable programme running since 2001. The programme includes selecting titles of microfilmed newspapers held at the national Library and sending these to a digitisation supplier.

One weakness of this programme is that there has not been any provision of funds for microfilming titles not already on film, or re-microfilming any poorly microfilmed titles. Where a title is only held on microfilm and no paper copy is in existence this is not an issue. But where some titles where the microfilming could be improved by re-filming, it is an issue. This can encourage digitisation of microfilms that could be improved by microfilming to a higher standard. I strongly agree with the British Library approach who have included in their digitisation funding process for the survey of microfilm collections, preparation and treatment of originals and re-microfilming content where the existing microfilm is not to an acceptable standard to support digitisation and effective OCR. The amount of time and resources required for effective assessment of originals and microfilm collections should never be underestimated and is often not considered in digitisation projects where there can be pressure to get content digitised and made accessible.

Our microfilming budget has been static for a number of years, and with the rising cost of microfilming by suppliers it is reducing our programme outputs. Our programme to microfilm early collections is also being hindered by the fact that current newspaper sizes are growing. Our programme of a half million pages being microfilmed each year was made up of 2/3rds early newspapers and 1/3rd current newspapers, but this is now half and half. These two factors have affected our ability to microfilm our early national newspaper collections that are often at risk.

«Papers Past» contains 41 titles, with an extensive geographical coverage of the country. From our earliest title in 1840, to a date that we consider to be safely out of copyright which is up to 1915. To date the Library has not made any agreements with publishers about digitising more recently published newspapers and is something we should explore.

The digital content is a static collection of TIFF images that requires a plug-in to view the pages; the collection has not been OCR'ed. The site has had half a million visits since its 2001 launch, and our users have been very keen to have the ability to keyword search the collection. After the last IFLA Newspapers Conference in Canberra last year I wrote a paper to the Library's executive team with an international perspective that discussed the priority of making the collection searchable.

In the paper Clark and I presented in Canberra last year, we recognised the shortcomings of our static online collection that could only be browsed by title-year-month-day, which have very limited search functionality. The pages of each newspaper are TIFF images close to 1 Megabyte each that is an access problem for many of our users. The good news is there has been additional funding from the Library's digitisation programme, where one of this year's priorities is a project to develop Papers Past into a more functional collection for our users, through OCR and improved online delivery. Our Innovation Centre staff is undertaking most of this project work, and I have been working closely with them in the Digitisation Programme Committee and Tender Evaluation team.

Before going out to the market with a «Request for Proposal» for this project, a number of pieces of work were undertaken to gather information and build on some learning opportunities. This background included:

- an environmental scan on online newspaper collections;
- some research on the users of our current collection;
- a discussion paper on page versus article level delivery (that this work actually came during the tender evaluation process);
- developing a tender evaluation plan.

All of this preliminary work was necessary to ensure we would be evaluating proposals in the light of what the Library and its users need from an online digital newspaper collection.

The environmental scan was undertaken to survey what institutional collections were currently out there live and accessible, how big they were, and what processing and delivery applications were being used. This allowed us to set the scene for our development, and to build up knowledge to make more informed decisions. From that work common features and functionality of systems could be identified, and if there were any standards being used.

Some of our findings included:

- Around 50 current online collections are accessible, we looked at about 30 of these, which were the most applicable to our project.
- There are now a wide variety of processing and delivery methods, but most use similar «user features»; such as browse by title, page or article level granularity, highlighted search terms, printing ability etc.
- There are a constantly increasing number of vendors providing products and services for meeting the needs of newspaper digitisation projects.
- There are a number of defacto standards emerging now, such as XML, METS/ALTO (METS provides metadata and structural information, while ALTO contains content and physical information).

The research on our users was undertaken to identify what their needs were, and to observe some researchers using more functional collections than our own. This helped us find out what they liked or disliked, and what they thought was important.

We used an online survey from the «Papers Past» website which provided over 200 responses, here we also learnt more about the type of visitors we have to the site.

We brought five experienced researchers into the Library who use online newspaper collections. We sat them down to observe them going through a number of set tasks on two digital newspaper collections that have more functionality than our own.

This information and survey results could then be fed back into our tender evaluation process, to assist us selecting the strongest proposals based on our users needs.

The issue of page level versus article level delivery came up frequently, so we circulated a discussion paper to get more input. This allowed for wider stakeholder interest to provide some clear direction of what was expected in the access to the collection. It is expected we will provide article level access. One local factor is that New Zealand is low down on the OECD list of broadband uptake due to a number of reasons and therefore many users still are using 56Kbps modems.

This is how our users described themselves in the online survey:

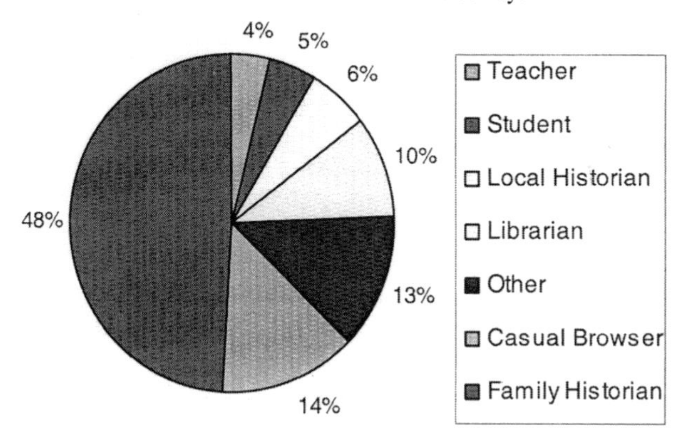

Fig. 1. Results of online survey

Half of them are family historians, the next biggest groups are casual browsers and «other» (there are some family historians in that «other» group too). Clearly from this we can say more than half our users are family historians. We often describe our users as researchers and it is interesting to see how they prefer to describe themselves.

With this supporting background information and a greater understanding, the Library posted an RfP in February. We received quite a number of responses. This probably indicates how much international interest and initiatives there are in the digitisation and delivery of newspaper and textual collections. Also an increase in the number of experienced commercial suppliers meeting that demand. Products and services abound, compared to 5, or even 3 years ago.

We consider the online delivery of newspapers to be made up of three parts:

- Part 1 – microfilming and or digitsation;
- Part 2 – OCR process;
- Part 3 – delivery and access application.

Microfilming and digitisation we have in hand with effective processes and a local micrographics service supplier, so our tender was structured to find suppliers for parts 2 and 3, the OCR and online delivery.

The RfP was broken into two parts and assessed in this way. This allowed suppliers to respond to one part only or to both. That way we did not eliminate suppliers who had expertise in one part, or could join with another vendor to respond to both parts.

It also allowed us to consider selecting the best part of a proposal if we desired.

We expect to choose our supplier very soon. We would like to process 100,000 pages hosted on a demonstrator later this year, with final development work on the delivery application to be made over the next 6 months or so. The main constraints to the project being; we have a short time frame due to budget availability, and as the Library will host the collection the solution must fit into our existing technical infrastructure.

From here we expect to move all of our existing content on «Papers Past» to the new delivery application to have one point of access for our users. We want to avoid a collection of static pages and a new collection of keyword searchable pages, which could confuse our users. Therefore we need a solution that can manage both a keyword search and a static page browse of the collection. For technical reasons our existing «Papers Past» collection of 1 million pages is at full capacity and this has also been a driver for building a new hosting solution.

The current collection will be OCR'ed incrementally, so for a time there will be a mix of static pages and text searchable pages until the whole collection is processed and becomes fully functional. This may take a number of years depending on the Libraries priorities and budget availability.

We expect to continue to build the collection with more titles and date ranges from our microfilm collections. We are also considering the digitisation of collections held in other New Zealand institutions where the title may be important. We also would like to ensure we can apply the OCR and delivery project processes to other textual collections such as serials and journals.

One day we may have more pages of New Zealand newspapers online than 120 sheep!

HISTORICAL MEMORY OF MEXICO (1722 – 2005)

Gerardo Valencia

National Digital Newspaper Library of Mexico
Hemeroteca Nacional Digital de México (HNDM)

The National Newspaper Library of Mexico

In the year 1884, the National Library of Mexico (BN) was established. Since 1929, the National Library is part of the National University (UNAM). The formal inauguration of the National Newspaper Library (HN) took place in 1944. In 1967, the Institute for Bibliographic Research (IIB) of the National Library opened its office, in order to promote the mission of both the BN and the HN.

Preservation and Conservation at the National Newspaper Library (HN)

The large volume of periodicals represents a huge challenge for conservation and preservation. The initiatives and programs aimed at improving conservation are:

- microfilming,
- re-binding and stabilization of collections,
- access policies and reference regulations,
- catalogues, inventories and other electronic services,
- building conditions for periodicals safeguarding, and
- digital subrogates (HNDM).

The Objectives of the National Digital Newspaper Library (HNDM)

The objectives of the National Digital Newspaper Library are to make a contribution to the objectives of the National Newspaper Library, to promote and favor preservation, conservation and diffusion of the country's periodicals heritage as well as supporting democratization of knowledge. In addition, HNDM is aiming at offering digital surrogate documents that contribute to minimize the use of originals, and additionally provide access to intellectual content free of time and space restraints.

HNDM is providing new ways of information storage, processing and diffusion, new and more efficient possibilities for retrieval of information contained in millions of pages and hundreds of newspaper titles. It offers a comprehensive newspaper collection – instead of individual collections – with a heritage value proportionally weighted in quality, diversity and number of included titles. It thereby provides a landscape view of the national everyday life.

Newspapers are digitized as a series of black and white page images in 1-bit 300 dpi resolution. The scans comprise the uncorrected, complete text in order to support searches. Images are delivered as full single-page PDF. Search terms appear highlighted (context only).

Improved access possibilities include simple and advanced search methods using phrases, simple words or combined terms with Boolean operators. Proximity, fuzzy and other expert search features are currently developed.

Several browsing options (free navigation) exist: Browsing by title, by place of publication or catalogue reference. Other options are currently developed (timelines, historical characters and events).

The Collections

The collections comprise almost seven million searchable images, more than 800 titles. The publications range from 1722 to January 2006. The newspapers represent every state of the country, among them two contemporary newspapers: *El Informador* from Guadalajara and *El Porvenir* from Monterrey.

In addition, HNDM administers the *Catalogue of Mexican Periodicals from the 19th Century (1822–1876)*. The catalogue offers a word search in the complete catalogue registries. Catalogue entries point to digitized pages and vice versa. A pseudonym dictionary and other reference works are in preparation.

Working Portal and User Evaluation

A working portal is in an evaluation stage since October 2005 in order to improve all available features and services. It will be available for direct use only at HN facilities. The entry gateway will be an intranet interface that encourages user input, especially feedback with proposals and opinions.

Here are some data from the user profile gained in the pilot study: As far as the study degree is concerned, fifty percent of the users are graduated, forty percent are undergraduates. Areas of study are social sciences and humanities (88%), biology, chemistry, medicine and health sciences (8%). 64% of the users are women.

Only seven percent of the users reported about a technical observation: The main inconvenience pointed out was the downloading time. Six percent of the users proposed improvements concerning services, firstly more and better browsing capabilities.

The Future of the HNDM

Among the immediate activities (actions in process) are measurements to extend the evaluation process to a larger number of users. It is intended to take into consideration the best proposals made by users and to change the portal graphic design.

In a mid-term perspective, it is planned to process and add the full microfilm collection from the Reserved Fund. Furthermore, it will be necessary to define the way the HNDM will be available to the general public, according to the decisions made by university authorities and the Advisory Committee. It is intended to find mechanisms which will make the HNDM self-sustainable.

How the Project Works

The HNDM is the product of a collaboration agreement between the UNAM, the IIB (HN) and the Mexican company Digix. Technical and operative decisions are discussed, designed, tested and approved by both the HN and Digix. Logistics and upper management decisions are made by the UNAM helped by the Advisory Committee and a Legal Committee. The fund raising for the project has been performed by the UNAM Foundation. For the last two years, the UNAM has allocated a specific budget to the HNDM.

Technical Requirements

The digitization process requires

- workflow control,
- high productivity scanners,
- custom-made software for:
  - cropping,
  - classification, and
  - quality control,
- technical trained staff, and
- 24x6 operations.

Efficient Optical Character Recognition (OCR) has to cope with

- a variable quality of originals,
- an impact of quality of characters on processing times and recognition rates,

and requires

- high performance computing concepts application to respond to processing power demands and workloads,
- a hardware and software engines selection, and
- a document management and OCR workflow application design.

On-line publishing requires

- access through XML-based metadata:
  - digital Inventories (free navigation) and
  - search engine (index of contents)
- a custom-made application development to integrate digital content with bibliographical entries,
- the use of platforms with strong commercial support, and
- a Service Oriented Architecture (SOA) on high capacity servers.

The storage of and access to digital contents requires:

- a three-level storage scheme :
  - online material, FC technology,
  - material being processed or with low use, SATA, and
  - backed-up material (raw source and final version), high capacity magnetic tapes in robotic library

Security and availability will be guaranteed by

- RAID 5, logical and physical redundancy in HDs,
- redundancy in power supplies, switches, Ethernet ports, and optical fiber,
- protection and backup of electrical supply, online UPS, and
- aggressive on-site support policies from providers, 365x24x7x4.

National Autonomous University of Mexico
(Universidad Nacional Autónoma de México)
Dr. Juan Ramón de la Fuente Ramírez, President
Dra. Mari Carmen Serra Puche, Humanities Area

Institute for Bibliographic Research
(Instituto de Investigaciones Bibliográficas)
Dr. Vicente Quirarte Castañeda, Director
Mtra. Guadalupe Curiel Defossé, Head of the National Newspaper Library

Contact:

Lorena Gutiérrez Schott, Head of Reserved Fund
lorena@biblional.bibliog.unam.mx

Ricardo J Jiménez
Head of Microfilming Unit
Responsible of technical issues of the HNDM
jimenezr@biblional.bibliog.unam.mx

Gerardo Valencia
Director of Technology, Digix
gerardo.valencia@digix.com.mx

THE DIGITIZATION OF CHILEAN NEWSPAPERS

Maritza Failla

National Library of Chile

1. Background Information

The Chilean National Library, one of Chile's first public institutions, was founded on August 19, 1813. Its Founding Proclamation, published in the official newspaper *El Monitor Araucano*, states that «every book shall be a precious gift, because each one is useful.» Since then, the National Library has been a depository of the knowledge, creation, culture and bibliographical heritage of Chile and the world, and available to all.

Although books are the expression of knowledge and creation, and serve as primary sources for social, political, historical and economic research, newspapers – reflecting social thought over time in all its complexity and diversity – have also proved to be as rich a source for researchers as books traditionally have been. By consulting and researching with newspapers, it is possible for us to go about discovering the identity of the Chilean nation, day by day and week by week. They show the changes and evolutions of our society as we become who we are today.

Therefore, the National Library has developed a collection of newspapers since its foundation, based on a policy that promotes:

a) The preservation and conservation of its collections;
b) The inclusion of nationally – and regionally – circulating newspapers;
c) The intention of completing those collections, and keeping them up-to-date;
d) The intention of making the collections available to the public as needed;
e) The intention of offering the collections to meet patrons' requests and allowing them to be viewed; and
f) The incorporation of technological innovations to offer more and better services.

The newspapers collection is supported by a norm in the Chilean Press Law obliging printers of newspapers and books to deposit 15 paper copies of each item printed in the National Library; the law also recommends that two more copies be deposited in a medium other than paper, such as CDs, videos, or other media.

2. Users

On average 3,500,000 references are given, and 90,000 people spend time in the National Library's reading rooms every year, consulting newspapers for research and other reasons. Residents of Santiago are not the only ones who utilize the reading rooms; residents of all of Chile's different regions come to the National Library, as well as foreigners. The Library offers the only complete collection of newspapers available to the public in the entire country. Different Chilean media companies also maintain complete collections of the newspapers they publish, but their collections are private, and therefore unavailable to the public.

Users may access the following services in the newspapers reading rooms:

a) Read paper-based national and regional newspapers;
b) Consult microfilms using machine readers;
c) Make photocopies;

d) Print microfilm copies, with the aid of trained staff (new machines will be installed this year, allowing patrons to make their own copies of microfilms);
e) Request scans of newspapers;
f) Make films; and
g) Copy rolls of microfilm.

Newspapers are an important source – and are generally the only reliable source – for judicial researchers, historians, thesis writers, and others. The conservation of the collections is very important to the process of making them available to these patrons.

3. Conserving and Preserving the Collections

The newspapers collection is one of the collections most requested by the people of Chile, which presents challenges that need to be addressed. We have two goals in this area: first, to diminish the lending and handling of newspapers, in order to assure that they will remain preserved in their paper-based form for future generations; and second, to make these newspapers available to the public without restriction, in order to meet patrons' needs for knowledge and information. The National Library has developed policies and strategies to reconcile these two objectives, while raising awareness of increasingly higher percentages of the collections.

The conservation and preservation policy states that efforts should be focused on:

a) Newspapers in more advanced stages of deterioration;
b) Older newspapers that are more likely to be requested by patrons;
c) More valuable newspapers; and
d) Newspapers often requested for research, consultation and information purposes.

Therefore, in accordance with established norms, the following strategies for conservation and preservation have been established:

a) The creation of second, or reserve, collections;
b) The microfilming of newspapers; and
c) The digitization of newspapers.

The Creation of Reserve Collections

Thanks to the Legal Deposit Law, we can place two copies on reserve. A warehouse has been built apart from the National Library facility and equipped with shelving to store those reserve collections. This guarantees security and back-up of the library's collections in the event of possible problems that could arise.

Newspaperss on Microfilm

Microfilming has been one of the main strategies for the conservation and preservation of the newspapers collections. There are three basic steps to the microfilming process: restoring newspapers and preparing them for microfilming; the microfilming process itself; and the storage of the newspapers that have been microfilmed in specially-manufactured, acid-free storage boxes.

In 2002, 2003, 2004 and 2005, the microfilming has been funded publicly, with monies that have gone towards hiring outside companies that specialize in microfilming to do it and the purchase of the storage boxes. At this point, there are 8,000,000 images.

Certain complications have arisen from this process, among them:

a) Only two Chilean companies offer reliable microfilming services, but even they do not have the necessary expertise in heritage items like newspapers.
b) National Library personnel have had to learn about the process along the way.
c) The supervision and control of the rolls of microfilm requires manpower and time.
d) The storage of masters and copies requires space, equipment and conservation measures.
e) Catalogues need to be modified to include information about microfilms, in order to make them more accessible to patrons.
f) Insufficient resources in proportion to the vast amount of material that still needs to be stored on microfilm. Yearly requests for additional funds are not always accepted. This leads to more of a back-up every year.
g) Copies from microfilm are more difficult to make than regular photocopies.
h) Patrons are restricted, as they must be in the reading rooms to consult microfilm resources and are obligated to use specialized equipment.
i) Reproductions on microfilm are not always satisfactory, due to the conditions of the originals.

Despite this, microfilm offers substantial advantages in terms of conservation and preservation, guaranteeing at least 100 years of use.

Digitizing Newspapers

Developments in information and communication technologies have given us new tools for storing, accessing and transmitting documents digitally, offering significant advantages and promising to solve some of the problems presented by the strategy of microfilm storage. Digitization allows patrons to access, browse and reproduce documents at their Internet-computers, from anywhere in the world and at any time.

The newspapers digitization policy has been focusing on the following areas:

a) National newspapers only;
b) Newspapers of the year; and
c) Commonly requested newspapers with historical and heritage value.

Although this is convenient for patrons and allows for conservation and preservation of original materials, it presents risks that need to be evaluated. Evaluating such risks is a complex task; highly-qualified experts would be needed to evaluate the cutting-edge technological resources involved. Therefore, this strategy is currently being analyzed and evaluated in light of the following factors:

a) The high cost of digitization, requiring the services of specialized companies.
b) The insufficiency and/or unavailability of expertise on the part of the providers of newspapers.
c) The prohibitive costs involved in purchasing servers, storage units and other necessities, and the risk that such materials would quickly become obsolete.
d) Problems with the electronic storage of vast volumes of images, as well as access, electronic cataloguing and back-ups.
e) The supervision of the digitization process is exhaustive and time-consuming.
f) The complexity of bibliographic material: different sizes, colors, paper type and quality, which all affect the fidelity of the digital copy.
g) Scanners are designed for standard-format documents and may not be able to completely scan larger documents.
h) The people doing the work of digitizing the documents need to be trained and constant-

ly supervised, which is exhausting and difficult.

i) Patrons consulting and manipulating the documents will be untrained in the use of such technologies.
j) An infinite number of possible software and hardware configurations.
k) Making copies may be complicated for patrons unfamiliar with the use of programs. Technical support will be needed to minimize patron errors.
l) Programs may rapidly go obsolete, meaning added costs for updates and maintenance.
m) Personnel must be trained in order to maximize and optimize use of resources for digitization.
n) Intellectual property and copyright issues. An intellectual property law is currently under debate in Chile, which would take newspapers into account. The norms and restrictions of this law will determine the library's digitization policies and the facilities it will offer the public for access and reproduction

The following are the technical standards for digitization: 300 dpi, non-compressed TIFF format, and medium-resolution PDF format for copies destined for publication.

Newspapers Digitization and Content Development

Since the year 2000, the National Library has carried out a project known as Internet Cultural and Educational Content Development, which has resulted in the websites www.memoriachilena.cl and www.chileparaninos.cl This project was conceived to offer Chileans and foreigners online, real-time access to the library's heritage collections, be they researchers, thesis writers, university and high school students or the general public.

True to its name, the «memoria chilena» (Chilean memory) website offers information about the creation, development and cultural heritage of the Chilean national identity, over time. The site is made up of Content Units (the development of a theme, fact, myth or story), with texts that link to newspapers, images, videos, books, photos, etc. Several of these Content Units have newspapers.

Newspapers selected for digitization in the Content Units are defined by the site's editorial team, and are intended to enrich and improve the said content. A total of 1,000,000 images – 10% of which are from press clippings – have been digitized as part of this process. The digitization guidelines have taken the following factors into account:

a) Press clippings from well-known journals specializing in literature and the social sciences;
b) Newspapers that cover important historical, social and political events in Chile and abroad; and
c) Newspapers that serve as primary sources for content, or are the only historical record of certain events.

The digitization has taken place in the National Library, using equipment owned by the facility and following international standards established by the technical team. The following issues often arise during this process:

a) The need for computer specialists to ensure that the hardware closely corresponds to content development and services to patrons, in terms of storage, operations, updates, security, databases, communications, backups, etc.
b) The constant evolution of information and communication technologies brings with it the risk of hardware and software obsolescence.
c) The personnel in charge of the projects need to be constantly trained, and it is not always possible to optimize the processes and resources involved.

d) The security of both equipment and information.
e) Varying patron knowledge of information and communication technologies – also known as the «digital divide» – leads to difficulties in patron access and use of equipment.
f) Qualified external personnel willing to work on content development, digitization, editing, etc. for reasonable prices are difficult to find.
g) Problems with storage and backup of electronic databases (and meta-databases), as well as access and cataloguing.
h) Copyright.
i) Updates to the site to meet the needs of an increasingly demanding public.
j) Issues related to intellectual property and restrictions on reproductions.

4. Towards the Virtual Library of the 21st Century

With the arrival of new information and communication technologies, the way the public receives information, learns, investigates, entertains itself and creates is constantly changing. Newspapers have not been immune to these changes, and not all of them are paper-based anymore; electronic newspapers are increasingly common today. Electronic newspapers bring with them certain advantages: they reach a much larger public, free of charge, in real time and available from anywhere in the world where there is a computer connected to the Internet. Will all newspapers take this form in the future? Issues of format, digitization, colors and resolution are no longer as pressing. However, the prospect of conserving and preserving these newspapers – which serve as the country's collective memory – has become more of an issue.

Currently, there are several nationwide, electronic newspapers in Chile: *El Mostrador*, *La Nación*, *La Tercera*, *La Segunda*, *El Rastro*, and *EMOL*. Of all of these, *El Mostrador* is the only one with a purely electronic format; the others also come in paper form as well as electronically.

By the Legal Deposit Law, some of these newspapers are turned in to the National Library in CD form. However, they present challenges related to storage, access to the public, and cataloguing as digital collections. The resulting process takes the following considerations into account:

a) Storing electronic media;
b) Policies for creating electronic collections;
c) Offering access to electronic media;
d) Cataloguing electronic media;
e) The lack of uniform, technical standards;
f) Backups;
g) Security;
h) Conservation and preservation;
i) Supporting software for the newspapers used; and
j) Intellectual property, use and reproduction of electronic newspapers.

The library is carrying out a project in 2006 entitled «Towards the Virtual Library of the 21st Century,» to address the challenges specified in the previous paragraph and establish development goals for the next five years.

The first step in this planning effort – known as the Virtual Library Economic and Technical Feasibility Evaluation – will specifically incorporate electronic newspapers. The main components of this phase are:

a) Analysis and Market Trends;
b) Legal Feasibility Studies;
c) Technical Feasibility Studies;
d) Economic Feasibility Studies; and
e) Financial Feasibility Studies.

The main activities in 2006 will be:

a) Research on Chilean and international market trends related to the production of online material, those who can produce it, the production and distribution process of the material, conditions and characteristics (ie., when and how it is produced), etc.
b) Research on technological and communicational means used for the production of online material, both in Chile and abroad.
c) Research on related legal matters: intellectual property considerations for online materials, as well as laws, norms, international agreements, conventions, etc.
d) Research on the successful creation of virtual libraries in foreign countries.
e) Research on the services currently offered by virtual libraries, and service trends.
f) Market studies of the demand for electronic newspapers, in order to rigorously review the requirements of potential users.
g) Analysis and evaluation of information collected.
h) Formulation of a detailed model of a virtual library, including resources, supply, demand, operations, services, support, etc.
i) Determination of the necessary costs involved in creating a model virtual library.
j) Technical, economic and financial evaluation of the model virtual library.
k) Corrections to that model.
l) Formulation of the Virtual Library itself, including resources, supply, demand, operations, services, support, etc.
m) Virtual Library Implementation Plan.

However the model Virtual Library will turn out, alliances between the Chilean National Library and the private sector will be a critical factor in its success. Collaboration and cooperation are basic prerequisites for working in the virtual world. The active participation of all involved is ideal.

Everyone has the right to information, knowledge, creation ... wherever, whenever and however they are needed.

COOPERATIVE DIGITIZATION AND DISSEMINATION OF WORLD NEWSPAPERS: A PROPOSAL

James Simon

Director of International Resources
Center for Research Libraries

Abstract

Through a century of major, sustained investment in acquisition, documentation and preservation, North American research libraries have amassed a large and valuable corpus of newspapers from around the world. Those libraries' aggregate holdings of newspapers in paper and micro-formats span four centuries and constitute a corpus of historical and cultural evidence that is not, and could not be, replicated elsewhere.

Various national libraries, including the British Library and the Library of Congress, have begun to undertake the digitization and Web presentation of back runs of newspapers from their countries. In addition a number of commercial publishers have expressed interest in digitizing selected major U.S. and foreign newspapers holdings of American libraries to enable public access.

It is doubtful that either the national or commercial projects are of a model suited to provide access to most newspapers from regions outside the developed world. In an effort to provide such access, CRL is exploring the feasibility of a collective, library-driven effort in collaboration with one or more electronic publishers to digitally reformat and disseminate newspapers from Latin America, Africa, the Middle East, and other world regions.

Introduction

Through a century of major, sustained investment in acquisition, documentation and preservation, North American research libraries have amassed a large and valuable corpus of newspapers from all regions of the world. Those libraries' aggregate holdings of newspapers in paper and micro-formats span four centuries and constitute a body of historical and cultural evidence that is not, and could not be, replicated elsewhere.

Microform, the chief means of access to these primary source materials, affords limited use and discoverability of the materials. Consequently various national libraries, including the Bibliotheque Nationale de France, British Library, Library and Archives Canada, Library of Congress, and the Österreichische Nationalbibliothek, have begun to digitize back runs of their respective domestic newspapers. These national projects are not likely to soon provide access to newspapers from regions outside of the United States, Canada, Europe and the United Kingdom, however.

The Center for Research Libraries and major North American research libraries are now contemplating the systematic, large scale digitization of world newspapers and news-related materials from their paper and microform holdings. They have recently approached a number of institutions with a mix of business models to explore this effort further.

Before I tackle this subject matter, a brief history of North American cooperative efforts with respect to foreign newspaper preservation and access is in order.

History

Cooperative foreign newspaper preservation in the United States began in 1938 at Harvard University, with grant funds received from the Rockefeller Foundation to select and microfilm a representative sample of international newspapers for preservation and distribution. In 1946, the Association for Research Libraries (ARL) began discussing the need for a nationally coordinated and cooperative plan to preserve library materials, and in 1956 the Foreign Newspaper Microfilm Project (FNMP) was established to provide worldwide coverage of representative foreign titles.

The Center for Research Libraries recognized the importance of international newspapers from its inception and in 1952 began original filming and purchases of 50 foreign newspapers. CRL became the repository and administrative coordinator of the newly founded FNMP due to its ability to maintain newspapers in ideal storage conditions, efficiently deliver materials to constituents, and handle other necessary administrative arrangements of the project.

By 1968, the number of available foreign newspaper titles and separate microfilming projects had proliferated so rapidly that the ARL Foreign Newspaper Microfilm Committee began seeking an expanded national approach to the coordinated coverage of international newspapers. ARL proposed an undertaking to include 2,000 titles and utilize resources of ARL, the Library of Congress, and other interested research institutions that had begun their own filming programs.[1] The Library of Congress took a lead role in this initiative, sponsoring a feasibility study and summary recommendations for action. In 1972, the Library of Congress expanded its newspaper preservation program and established the position of coordinator of foreign newspaper microfilming. It produced several publications important for sharing information about newspaper preservation, including the *Newspapers in Microform* union list and a new publication titled *Foreign Newspaper Report*. This title provided a clearinghouse of information on newspaper microfilming from nonprofit and commercial publishers.[2] It was a critical tool for sharing news on title changes, suspensions or cessation, and filming announcements for new titles.

Eventually, the increasing attention to the need for preservation strategies for domestic newspapers shifted priorities away from international titles. Though the United States Newspaper Program attracted increasing funds on a national scale, CRL and the FNMP maintained their role as guardians of international news sources. In 1982, CRL officially took over the full responsibility of the FNMP and absorbed the program into its general operations.

In a renewed effort in 1987, the NEH and other organizations sponsored the «First International Symposium on Newspaper Preservation and Access.» The conference brought together over 100 librarians, scholars, and information professionals to gather information on newspaper collections in libraries around the world and to focus on solutions to the numerous and varied challenges to newspaper collection and preservation. Ten years later, the Center for Research Libraries convened the «Symposium on Access to and Preservation

---

1 These institutions included Hoover Institution, Cornell University, University of Florida, New York Public Library, and the University of California at Berkeley. Other nonprofit and commercial institutions also began filming foreign newspapers.

2 The Foreign Newspaper Report subsumed the function of circular letters to the FNMP subscribers. Beginning in 1973, it came out three times a year; the title was expanded to Foreign Newspaper and Gazette Report the next year, changed again to Newspaper and Gazette Report in 1976, and replaced by the National Preservation Report in 1979.

of Global Newspapers» (Washington, D.C., May 1997). The 1997 symposium sought to revisit the issue of newspaper collections with an ambitious agenda exploring and defining problems of collecting, storing, preserving, and providing access to international newspapers. As a direct result of this conference, the International Coalition on Newspapers (ICON) was created.

In 1998, a working group was formed to further explore the complex factors affecting foreign newspaper collection and access. With support from the Andrew W. Mellon Foundation, the group issued a set of recommendations for a permanent body to monitor and coordinate an international effort of newspaper acquisition and preservation. In 1999, a permanent ICON steering committee was formed from among the participants. Charter members included such prominent institutions as the Library of Congress, British Library, National Library of Canada, New York Public Library, University of Illinois, and the University of Washington. The Center for Research Libraries was selected as the administrative home of the project.

Today ICON is a multi-institutional cooperative effort to increase the availability of international newspaper collections by improving both bibliographic and physical access to these resources, and to preserve global cultural heritage through the preservation of international newspaper collections held in the United States and abroad. ICON is comprised of the foremost experts in global newspaper acquisition and preservation. It involves principals from key sectors of the information community: academic institutions, research and national libraries, scholarly and professional societies, commercial publishers and micropublishers, and funding agencies.

ICON's goals are international in scope, collaborative in nature, and long-term and multiphased in range.

- To amass information on the collection and preservation status of the world's newspapers;
- To provide access to an unprecedented array of resources and information on newspaper holdings and conditions;
- To increase the availability of humanistic resources and materials to the scholarly community in the U.S. and abroad through coordinated foreign newspaper collection, indexing, and preservation;
- To preserve global cultural and intellectual resources through cooperative microfilming efforts and through the exploration of alternative preservation models (e.g., digitization);
- To broker international collaborative partnerships and efforts through a structured framework and coordinated oversight; and
- To provide an ongoing forum for discussion of issues relating to global newspapers and to increase awareness and support of preservation and access to newspapers worldwide.

The National Endowment for the Humanities has been instrumental in assisting with the objectives of ICON. A grant in 2000 launched ICON's long-term preservation and access initiatives. The core components of the funded effort were to create an online Database of International Newspapers and to preserve on microfilm a set of representative newspaper titles. Subsequent grant phases in 2002 and 2004 have expanded the efforts of the project, leading to a number of significant outcomes.

The database is freely available on the Web and stands as the most significant outcome of the ICON project to date. Over 22,000 bibliographic records and 12,000 holdings records are available, and input is ongoing.

Preservation microfilm has resulted in more than 840 reels and 45 newspaper titles preserved from Africa, Latin America, Middle East, Eastern Europe, and others.

The project has also focused on the creation of new bibliographic records for newspapers in order to increase access and awareness of foreign titles. With funding to distributed institutions to create new records, ICON is serving a national and international need for better information relating to newspapers published outside the United States.

It should be stated up front that the proposed cooperative digitization effort is not currently an official effort under the jurisdiction of ICON. Indeed, from the outset, ICON has maintained its core mission of long-term preservation of news resources and has not yet endorsed digitization as a viable preservation means. However, ICON members and the advisory committee have played a significant role in shaping the proposed effort and support it as a parallel activity to newspaper preservation.

World News Archive

The proposed initiative, tentatively titled the «World News Archive,» strives to make the holdings of world newspapers easily accessible in digital format to scholarly communities in North America and throughout the world. CRL and participating institutions («Affiliates») propose to focus, initially, on newspapers from a single region: Latin America and the Caribbean. The number of titles digitized will be scaled to the funds and resources available to CRL, Affiliates, and partner organization(s). The effort assumes that the arrangement with the partner organization(s) will be ongoing and may eventually encompass newspapers and news-related materials from other world regions as well.

Holdings will be compiled and/or combined from the strengths of participating institutions. Thus far, nine major research institutions have expressed interest in joining the effort, including some institutions with the most extensive research collections of newspapers (New York Public Library, for instance has more than 11,500 newspaper titles, 1/3 to 1/2 of which are foreign). CRL holds more than 7,000 foreign titles in varying runs.

In terms of scope, we are being deliberately vague with participants and potential partner organizations. At this point, the effort is still under development, and the scale of the initial phase of the project will have to be determined on the basis of the nature, degree, and quality of publisher interest. The long-term vision is that the collection will be comprehensive in its scope, including:

- Small independent newspapers as well as major dailies;
- In-copyright and out-of-copyright material; and
- High-use material as well as culturally significant materials in lesser demand.

The precise scope of the endeavor will ultimately be determined by mutual agreement between CRL and Affiliates and the partner organization(s).

The venture will promote the application and adoption of international standards and best practices to digitization projects. CRL and Affiliates will determine the minimum standards and specifications for the digital conversion and for the production of metadata for the newspapers, and the quality, scope, and functionality of the digital resource to be produced. In general the standards and specifications will be compatible with those developed for the national projects underway. This is important so that we aim to drive towards a de facto standard and to open the possibility of interoperability among existing and future projects.

We aim to collectively take the initiative in the migration of our news collections content from microform and paper to digital and to recruit appropriate partners in the commercial sector who might assist in the effort. The mechanism for getting this done is still in flux. CRL has issued a request for general proposals to a variety of organizations, electronic publishers, aggregators, and other entities that have expressed interest in distributing digital newspaper content from libraries. The Request for Information, or «RFI,» asks for written proposals from potential partner organizations, essentially expressions of interest in participating in this endeavor.

Respondents have been asked to respond to a number of issues, including the proposed scope of their interest,[3] the services they propose to provide to the endeavor (such as digital conversion, markup, metadata production, exposure, presentation, marketing), and the nature and level of their expected return on investment. Organizations may propose to contribute a wide array of services and resources to the endeavor or a limited number of specialized services. Proposals may be submitted by individual organizations or by several organizations working in tandem. The digital resources developed under the proposed endeavor will be made available exclusively through the partnership for a specified period of time.

In choosing its partners, CRL and Affiliates will favor organizations that bring to the endeavor the greatest combination of competency and experience in the production and distribution of digital resources, and commitment of in-kind and financial investment to the project.

CRL and its Affiliates expect to derive similar return on their investment, be it in the form of increased access to research resources for their constituent communities, financial compensation for costs incurred, or some combination of the two.

It is the balance of these expected returns that will prove, in my mind, most interesting. On the one hand, a purely philanthropic endeavor would provide the widest access to the material (generally federal- or foundation-supported efforts favor open access). Given the scope and cost of such an investment, this option, while most desirable, is unlikely. On the other hand, a purely commercial investment would seem to be more likely to occur, and at a lower cost for the donating institution, but not desirable from the standpoint of the educational community that is seeking to protect its assets for the scholarly commons. In order to safeguard the rights and benefits, it seems apparent that co-investment by the educational and commercial sector will be necessary. What that blend will be is the subject to negotiations over the next several months.

The interests that the Center for Research Libraries and Affiliates seek to protect include:

Rights

The consortium will clear with copyright owners and will secure all rights necessary to permit digital conversion and dissemination of the selected newspapers to scholarly users. CRL and Affiliates will provide to the partner organization a limited license for specified

---

3 Prospective partners may indicate the scale and scope of the undertaking in which they are willing to invest and participate. This can be expressed in terms of an estimated number of titles or estimated total number of pages/frames to be digitized, or the chronological and/or geographical range of materials the prospective partner proposes to convert under the endeavor. (A range might include, for example, Cuban newspapers published between 1890 and 1960, or Mexican newspapers produced before 1900.)

uses of the digitized news content, which shall last for a specific duration. The scope and duration of the license will be negotiated and will be dependent upon the scale of the partner organization's investment in the endeavor. The license will be renewable periodically by mutual agreement.

Ownership

CRL and Affiliates will receive escrow copies of all digital files and associated metadata for preservation purposes, and will reserve the right, forward from a specified date to be determined by mutual agreement between CRL and the partner organization, to make those files available to their respective constituencies. All contracts will stipulate that, after a mutually agreed upon and specified period, CRL and Affiliates or their designated agent will thenceforth be free to make any and all possible uses of the digital files and related metadata created under the project from their respective holdings.

Transparency

Rights and incentives to participate shall be disclosed to the interested parties and stakeholders.

Pricing

Because the Affiliates' respective constituencies have a vested interest in the availability of the source materials, and have in many instances funded the preservation of those materials, it may be appropriate to provide preferential pricing of the resultant digital resources for certain markets. CRL and Affiliates might impose upon distribution of World News Archive resources conditions regarding pricing that are preferential to certain constituencies. Preference might be given by establishing pricing tiers or even specific rates that favor such markets as independent and academic research libraries, libraries and universities in developing regions, and so forth.

The timeframe for the kickoff of the endeavor is short. The RFI has been issued, and we are seeking to have submissions from interested institutions by July 9, 2006. An informational session has been organized on June 6 At the Center for Research Libraries. Second phase negotiations are targeted for the fall of this year, with final selection for January-February 2007.

Finally, we are seeking to work with institutions and organizations with the appropriate expertise and efficiencies to make this a sustainable endeavor. This may include educational or research institutions in other regions. Certainly we are sensitive to the need for access to these resources in the region, and we do not want to duplicate work underway. So, for this group, I would encourage you to share with us your experiences and knowledge of successful practices. We will continue to communicate progress of the discussions through the IFLA Newspaper Section.

THE U.S. NATIONAL DIGITAL NEWSPAPER PROGRAM: THINKING AHEAD, DESIGNING NOW PART I: PROGRAM DEVELOPMENT

Helen Aguera

Senior Program Officer
U.S. National Endowment for the Humanities

As you may know, the National Endowment for the Humanities (or NEH) is an independent agency of the United States government that accomplishes its mission of promoting excellence in the humanities by making grants for projects in four funding areas: preserving and providing access to cultural resources, scholarly research, education, and public programs. While funded projects generally focus on topics related to United States history and culture, the Endowment supports international projects in which American scholars participate such as bibliographic databases, digital archives, and reference works. Cooperative efforts that benefit scholars worldwide are also funded. For instance, through awards to the International Coalition on Newspapers Project (iCON) housed at the Center for Research Libraries, NEH has facilitated the work of preserving and improving access to newspapers from around the globe.

The NEH has had a long-term commitment to preserving and making accessible historical newspapers published in the United States for their importance as source material to various humanities disciplines. Since the 1980s, the Endowment has conducted the United States Newspaper Program (USNP for short). Through USNP, state projects-usually housed at the major newspaper repository in a state-have received grants to organize and manage the inventorying and cataloging of all newspaper holdings scattered throughout each state. The projects have also preserved in microfilm selected state newspapers, which are made available to researchers through inter-library loan. As a partner in this program, the Library of Congress has provided through the years training and technical advice to the state projects, and monitored the quality of the bibliographic records. The bibliographic information about titles is stored in the CONSER database managed by LC and the holdings records are provided by OCLC.

The collective accomplishments of the USNP have been vast. When the program comes to conclusion in 2007, or shortly after, there will be records for state newspapers published in every state, Puerto Rico, the Virgin Islands, and the District of Columbia. Ultimately, users will have access to bibliographic records for over 140,000 newspaper titles and over 70 million pages of newsprint in microfilm. NEH funding during the history of this program will exceed $54 million. It is our expectation that states will maintain the database of bibliographic information and continue to film selected current titles.

As we were coming to the end of USNP, we began to plan for a new program to provide enhanced access to newspapers by digitizing selected titles already preserved in microfilm. This program is now known as the National Digital Newspaper Program or NDNP. Because no single institution in the United States has a complete collection of American newspapers, we understood that this program had to be a distributed effort that involved state institutions in applying a uniform set of selection criteria in order to create a geographically representative collection. Since the Library of Congress is a national repository with extensive newspaper holdings and a commitment to their long-term preservation, it was logical for the NEH to form another partnership with the Library. Consequently, on March 31, 2004, the Endowment signed an agreement with LC to create a digital resource of historical newspapers, which we are currently calling «American Chronicle.» Under the terms of this partnership, the Endowment will make awards to state projects to select important newspapers from their collections and digitize them. The Library will host the aggregated digital files and associated metadata, including optically converted text, to support basic access to newspaper pages through chronological and keyword searches. While LC will be aggregating information provided by the state projects for cross-searching, the state partners will be free to repurpose the newspaper files created with NDNP funding to provide enhanced access. They can integrate them in other state or regional projects to address the needs of local users. However, the funding needed to develop local interfaces or to do additional processing will be the responsibility of the state projects. The NDNP is part of a special NEH initiative called «We the People» that aims to explore significant events and themes in our nation's history. No other source is richer for this purpose than historical newspapers.

Given the large number of newspaper titles available for digitization, American Chronicle will focus on the extensive and crucial period of the nation's history from 1836 to 1922, thus complementing other digital resources that cover earlier periods of the country's history. It will also be limited to newspapers that are in the public domain. In creating NDNP, we understood that we had to proceed in various phases, since digitizing millions of pages would require a long-term program (of fifteen to twenty years) to fund institutions in every state and territory of the Union. Because the title aggregation is being done to allow cross-searching of selected state papers, we decided to focus initially on digitizing titles published in the early twenty century, a time when all states had an active press that could be represented in the repository. As the program developed, we would expand the chronological coverage starting with the late nineteenth century and eventually going back to the 1830s. In this way, NDNP would provide broad geographic representation as well as focused searching in time clusters rather than scattered access through the entire period.

In addition, we thought it important that American Chronicle repurpose the rich bibliographic and holdings information compiled through USNP so that users can find out about the location of titles available in microfilm and in print. This tool will provide an important service to users since most newspapers will not be digitized in the near future. Moreover, this information can help institutions embarking in a newspaper digitization effort to identify extant newspapers in analog formats.

In May 2005, the NDNP began its development phase by making awards to six state projects that are selecting newspapers published in California, Florida, Kentucky, New York, Utah, and Virginia during the decade of 1900 to 1910. These projects are currently digitizing a minimum of 100,000 pages, according to the technical guidelines outlined by the Library of Congress, and will be contributing to the evaluation of the test bed results. A prototype containing a sampling of the aggregated titles will be launched in September 2006. In addition, the evaluation of the test bed will inform refinements in the program guidelines and technical specifications.

My colleagues at LC will later explain the preservation framework they are creating for American Chronicle and their work in aggregating the materials produced by the various projects and the Library, which is also contributing newspapers from its own collection. Representatives from two of the participating state projects, California and Kentucky, will be explaining their experience as state partners during the development phase.

Let me say a few words about our assumptions in projecting future phases of NDNP. We know that technology will change and, therefore, the system that we design will have to take advantage of new ways of creating and processing data for enhancing access. While no one knows what the optimal way of preserving digital data will be, we can minimize the effort of providing persistent information by proceeding in stages and capitalizing on lessons learned at each stage, beginning with the development phase. The solutions that state projects will find to the challenges they face in contributing pages to American Chronicle will help us guide new projects on how to proceed with greater efficiency. LC's work on aggregating the information and in addressing issues of digital preservation, including their experience in the National Digital Information Infrastructure and Preservation Program (NDIIPP), will help NDNP ensure long-term access to digitized newspapers. For its part, NEH will be able to manage more effectively the funding it can dedicate to newspaper digitization as part of its support for preservation and access activities.

What are some of the characteristics of future projects? Since we do not anticipate funding more than one project per state, the successful projects are likely to be collaborative efforts that involve partners with access to negative microfilm of state newspapers and partners that have the necessary infrastructure to do large conversion projects and may have experience in digitizing serial formats. NEH will make an award to one institution, which in turn can subcontract to other participants, as necessary.

Successful projects would be those that have an advisory board composed of scholars, teachers, librarians, and archivists involved in the development of selection criteria for state titles. These criteria should follow some basic principles. Titles should:

- reflect the political, economic, and cultural history of the state (Such newspapers usually have statewide or regional influence. Preference should be given to titles that are recognized as a «paper of record» at the state or county level and that contain published legal notices, news of state and regional governmental affairs, and announcements of community news and events.);
- Papers should provide state coverage or at least multi-county coverage of the majority of the population areas; and
- Titles should have a significant chronological span (continuity is preferred over short runs or scattered issues).

In addition, special consideration should be given to papers meeting these criteria that are not available in digital form and are also «orphan» titles. Papers that are no longer published or do not have a recognized owner are less likely to be included in other digitization efforts. By making available such papers, NDNP can ensure that users have access to earlier titles that had broad circulation.

What costs will NDNP support? The costs of title selection, metadata creation, image capture and processing by a vendor (or perhaps doing it in-house), quality control work, and delivery of files to LC. Our expectation is that we would have a new competition each year until all states and territories have contributed material to American Chronicle. For the next deadline of November 1 we are now revising the guidelines, which will be made available through the NEH and LC web sites.

THE U.S. NATIONAL DIGITAL NEWSPAPER PROGRAM: THINKING AHEAD, DESIGNING NOW PART II: PRESERVATION PLANNING

Mark Sweeney

Program Manager
National Digital Newspaper Program

The National Digital Newspaper Program (NDNP) is a distributed effort to enhance access to America's newspapers through digital technology. One of the roles played by the Library of Congress to facilitate this access is preservation.

Newspapers have always presented significant preservation challenges for libraries – poor quality ink and paper, the size and volume of collections, the poor storage space available, and inherent weaknesses of the means to preserve the information content – whether through binding, microfilming, and now digitization, the most fragile of all formats.

While we are all focused on providing enhanced access to today's users of historic newspapers, how will we ensure that today's digital conversion investment benefits future generations of users? In developing the NDNP, the National Endowment for the Humanities (NEH) and the Library of Congress (LC) were mindful of several principles that guided our planning:

- aggregate, serve, and preserve;
- consistent with missions and philosophies of NEH and LC;
- open and perpetual access to the general public and scholarly community;
- take care to preserve the asset that NDNP builds;
- must demonstrate good use of taxpayer $;
- phased development;
- build incrementally – don't close off options.

We understood that it would be necessary for us to take into account all elements of the digital lifecycle if we were to going to be able of achieve NEH's requirement of long-term/perpetual access to the content created over the life of the program.

We needed to establish sound technical specifications for the creation of digital assets that could be efficiently aggregated from multiple sources, allowing basic public access, and we would need to preserve the content for future generations of users. High quality digital content stored in a poor environment will not ensure long-term access.

This project is consistent with the missions of our two agencies, LC and NEH, by making the assets created through federal funds freely accessible to many different users. We had to be good stewards of both the digital content as well as the federal funds supporting the program.

This effort called for a phased development approach in which we build incrementally upon existing expertise and best practices while recognizing that there are many different options that can be exercised now and in the future. To the best of our ability we want to leave the door open to future options.

So what will the system be like? The best way to describe the system that we envisioned and are building for the NDNP is OPEN:

- freely accessible (a public resource);
- available to use and re-use;
- deep linking and persistent identification to support citation;
- open technical formats;
- interoperable through support for standard protocols;
- modular architecture;
- software based on open source code to degree possible.

We envision an «open» system because we know that the only thing that is certain about the future is CHANGE. We want to be positioned to take advantage of new technology to meet changing user needs. We expect the technology to improve and change:

- Access capabilities will improve and get cheaper.
- OCR will improve.
- Accuracy of automated article segmentation will improve.
- Availability of open source tools will expand.

User expectations will also evolve, in ways we may or may not be able to predict. What will scholars want? Text mining and time and place analysis are highly desirable by the research community. What will new user communities want? Difficult to predict, but certainly PDA access and learning tool integration will be expected.

Preservation models will also evolve and expectations will likely change, but build on the core elements of openness, trust, standard tools, and stability.

With an assumption of CHANGE and a program lifetime of 20 or more years, how do we plan for the future? We agree that content is more important than «system» of today, so the «system» is designed to be expandable. The «system» must be modular and upgradeable. Interoperability is a key element since it is intended to be a resource that stands alone but plays well with others.

The phased development approach is deliberate. It creates an environment with opportunities for learning and a way to validate assumptions. The early development phase is an opportunity to develop best practices that could lead to standards and builds a corpus that is of value for technical experimentation.

Certain practical concerns guided our deliberations as well. While we recognize that there may be situations in which it is advantageous to purchase «out-of-the box» solutions for providing access to digital collections, the unique Library of Congress responsibility is to sustain NDNP content created over a very long time frame. That necessitated that we develop our own repository, keeping in mind that the preservation of digital objects for future users was as important as providing access today.

We carefully analyzed the technical options, recognizing the need to:

- think carefully about formats;
- detail specifications to assure consistency;
- develop means to validate conformance;
- incorporate metadata to understand context and circumstances of creation.

In addition, we made a conscious effort to build on LC's expertise and investment in metadata schemes, repository models, and emerging image formats. LC's development, enhancement, and implementation of METS, PREMIS, FEDORA, JPEG2000 provided valuable experience useful for NDNP. Likewise our experience with large-scale and distributed digitization and aggregation, learned through such projects as the Stars and Stripes digitization project as well as other NDIIPP projects, has proven invaluable for NDNP.

Finally, we expect to learn from our awardees as we work with them through a distributed content creation and central aggregation model. Awardees have been given wide latitude in selecting content and the means of creating the data within tight technical specifications. We fully expect that those technical specifications will change as we collectively gain more experience working through different digital conversion workflows and interact with a variety of vendors.

Awardees have also been afforded the opportunity to retain a copy of the data they produce to experiment with, to enhance, and to aggregate with other digital content that falls out-of-scope for NDNP. We will learn from their efforts and if possible incorporate them into our future plans.

THE U.S. NATIONAL DIGITAL NEWSPAPER PROGRAM: THINKING AHEAD, DESIGNING NOW PART III: TECHNICAL SPECIFICATIONS

Ray Murray

Digital Conversion Specialist
Library of Congress

Archival Needs, Data Needs

In order to implement a digital program, specific choices need to be made. With a mindset toward preservation, the Library of Congress chose to follow the philosophy of the Open Archival Information System (OAIS) Model.

An OAIS repository can be seen as interacting with discrete groups of actors, including: producers, managers and consumers. Each group has different roles with respect to the repository, so the repository will present different options to each, perhaps even through different interfaces.

Producers create the data that is stored by the repository. When interacting with producers, the repository needs to ingest the data. The vehicle for this interaction is the Submission Information Package (SIP).

Managers need to ensure that the data is stable over the long term. The repository can also be seen as managing the data internally, storing it in the form of an Archival Information Package (AIP).

Consumers are those end-users that are interested in the data within the repository. To satisfy them, the repository needs a mechanism to distribute the data. This vehicle is the Distribution Information Package or DIP.

Information Object, Data Object

A newspaper on either paper or microfilm does not innately suggest how it should be stored in a digital repository. This information object must be transformed into a data object – a digital surrogate – in order to be ingested into the repository. There are choices to be made on exactly how this is done, many different ways by which one could accomplish this.

The choices made for NDNP result in a SIP with five types of data file for each newspaper page. The archival master is a TIFF file. A JPEG 2000 file is used as a production master. A PDF version is also stored. Optical Character Recognition (OCR) text for the page is ingested in a simplified ALTO format. A metadata file carries structural metadata, preservation metadata, and validation information.

Archival Master: TIFF

For Phase I of the NDNP, a conservative approach was taken with respect to the archival master digital image. Specifications were that it was to conform with TIFF 6.0, be 8-bit uncompressed grayscale, 400 dpi preferred. Grayscale was used rather than bitonal, to allow dynamic threshholding during the OCR process. This choice also leaves the door open for future reprocessing of the OCR that take positive advantage of the subtleties of a grayscale image.

Additional TIFF tags, above and beyond those standard in TIFF 6.0, were required for preservation purposes. These have potential to help in identifying lost files – those that have become dissociated from their metadata or file structures. The additional preservation information in the TIFF tags will also inform migrations to future file formats.

Production Master: JPEG 2000

Prior to NDNP, the Library of Congress did not have a great deal of experience using JPEG 2000 files. Because of this the Library of Congress sought the expertise of Rob Buckley of Xerox Labs, working with him to develop a profile for JPEG 2000 suitable for a production master for digitized historical newspapers. The specification decided upon conforms with JPEG 2000, Part 1, and uses a 9-7 irreversible (lossy) filter to compress the file to 1/8 the size of the original TIFF.

For preservation purposes, RDF/Dublin Core metadata was specified to be included in the file header an XML box.

The JPEG 2000 specification for NDNP was designed only with production use of the file in mind; the specifications for a JPEG 2000 file as an archival master would necessarily be different.

Derivative: PDF

The PDF file was specified for NDNP to be compatible with Acrobat 5.0 (PDF 1.4) or later. It contains the newspaper page image with text behind, to allow standalone text searching of a downloaded PDF file.

Once again for preservation purposes, XMP/RDF/Dublin Core metadata was specified to be included in the PDF file header.

OCR Text: ALTO

Initially, NDNP sought to design a format for the OCR text that would be independent of the OCR engine used to create it. It would be an open file structure, preferably XML-based.

It would also be important that the OCR data would map the text to its position on the page. With approximately 5000 words on a typical newspaper page, being able to locate and highlight a word found in a text search was seen as an essential capability of the system.

In fact there already existed such a format, the Analyzed Layout and Text Object (ALTO) format, a product of the EU-funded METAe project. Since ALTO had more capabilities than needed, a simplified form was used for NDNP.

Structural Metadata

The structural metadata for NDNP was build using the Metadata Encoding and Transmission Standard (METS), developed and maintained by the Library of Congress. It includes information on titles, issues, pages and microfilm reels.

The title METS Object is based on the MARC record for the titles. Bibliographic records for 140,000 newspaper titles published in the United States, many created through USNP funding, were ingested into the NDNP repository.

The holdings data for all titles was also incorporated into the data structure. The repository will have a directory function, where consumers can find historical newspapers whether they are in digital form, on microfilm, or in the original. This directory will also locate master microfilm, for institutions interested in digitizing from microfilm.

The issue METS Object incorporates metadata on the issue and its constituent pages. It was designed to allow multiple editions on the same date. Its data structure also can record missing issues and missing pages, making use of the collation work that was recorded on the original microfilm.

The reel METS document includes technical metadata about the microfilm, such as the camera's effective reduction ratio, resolution quality of the film and photographic emulsion density. This information can be used to analyze the preservation process from paper to microfilm, as well as the conversion process from microfilm to digital. One avenue of questions concerns how the characteristics of the film correlate with the quality of the digital end product, especially with respect to OCR accuracy.

Validating the SIP

A major precept of the OAIS repository model is to know the nature of the data going into it, and to apply strong quality standards to the data prior to ingestion.

Toward that end, NDNP developed its own Digital Viewer and Validator (DVV). This software program allows users to validate NDNP data for compliance to specifications in an automated way, and to view the data to examine its qualitative aspects. The DVV is built on the open-source JHOVE software developed at Harvard, and extends its capabilities for the specific needs of NDNP.

When validation is run by the DVV, it creates digital signatures that sign the files as having passed validation. The signature incorporates a checksum, so it also can vouch for the bit-by-bit integrity of a file from that point forward. The validation process also adds PREMIS and MIX preservation metadata to the metadata files.

With the preservation goals of NDNP, it is critically important to know the overall Submission Information Package is valid. Therefore it is only after the validation process has been successfully completed that the SIP is ingested. Then the data can become available to all the other capabilities of the NDNP repository.

THE U.S. NATIONAL DIGITAL NEWSPAPER PROGRAM: THINKING AHEAD, DESIGNING NOW PART IV: REPOSITORY DEVELOPMENT

George Schlukbier

Technical Project Manager,
National Digital Newspaper Program

The National Digital Newspaper repository was built using a variety of organizing tools, all supporting the Open Archival Information System (OAIS) model. The program uses Project Management or the PMI process in conjunction with open source tools and applications. It also uses Agile Software Development methodology, Subversion for source control, and Mantis for bug tracking. The team also used a wiki for communication.

Designers of the repository were guided by the needs of many different users and uses of the system. Below is the intended structure of the repository that will support the OAI preservation model.

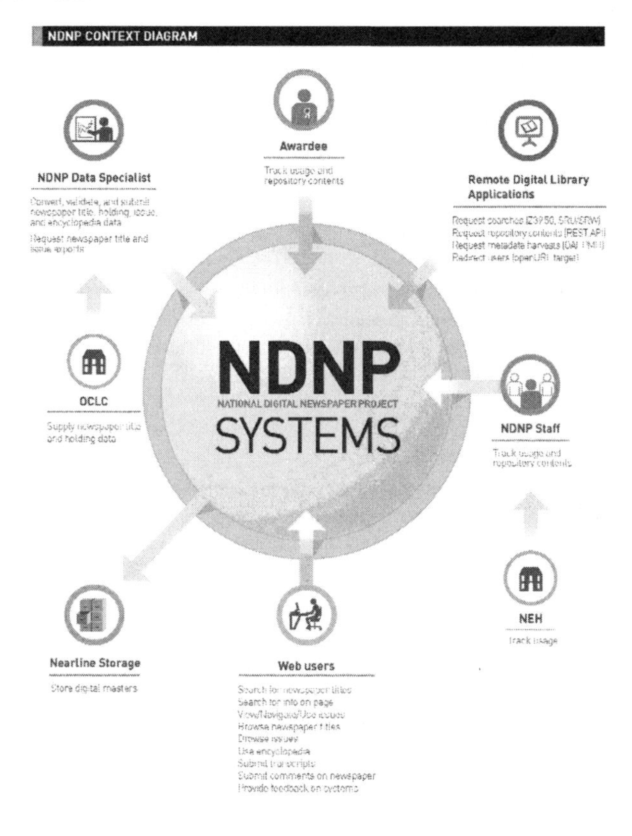

Fig. 1

As mentioned by other NDNP speakers, interoperability is of paramount importance for the repository, and influenced the decision to build an open source system. Such a system will ensure that this twenty-year program will have enduring value as software and hardware inevitably change. The future of interoperability begins with standards, and designers of the repository have defined and made publicly available the standards to be implemented and developed (JPEG, XML, METS/MODS, TIFF, ALTO, JPEG2000, PDF).

Standards are also needed for data migration. We need to be able to migrate these objects: Newspaper Titles, Issues and Pages with all the structural and descriptive metadata intact. So how best can migration of massive amounts of objects be achieved and maintained within a repository system?

The NDNP system is built in Modules: Ingest, Facade, Search, Repository and Disseminations. We will discuss these Modules at a high level.

API's

The system uses a variety of application program interfaces, or API's. An API is a set of routines, protocols, and tools for building software applications. A good API makes it easier to develop a program by providing all the building blocks. Within an open system, API's allow remote systems and users to gain access to the repository.

One set of API's are web exposed API's, and the ones used in the NDNP repository include:

- Search API-SRW[1] with extensions
- Access API
- Ingest API
- Relations API
- (tbd) Export API
- (tbd) OAI-PMH to enable Metadata Harvesting[2]
- (tbd) Client library.

Through API's the NDNP system may «expose» its object repository so that other libraries, institutions, or commercial group can send web service requests and query the NDNP. The opportunities are endless if you build an «open system» that uses standards and provide API's for remote system and user access.

Data Flow

We designed the system to handle data and requests. NDNP awardees input data which is ultimately used to respond to user requests. Upon receipt by the Library, the data is processed through what we call a «staging area» where the data is temporarily stored, validated to ensure accurate transfer, normalized and ultimately ingested. The diagram below best explains the process (Figure 2).

We also build a Validation Tool called the DVV which helps ensure that all the complicated information submitted is consistent it is structure and conforms to our data model.

1 SRW is a variation of SRU. Messages are conveyed from client to server, not by a URL, but instead using XML over HTTP via the W3C recommendation, SOAP, which specifies how to wrap an XML message within an XML envelope. The SRW specification tries to adhere to the Web Services Interoperability profile.

2 Open Archives Initiative Protocol for Metadata Harvesting (OAI-PMH).

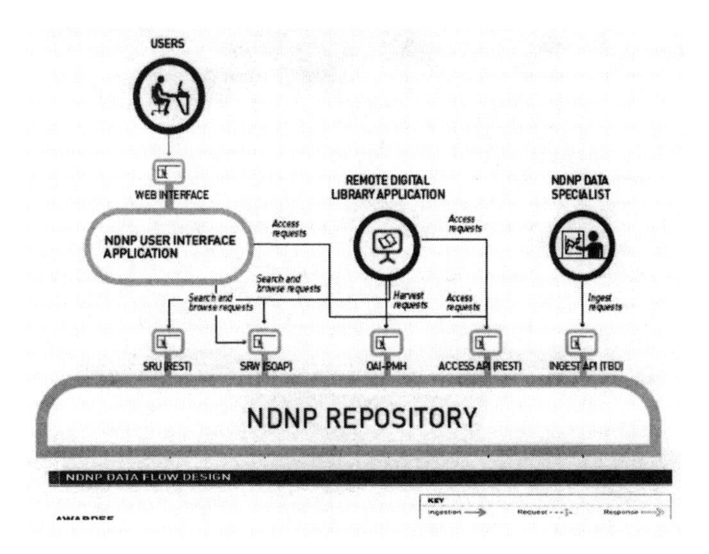

Fig. 2

The Module Approach

A modular approach gives us the flexibility to upgrade or change any one of the modules without having to re-architect or re-build the system. Four separate modules make up the system: Search System, Facade, Dissemination Services, and Fedora Repository (Figure 3).

The importance of the AIP's is obvious: we use them to deliver the information throughout the system. The result is that the information can be accessed through the User Interface.

A number of Dissemination Information Packages allow data to flow between users and the repository. Like SIP's, these conform to the technical language of OAIS for preservation purposes. Thus, the NDNP repository is a freely accessible system AND is representative of the «best of practices» for digital preservation at LC.

As the diagram above illustrates, all changing format requests such as Z39.50 search API's, and SRW APIs and SRUs API's outside of the Repository. This means we do not have to change our basic storage system to handle new standards. The Facade serves as a barrier between changing applications and the NDNP repository.

The Fedora repository is our «black box,» a file management system that is more open than DSPACE (the other object repository being used for «open source» digital preservation projects). Fedora, Flexible Extensible Digital Object Repository Architecture,[3] is an open source digital library plumbing system. It was developed as a joint venture between the University of Virginia and Cornell University, funded by Mellon Foundation. It is characterized by low-level storage and digital object polymorphism. Digital Object Polymorphism is an Object Programming term meaning an object can have more than one meaning.

---

1 For more information about Fedora, see: http://fedora.info.

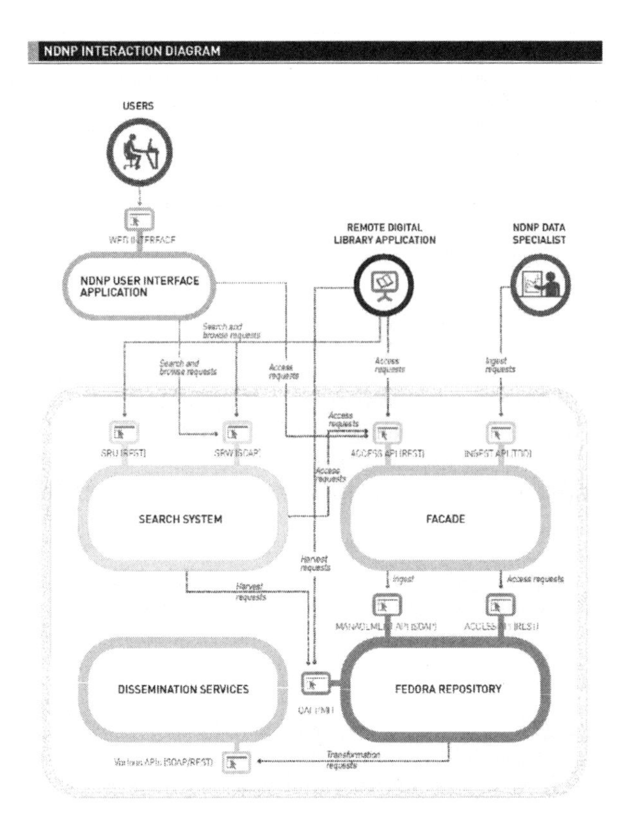
NDNP INTERACTION DIAGRAM
USERS
REMOTE DIGITAL LIBRARY APPLICATION
NDNP DATA SPECIALIST
NDNP USER INTERFACE APPLICATION
SEARCH SYSTEM
FACADE
DISSEMINATION SERVICES
FEDORA REPOSITORY

Fig. 3

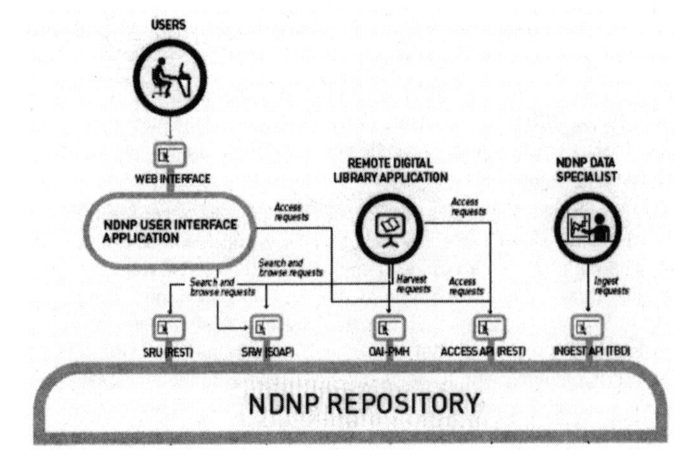
USERS
WEB INTERFACE
REMOTE DIGITAL LIBRARY APPLICATION
NDNP DATA SPECIALIST
NDNP USER INTERFACE APPLICATION
Access requests
Search and browse requests
Harvest requests
Ingest requests
SRU (REST)
SRW (SOAP)
OAI-PMH
ACCESS API (REST)
INGEST API (TBD)
NDNP REPOSITORY

Fig. 4

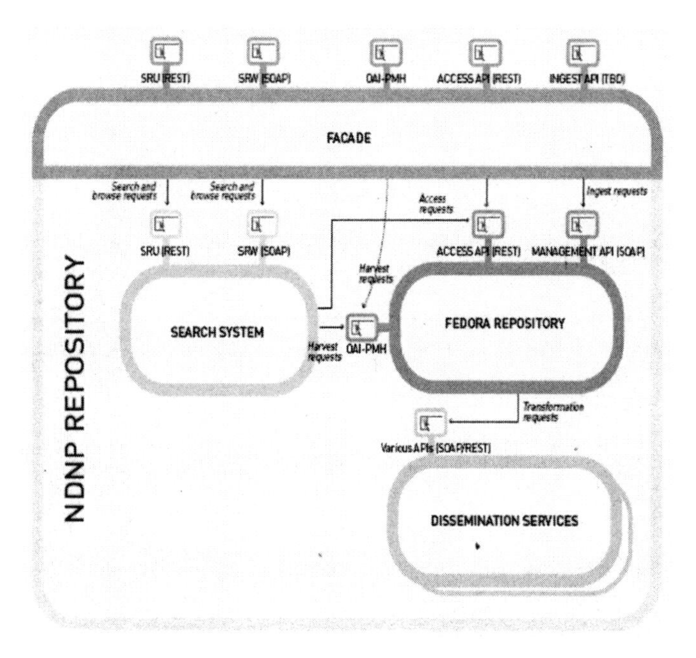

Fig. 5

Facade was a clever Architectural layer because it allows us to keep all the constantly changing web services requests outside of Fedora so we can use a variety of tools to translate requests and disseminations without having to change our Fedora model.

This modular approach to the NDNP system provides greatest flexibility for such a long term project. This flexibility will allow us to take advantage of technological and standards innovations that are sure to evolve over the twenty-year life span of the project.

UTAH DIGITAL NEWSPAPERS AND MOUNTAIN WEST DIGITAL LIBRARY

Kenning Arlitsch

J. Willard Marriott Library

Utah Digital Newspapers &
Mountain West Digital Library

UTAH ACADEMIC LIBRARY CONSORTIUM

Leveraging State-
Wide Cooperation

May 16, 2006

Kenning Arlitsch, Head of IT
J. Willard Marriott Library

MWDL Defined

State-wide program founded in 2002

Political, technical infrastructure

Aggregates metadata

- Single search
- Currently 400,000+ objects
  - o Excluding newspapers

Groundwork for other state-wide efforts

- Utah Digital Newspapers
  - o Distributed holdings across state
- Utah Institutional Repository

The University of Utah

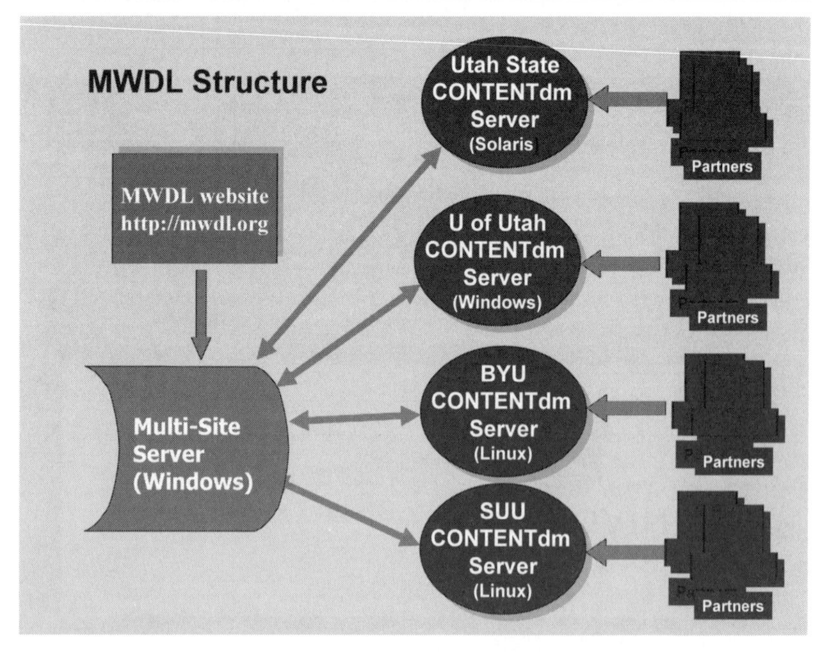

This graphic shows the technical structure of the MWDL. The ovals in the middle of the screen represent the regional digitization centers in Utah. Each center runs its own CONTENTdm server on Windows, Linux, or UNIX Solaris. Each center supports multiple partners who wish to create digital projects by offering fee-based scanning services and by offering space on their CONTENTdm servers. The Multi-Site Server, running at the University of Utah, harvests metadata from the regional centers and creates a single searchable index, which is accessed through the MWDL website.

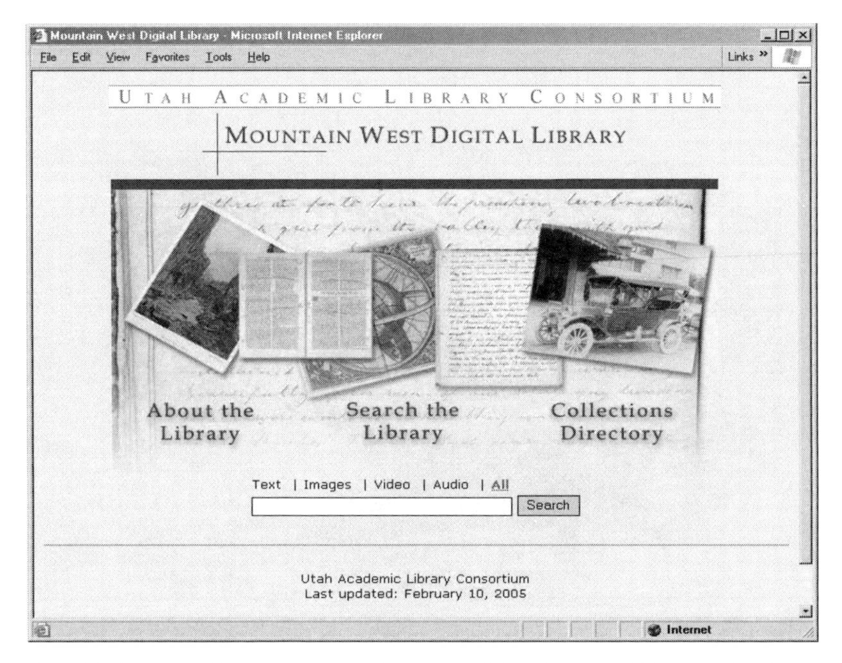

The result looks something like this to the end user. They view the MWDL website and click "Search the Library"…

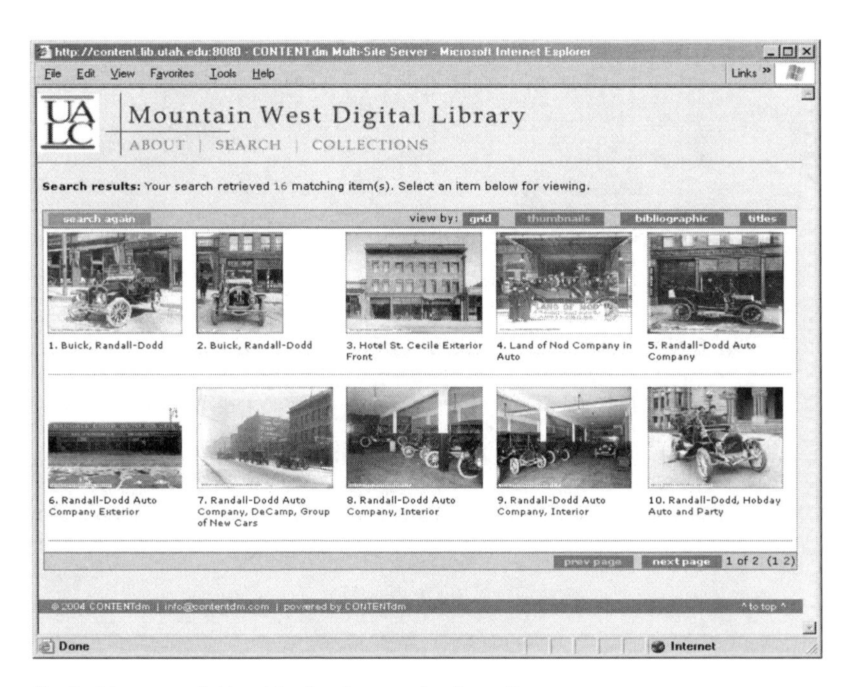

Thumbnail images are called in real-time from the server where they reside.

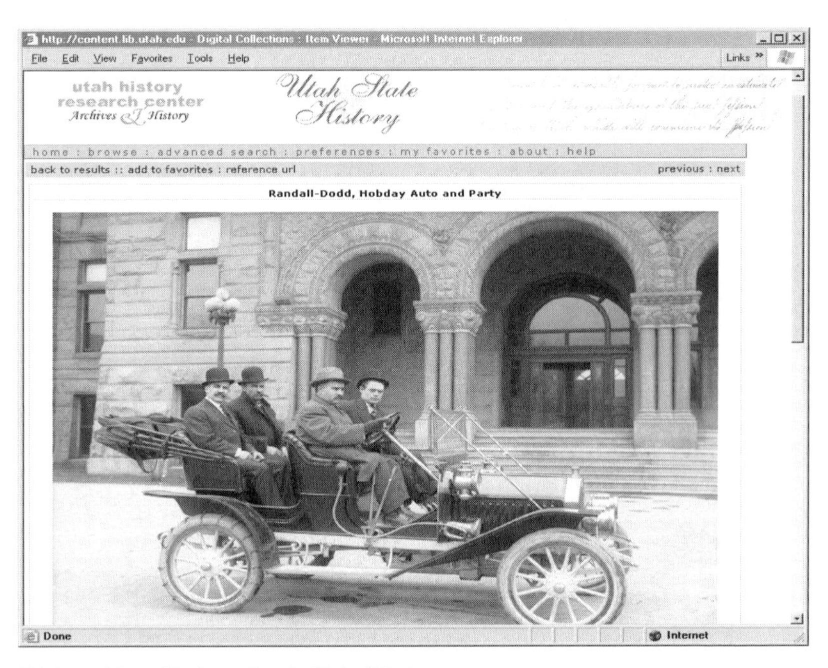

This is one of the resulting images from the Shipler Collection..

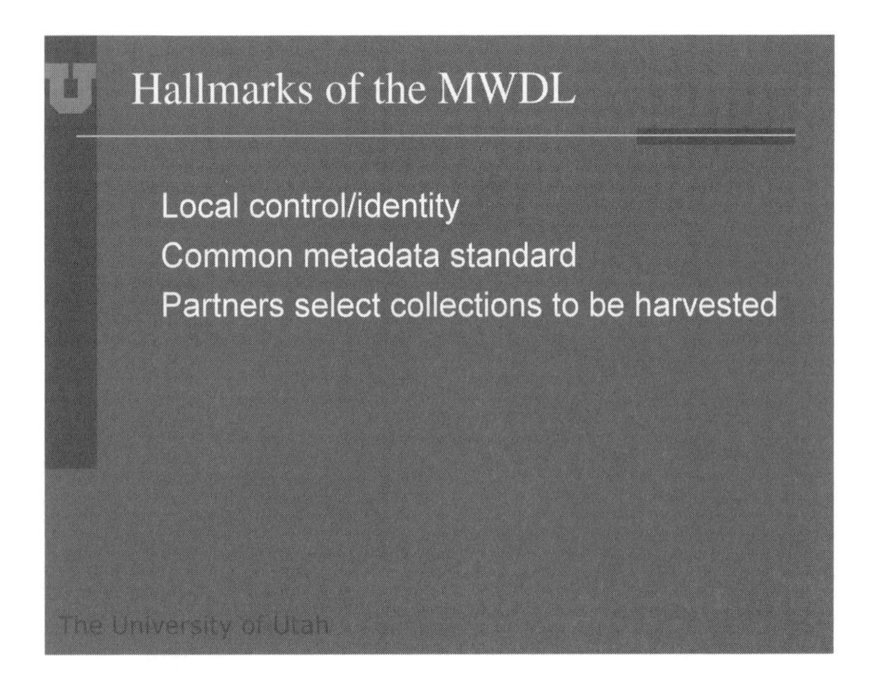

http://www.lib.utah.edu - Karl Bodmer Aquatint Collection - Microsoft Internet Explorer
File Edit View Favorites Tools Help
Links
The Karl Bodmer Aquatint Collection
About
Search
Browse
MARRIOTT LIBRARY
RARE BOOKS
DIGITAL TECHNOLOGIES
THE UNIVERSITY OF UTAH
Done
Internet

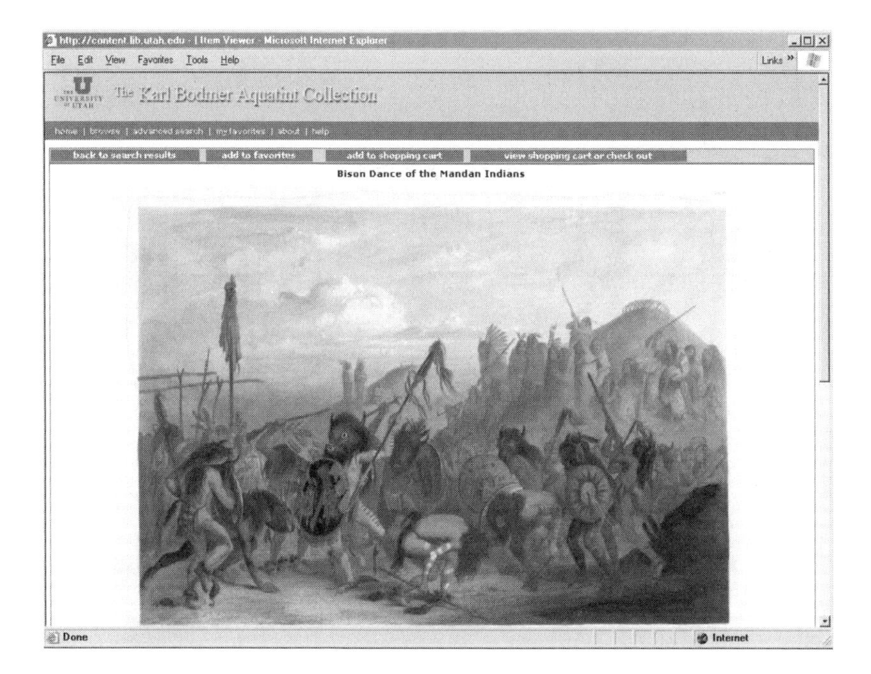
File Edit View Favorites Tools Help
Links
The Karl Bodmer Aquatint Collection
home | browse | advanced search | my favorites | about | help
back to search results
add to favorites
add to shopping cart
view shopping cart or check out
Bison Dance of the Mandan Indians
Done
Internet

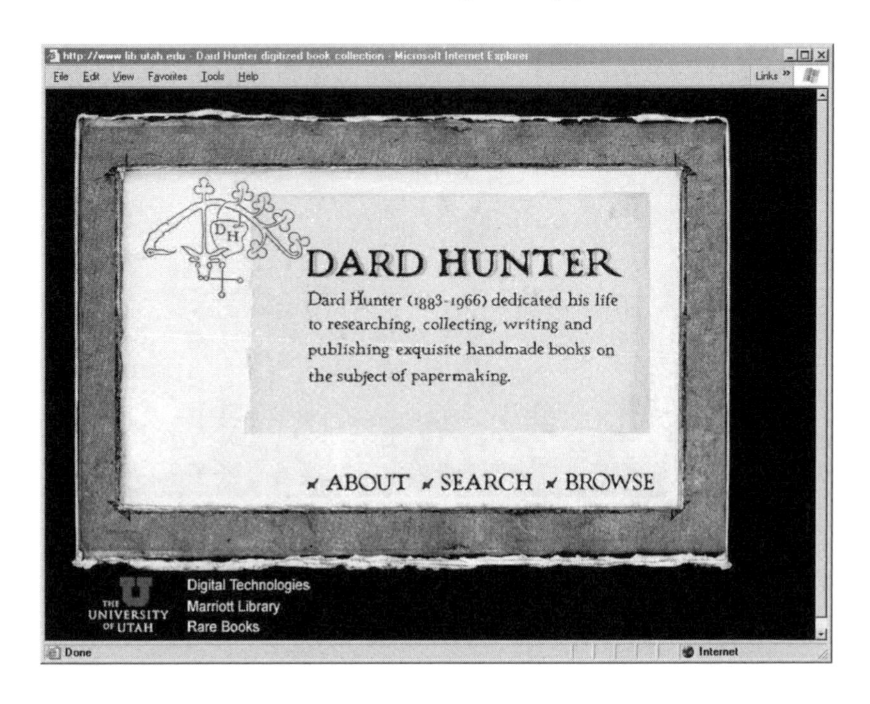

http://www.lib.utah.edu - Dard Hunter digitized book collection - Microsoft Internet Explorer
File Edit View Favorites Tools Help
Links
DH
DARD HUNTER
Dard Hunter (1883-1966) dedicated his life to researching, collecting, writing and publishing exquisite handmade books on the subject of papermaking.
ABOUT SEARCH BROWSE
THE UNIVERSITY OF UTAH
Digital Technologies
Marriott Library
Rare Books
Done
Internet

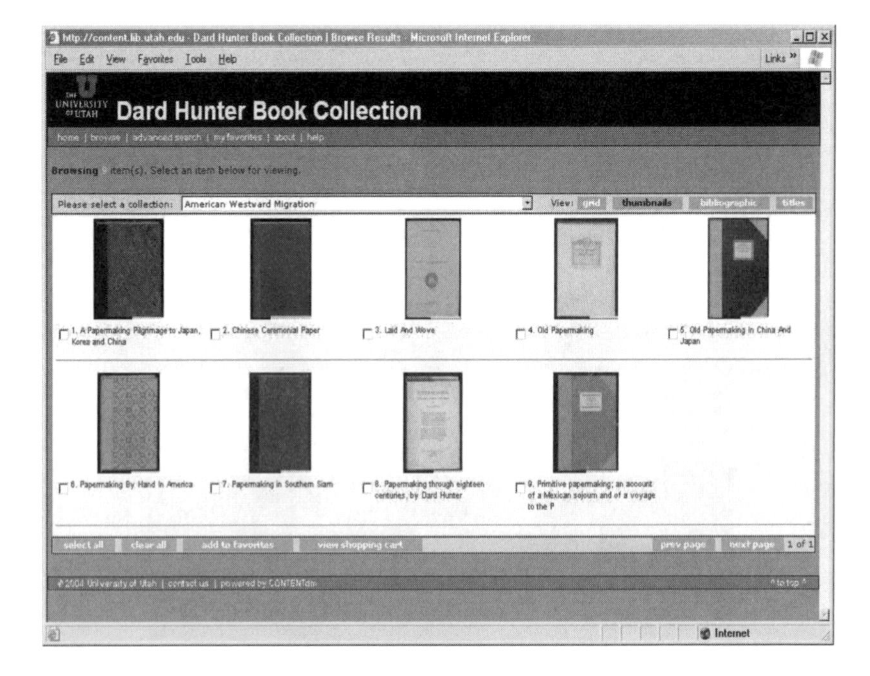

http://content.lib.utah.edu - Dard Hunter Book Collection | Browse Results - Microsoft Internet Explorer
File Edit View Favorites Tools Help
Links
THE UNIVERSITY OF UTAH
Dard Hunter Book Collection
Please select a collection:
American Westward Migration
View:
thumbnails
1. A Papermaking Pilgrimage to Japan, Korea and China
2. Chinese Ceremonial Paper
3. Laid And Wove
4. Old Papermaking
5. Old Papermaking In China And Japan
6. Papermaking By Hand In America
7. Papermaking In Southern Siam
8. Papermaking through eighteen centuries, by Dard Hunter
9. Primitive papermaking; an account of a Mexican sojourn and of a voyage to the P
Internet

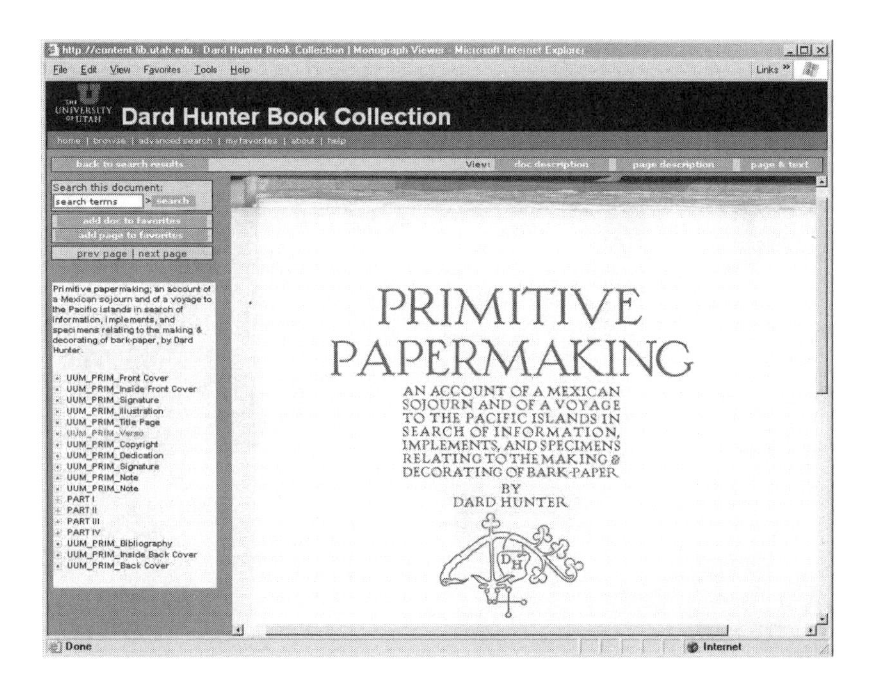
Dard Hunter Book Collection
home | browse | advanced search | my favorites | about | help
back to search results
View: doc description page description page & text
Search this document:
search terms
add doc to favorites
add page to favorites
prev page | next page
Primitive papermaking; an account of a Mexican sojourn and of a voyage to the Pacific islands in search of information, implements, and specimens relating to the making & decorating of bark-paper, by Dard Hunter.
UUM_PRIM_Front Cover
UUM_PRIM_Inside Front Cover
UUM_PRIM_Signature
UUM_PRIM_Illustration
UUM_PRIM_Title Page
UUM_PRIM_Verso
UUM_PRIM_Copyright
UUM_PRIM_Dedication
UUM_PRIM_Signature
UUM_PRIM_Note
UUM_PRIM_Note
PART I
PART II
PART III
PART IV
UUM_PRIM_Bibliography
UUM_PRIM_Inside Back Cover
UUM_PRIM_Back Cover
PRIMITIVE PAPERMAKING
AN ACCOUNT OF A MEXICAN SOJOURN AND OF A VOYAGE TO THE PACIFIC ISLANDS IN SEARCH OF INFORMATION, IMPLEMENTS, AND SPECIMENS RELATING TO THE MAKING & DECORATING OF BARK-PAPER
BY
DARD HUNTER
Done
Internet

Sanborn® Fire Insurance Maps - Microsoft Internet Explorer
J. Willard Marriott Library Digital Technologies
Sanborn® Fire Insurance Maps
BROWSE MAPS
ABOUT COLLECTION
SEARCH
THE UNIVERSITY OF UTAH
About the Sanborn Map® Collection | Browse the Maps | Search the Maps
Digital Technologies | Marriott Library | University of Utah
Internet

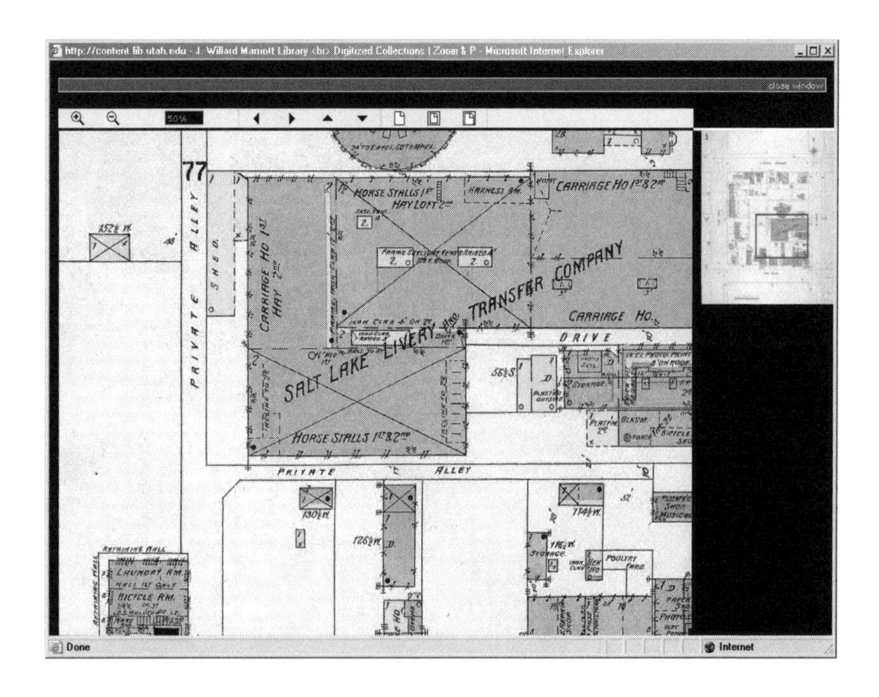
Done
Internet
SALT LAKE LIVERY AND TRANSFER COMPANY
CARRIAGE HO.
HORSE STALLS 1ST & 2ND
PRIVATE ALLEY
DRIVE

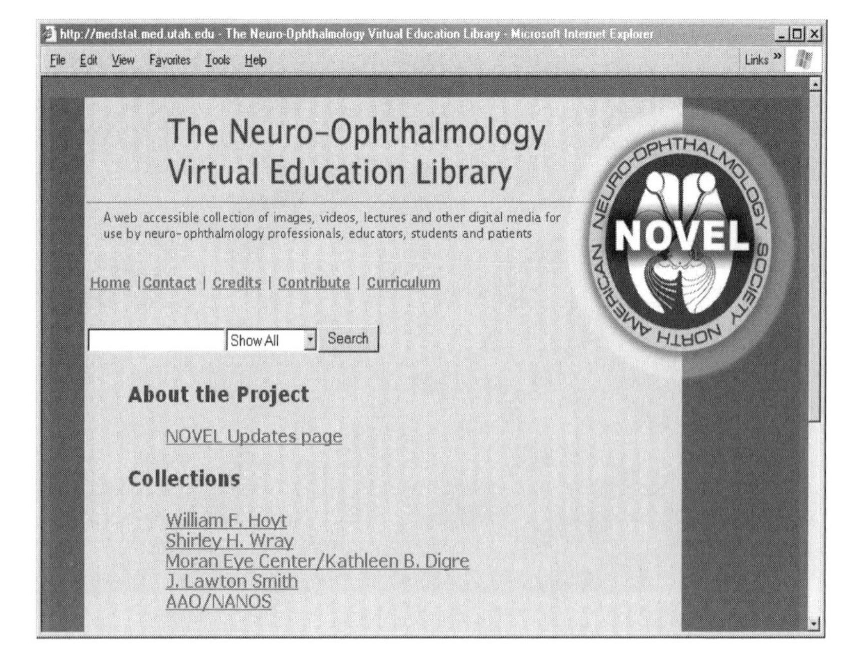
http://medstat.med.utah.edu - The Neuro-Ophthalmology Virtual Education Library - Microsoft Internet Explorer
File Edit View Favorites Tools Help
Links
The Neuro-Ophthalmology
Virtual Education Library
A web accessible collection of images, videos, lectures and other digital media for use by neuro-ophthalmology professionals, educators, students and patients
Home | Contact | Credits | Contribute | Curriculum
Show All
Search
About the Project
NOVEL Updates page
Collections
William F. Hoyt
Shirley H. Wray
Moran Eye Center/Kathleen B. Digre
J. Lawton Smith
AAO/NANOS
NOVEL
NORTH AMERICAN NEURO-OPHTHALMOLOGY SOCIETY

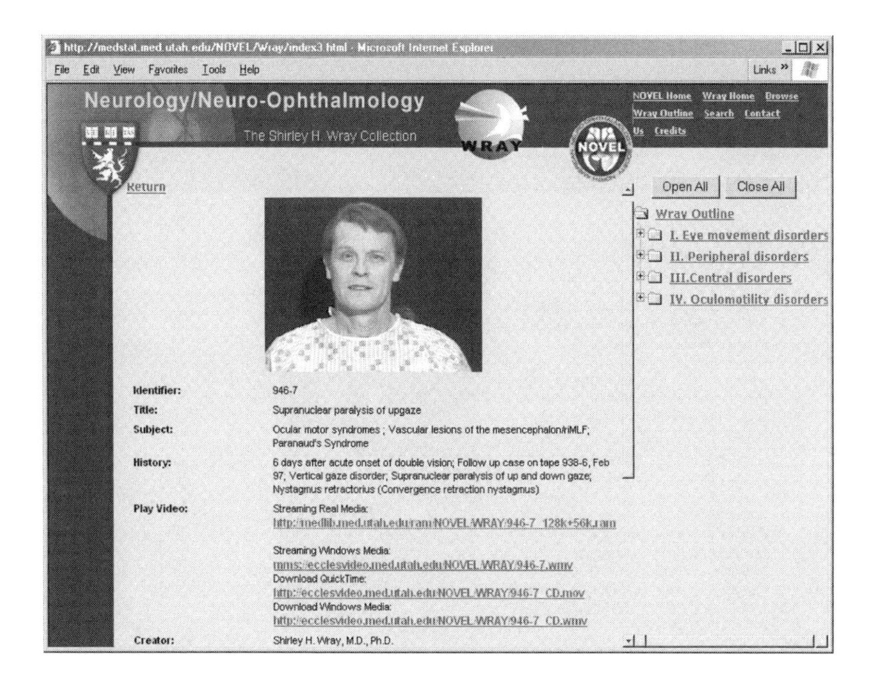

http://medstat.med.utah.edu/NOVEL/Wray/index3.html - Microsoft Internet Explorer
File Edit View Favorites Tools Help
Links
Neurology/Neuro-Ophthalmology
The Shirley H. Wray Collection
WRAY
NOVEL
NOVEL Home Wray Home Browse Wray Outline Search Contact Us Credits
Return
Open All
Close All
Wray Outline
I. Eye movement disorders
II. Peripheral disorders
III.Central disorders
IV. Oculomotility disorders
Identifier: 946-7
Title: Supranuclear paralysis of upgaze
Subject: Ocular motor syndromes ; Vascular lesions of the mesencephalon/riMLF; Paranaud's Syndrome
History: 6 days after acute onset of double vision; Follow up case on tape 938-6, Feb 97; Vertical gaze disorder; Supranuclear paralysis of up and down gaze; Nystagmus retractorius (Convergence retraction nystagmus)
Play Video: Streaming Real Media:
http://medlib.med.utah.edu/ram/NOVEL/WRAY/946-7_128k+56k.ram
Streaming Windows Media:
mms://ecclesvideo.med.utah.edu/NOVEL/WRAY/946-7.wmv
Download QuickTime:
http://ecclesvideo.med.utah.edu/NOVEL/WRAY/946-7_CD.mov
Download Windows Media:
http://ecclesvideo.med.utah.edu/NOVEL/WRAY/946-7_CD.wmv
Creator: Shirley H. Wray, M.D., Ph.D.

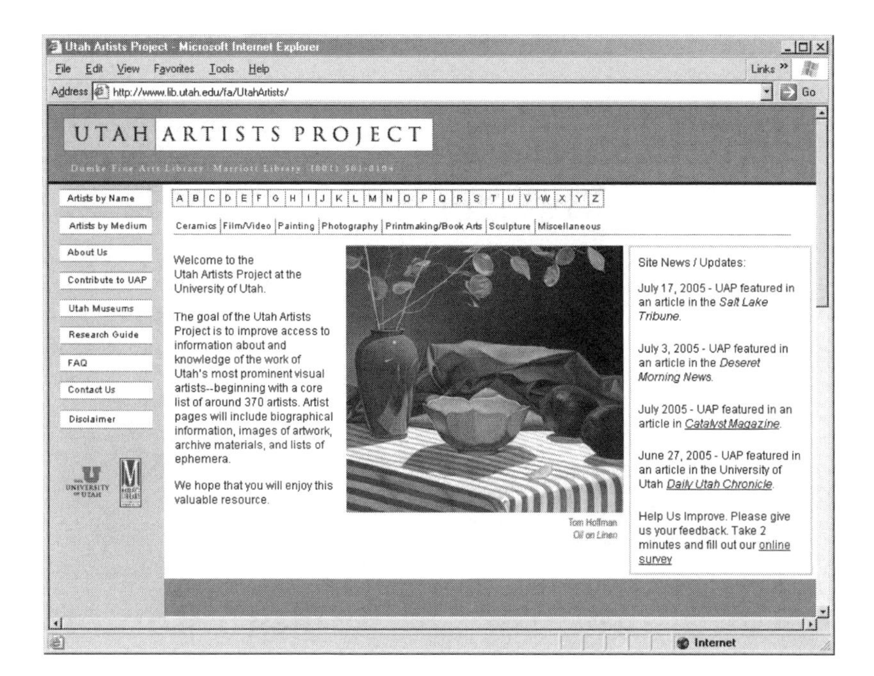

Utah Artists Project - Microsoft Internet Explorer
File Edit View Favorites Tools Help
Links
Address http://www.lib.utah.edu/fa/UtahArtists/
Go
UTAH ARTISTS PROJECT
Artists by Name
Artists by Medium
About Us
Contribute to UAP
Utah Museums
Research Guide
FAQ
Contact Us
Disclaimer
A B C D E F G H I J K L M N O P Q R S T U V W X Y Z
Ceramics Film/Video Painting Photography Printmaking/Book Arts Sculpture Miscellaneous
Welcome to the Utah Artists Project at the University of Utah.
The goal of the Utah Artists Project is to improve access to information about and knowledge of the work of Utah's most prominent visual artists--beginning with a core list of around 370 artists. Artist pages will include biographical information, images of artwork, archive materials, and lists of ephemera.
We hope that you will enjoy this valuable resource.
Tom Hoffman
Oil on Linen
Site News / Updates:
July 17, 2005 - UAP featured in an article in the Salt Lake Tribune.
July 3, 2005 - UAP featured in an article in the Deseret Morning News.
July 2005 - UAP featured in an article in Catalyst Magazine.
June 27, 2005 - UAP featured in an article in the University of Utah Daily Utah Chronicle.
Help Us Improve. Please give us your feedback. Take 2 minutes and fill out our online survey
Internet

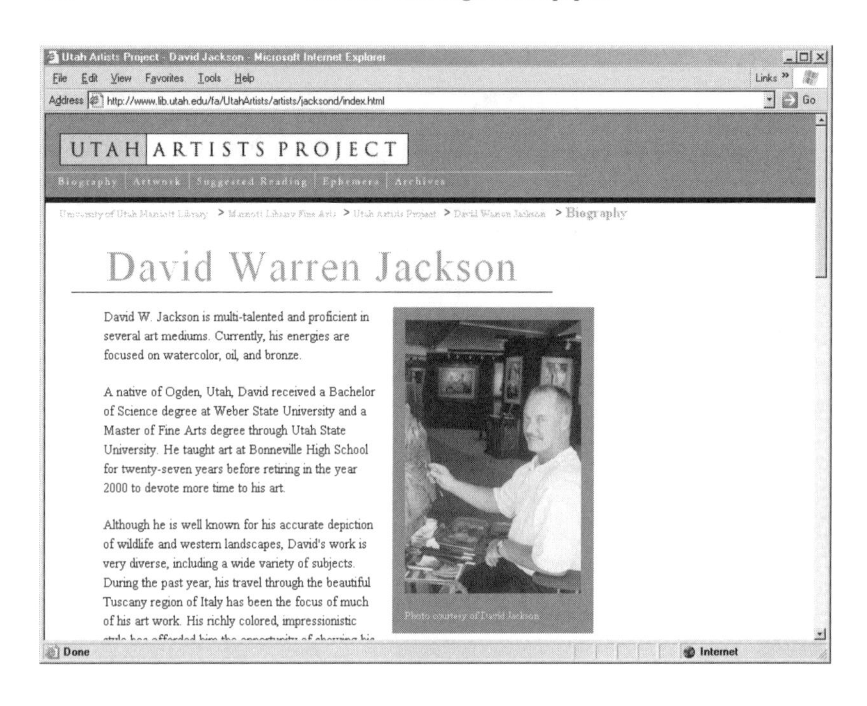
Utah Artists Project - David Jackson - Microsoft Internet Explorer
File Edit View Favorites Tools Help
Links
Address http://www.lib.utah.edu/fa/UtahArtists/artists/jacksond/index.html
Go
UTAH ARTISTS PROJECT
Biography | Artwork | Suggested Reading | Ephemera | Archives
> Biography
David Warren Jackson
David W. Jackson is multi-talented and proficient in several art mediums. Currently, his energies are focused on watercolor, oil, and bronze.
A native of Ogden, Utah, David received a Bachelor of Science degree at Weber State University and a Master of Fine Arts degree through Utah State University. He taught art at Bonneville High School for twenty-seven years before retiring in the year 2000 to devote more time to his art.
Although he is well known for his accurate depiction of wildlife and western landscapes, David's work is very diverse, including a wide variety of subjects. During the past year, his travel through the beautiful Tuscany region of Italy has been the focus of much of his art work. His richly colored, impressionistic
Photo courtesy of David Jackson
Done
Internet

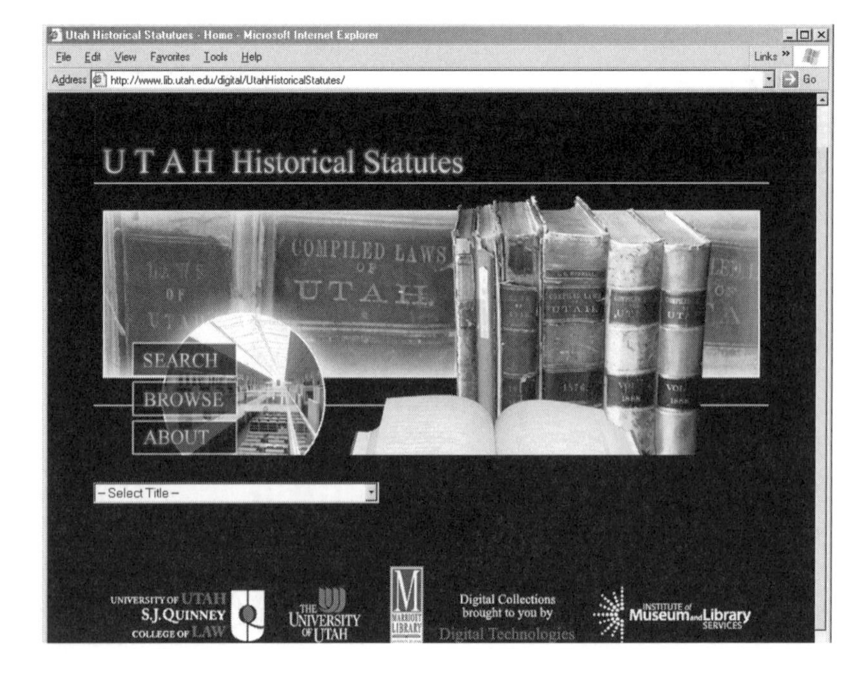
Utah Historical Statutues - Home - Microsoft Internet Explorer
File Edit View Favorites Tools Help
Links
Address http://www.lib.utah.edu/digital/UtahHistoricalStatutes/
Go
UTAH Historical Statutes
COMPILED LAWS OF UTAH
SEARCH
BROWSE
ABOUT
– Select Title –
UNIVERSITY OF UTAH
S.J. QUINNEY
COLLEGE OF LAW
THE UNIVERSITY OF UTAH
MARRIOTT LIBRARY
Digital Collections brought to you by
Digital Technologies
INSTITUTE of Museum and Library SERVICES

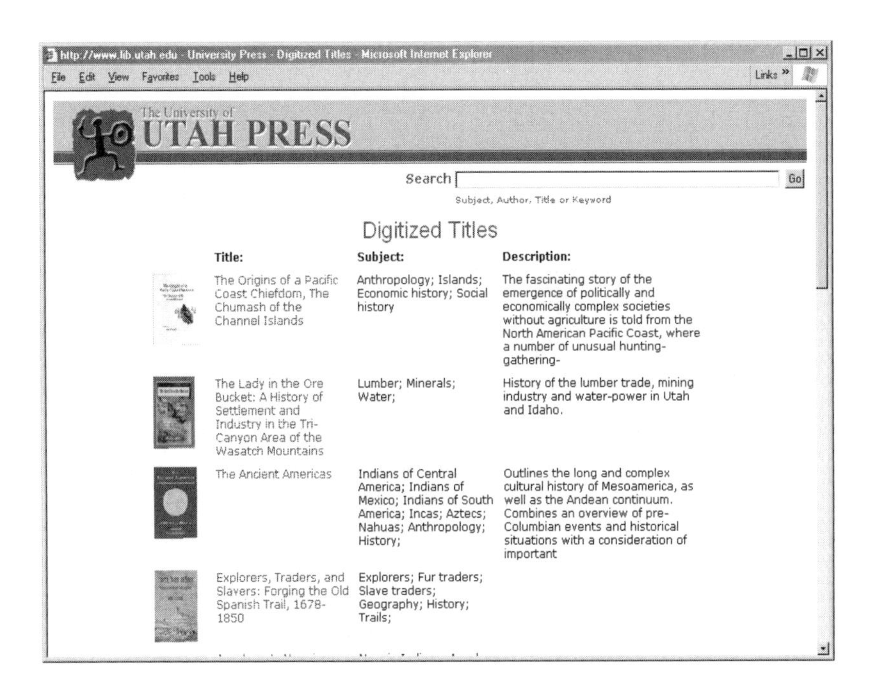
http://www.lib.utah.edu - University Press - Digitized Titles - Microsoft Internet Explorer
File Edit View Favorites Tools Help
Links
The University of
UTAH PRESS
Search
Go
Subject, Author, Title or Keyword
Digitized Titles
Title:
Subject:
Description:
The Origins of a Pacific Coast Chiefdom, The Chumash of the Channel Islands
Anthropology; Islands; Economic history; Social history
The fascinating story of the emergence of politically and economically complex societies without agriculture is told from the North American Pacific Coast, where a number of unusual hunting-gathering-
The Lady in the Ore Bucket: A History of Settlement and Industry in the Tri-Canyon Area of the Wasatch Mountains
Lumber; Minerals; Water;
History of the lumber trade, mining industry and water-power in Utah and Idaho.
The Ancient Americas
Indians of Central America; Indians of Mexico; Indians of South America; Incas; Aztecs; Nahuas; Anthropology; History;
Outlines the long and complex cultural history of Mesoamerica, as well as the Andean continuum. Combines an overview of pre-Columbian events and historical situations with a consideration of important
Explorers, Traders, and Slavers: Forging the Old Spanish Trail, 1678-1850
Explorers; Fur traders; Slave traders; Geography; History; Trails;

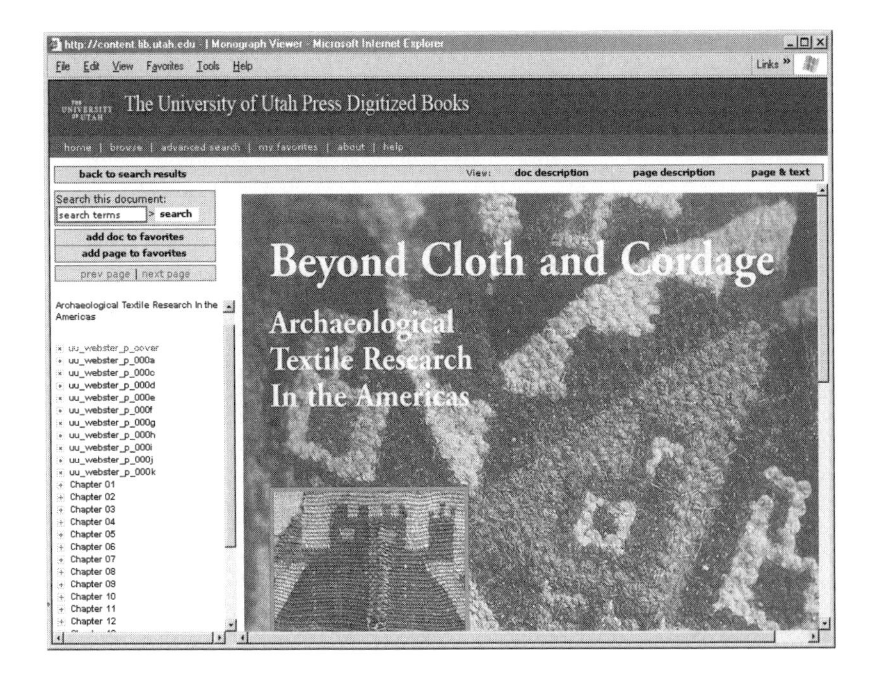
http://content.lib.utah.edu - | Monograph Viewer - Microsoft Internet Explorer
File Edit View Favorites Tools Help
Links
The University of Utah Press Digitized Books
home | browse | advanced search | my favorites | about | help
back to search results
View:
doc description
page description
page & text
Search this document:
search terms
search
add doc to favorites
add page to favorites
prev page | next page
Archaeological Textile Research In the Americas
uu_webster_p_cover
uu_webster_p_000a
uu_webster_p_000c
uu_webster_p_000d
uu_webster_p_000e
uu_webster_p_000f
uu_webster_p_000g
uu_webster_p_000h
uu_webster_p_000i
uu_webster_p_000j
uu_webster_p_000k
Chapter 01
Chapter 02
Chapter 03
Chapter 04
Chapter 05
Chapter 06
Chapter 07
Chapter 08
Chapter 09
Chapter 10
Chapter 11
Chapter 12
Beyond Cloth and Cordage
Archaeological Textile Research In the Americas

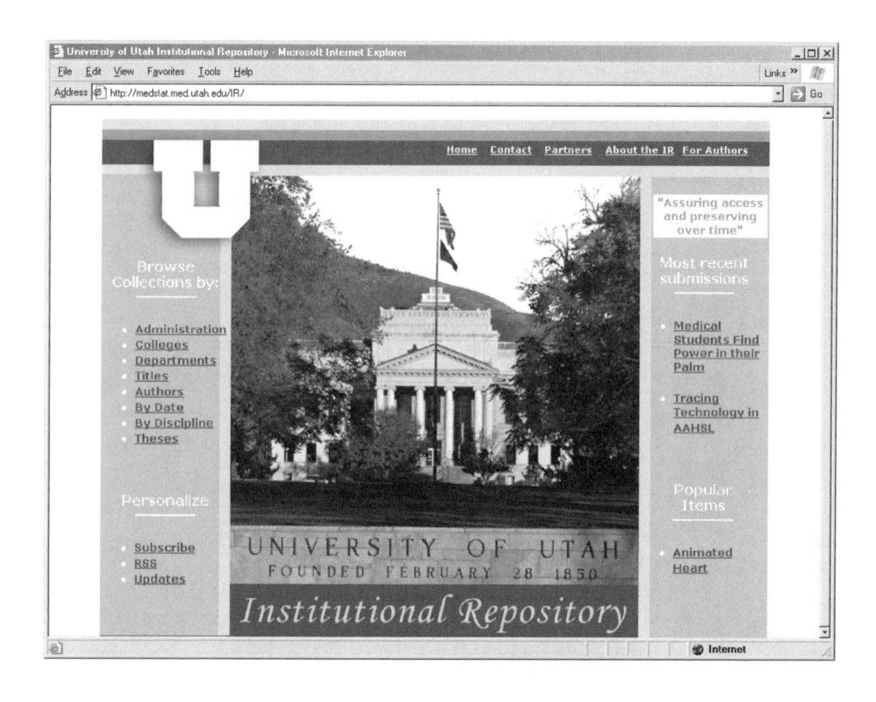
University of Utah Institutional Repository - Microsoft Internet Explorer
File Edit View Favorites Tools Help
Address http://medstat.med.utah.edu/IR/
Home Contact Partners About the IR For Authors
"Assuring access and preserving over time"
Browse Collections by:
Administration
Colleges
Departments
Titles
Authors
By Date
By Discipline
Theses
Personalize
Subscribe
RSS
Updates
Most recent submissions
Medical Students Find Power in their Palm
Tracing Technology in AAHSL
Popular Items
Animated Heart
UNIVERSITY OF UTAH
FOUNDED FEBRUARY 28 1850
Institutional Repository
Internet

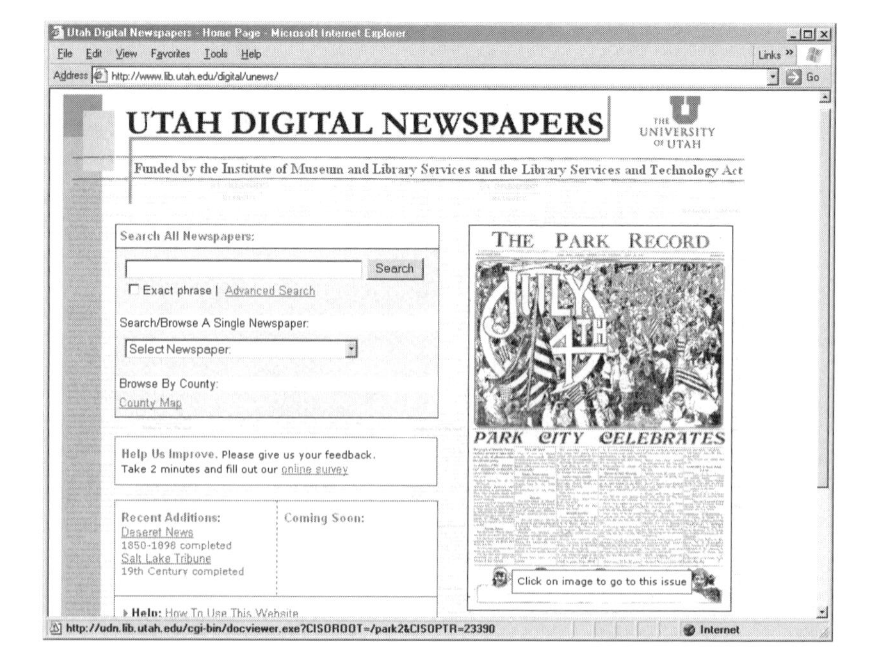
Utah Digital Newspapers - Home Page - Microsoft Internet Explorer
File Edit View Favorites Tools Help
Address http://www.lib.utah.edu/digital/unews/
UTAH DIGITAL NEWSPAPERS
THE UNIVERSITY OF UTAH
Funded by the Institute of Museum and Library Services and the Library Services and Technology Act
Search All Newspapers:
Search
Exact phrase | Advanced Search
Search/Browse A Single Newspaper:
Select Newspaper
Browse By County:
County Map
Help Us Improve. Please give us your feedback.
Take 2 minutes and fill out our online survey
Recent Additions:
Deseret News
1850-1898 completed
Salt Lake Tribune
19th Century completed
Coming Soon:
Help: How To Use This Website
THE PARK RECORD
JULY 4TH
PARK CITY CELEBRATES
Click on image to go to this issue
http://udn.lib.utah.edu/cgi-bin/docviewer.exe?CISOROOT=/park2&CISOPTR=23390
Internet

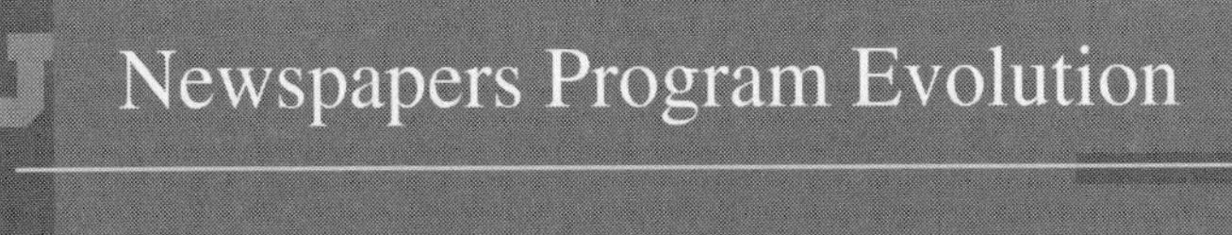

1951 – UU microfilming Utah newspapers
1983 – USNP grant award from NEH
2000 – Established Digitization Center
- Several successful digital projects
  - Maps, photographs, documents, books

2001 – LSTA R&D grant for newspapers
2003 – Second LSTA grant
2003 – IMLS grant
2005 - NDNP grant
2003-2006 – Grassroots funding efforts

The University of Utah

First LSTA Grant

Proposal:
- R&D newspaper digitization
- Benefit to entire state
- Digitize three weekly titles – ~30 yrs each
  - 30,000 pages total

Awarded $93K in fall 2001

The University of Utah

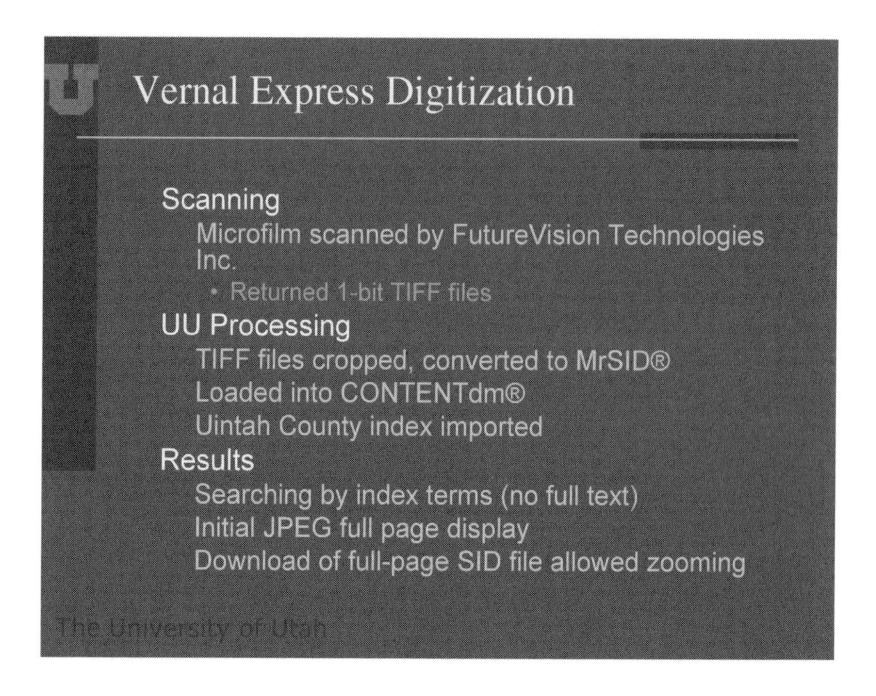
Vernal Express Digitization
Scanning
Microfilm scanned by FutureVision Technologies Inc.
• Returned 1-bit TIFF files
UU Processing
TIFF files cropped, converted to MrSID®
Loaded into CONTENTdm®
Uintah County index imported
Results
Searching by index terms (no full text)
Initial JPEG full page display
Download of full-page SID file allowed zooming
The University of Utah

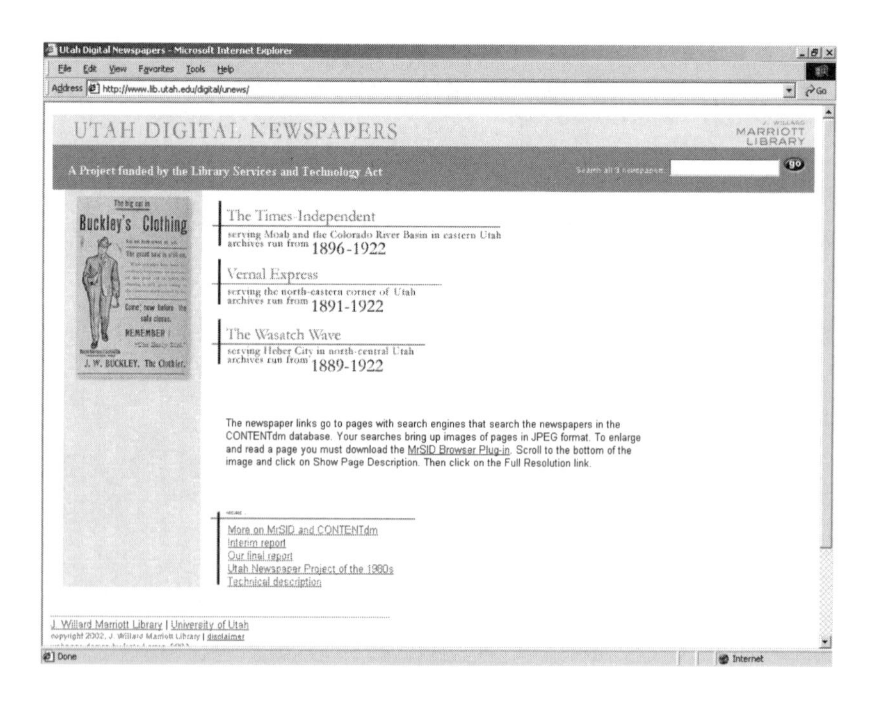
Utah Digital Newspapers - Microsoft Internet Explorer
File Edit View Favorites Tools Help
Address http://www.lib.utah.edu/digital/unews/
UTAH DIGITAL NEWSPAPERS
MARRIOTT LIBRARY
A Project funded by the Library Services and Technology Act
go
Buckley's Clothing
J. W. BUCKLEY, The Clothier.
The Times-Independent
serving Moab and the Colorado River Basin in eastern Utah
archives run from 1896-1922
Vernal Express
serving the north-eastern corner of Utah
archives run from 1891-1922
The Wasatch Wave
serving Heber City in north-central Utah
archives run from 1889-1922
The newspaper links go to pages with search engines that search the newspapers in the CONTENTdm database. Your searches bring up images of pages in JPEG format. To enlarge and read a page you must download the MrSID Browser Plug-in. Scroll to the bottom of the image and click on Show Page Description. Then click on the Full Resolution link.
More on MrSID and CONTENTdm
Interim report
Our final report
Utah Newspaper Project of the 1980s
Technical description
J. Willard Marriott Library | University of Utah
Done
Internet

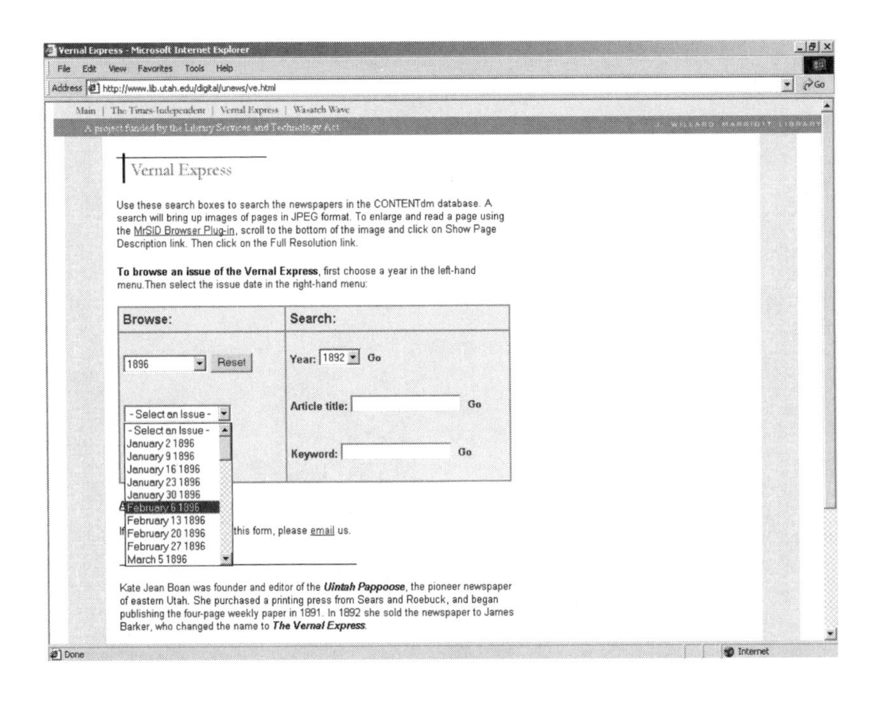
Vernal Express - Microsoft Internet Explorer
File Edit View Favorites Tools Help
Address http://www.lib.utah.edu/digital/unews/ve.html
Go
Main | The Times-Independent | Vernal Express | Wasatch Wave
A project funded by the Library Services and Technology Act
J. WILLARD MARRIOTT LIBRARY
Vernal Express
Use these search boxes to search the newspapers in the CONTENTdm database. A search will bring up images of pages in JPEG format. To enlarge and read a page using the MrSID Browser Plug-in, scroll to the bottom of the image and click on Show Page Description link. Then click on the Full Resolution link.
To browse an issue of the Vernal Express, first choose a year in the left-hand menu.Then select the issue date in the right-hand menu:
Browse:
Search:
1896
Reset
Year: 1892
Go
Article title:
Go
Keyword:
Go
- Select an Issue -
- Select an Issue -
January 2 1896
January 9 1896
January 16 1896
January 23 1896
January 30 1896
February 6 1896
February 13 1896
February 20 1896
February 27 1896
March 5 1896
this form, please email us.
Kate Jean Boan was founder and editor of the Uintah Pappoose, the pioneer newspaper of eastern Utah. She purchased a printing press from Sears and Roebuck, and began publishing the four-page weekly paper in 1891. In 1892 she sold the newspaper to James Barker, who changed the name to The Vernal Express.
Done
Internet

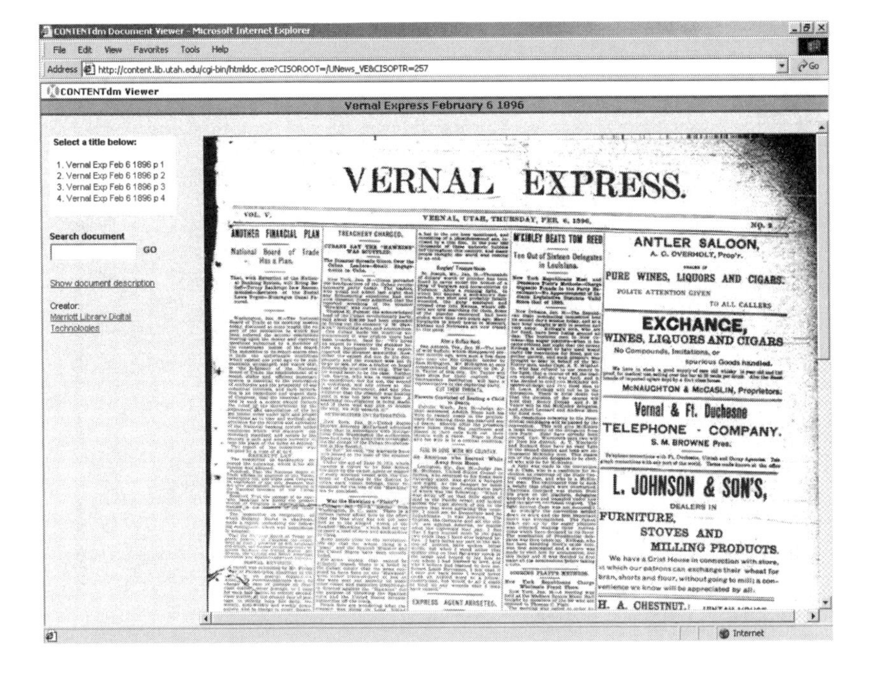
CONTENTdm Document Viewer - Microsoft Internet Explorer
File Edit View Favorites Tools Help
Address http://content.lib.utah.edu/cgi-bin/htmldoc.exe?CISOROOT=/UNews_VE&CISOPTR=257
Go
CONTENTdm Viewer
Vernal Express February 6 1896
Select a title below:
1. Vernal Exp Feb 6 1896 p 1
2. Vernal Exp Feb 6 1896 p 2
3. Vernal Exp Feb 6 1896 p 3
4. Vernal Exp Feb 6 1896 p 4
Search document
GO
Show document description
Creator:
Marriott Library Digital Technologies
VERNAL EXPRESS.
VOL. V.
VERNAL, UTAH, THURSDAY, FEB. 6, 1896.
NO. 2
ANOTHER FINANCIAL PLAN
National Board of Trade Has a Plan.
TREACHERY CHARGED.
M'KINLEY BEATS TOM REED
Ten Out of Sixteen Delegates in Louisiana.
ANTLER SALOON,
A. C. OVERHOLT, Prop'r.
PURE WINES, LIQUORS AND CIGARS.
POLITE ATTENTION GIVEN
TO ALL CALLERS
EXCHANGE,
WINES, LIQUORS AND CIGARS
No Compounds, Imitations, or
spurious Goods handled.
McNAUGHTON & McCASLIN, Proprietors.
Vernal & Ft. Duchesne
TELEPHONE - COMPANY.
S. M. BROWNE Pres.
L. JOHNSON & SON'S,
DEALERS IN
FURNITURE,
STOVES AND
MILLING PRODUCTS.
We have a Grist House in connection with store, at which our patrons can exchange their wheat for bran, shorts and flour, without going to mill; a convenience we know will be appreciated by all.
H. A. CHESTNUT.
Internet

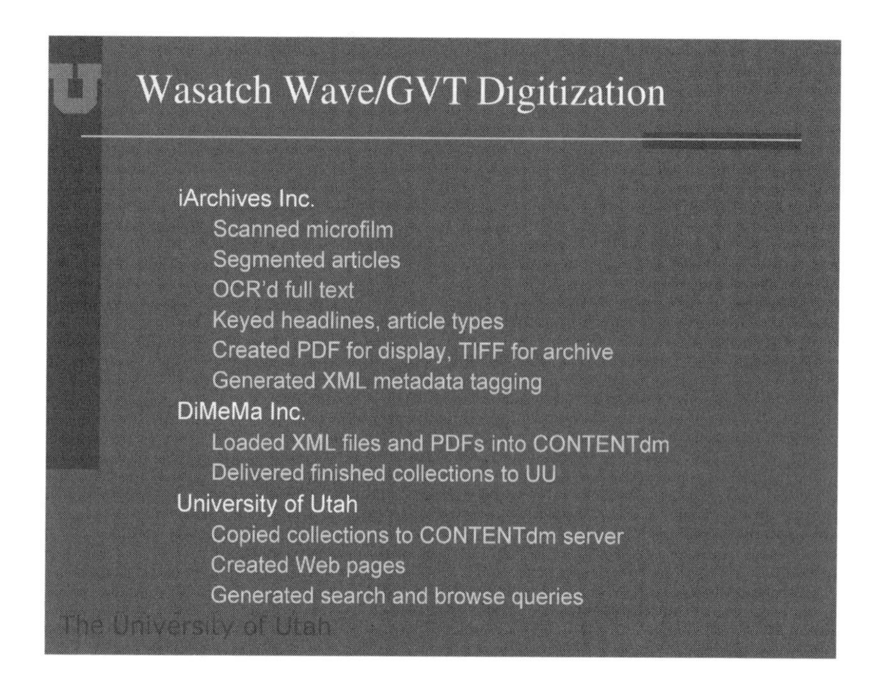
Wasatch Wave/GVT Digitization
iArchives Inc.
Scanned microfilm
Segmented articles
OCR'd full text
Keyed headlines, article types
Created PDF for display, TIFF for archive
Generated XML metadata tagging
DiMeMa Inc.
Loaded XML files and PDFs into CONTENTdm
Delivered finished collections to UU
University of Utah
Copied collections to CONTENTdm server
Created Web pages
Generated search and browse queries
The University of Utah

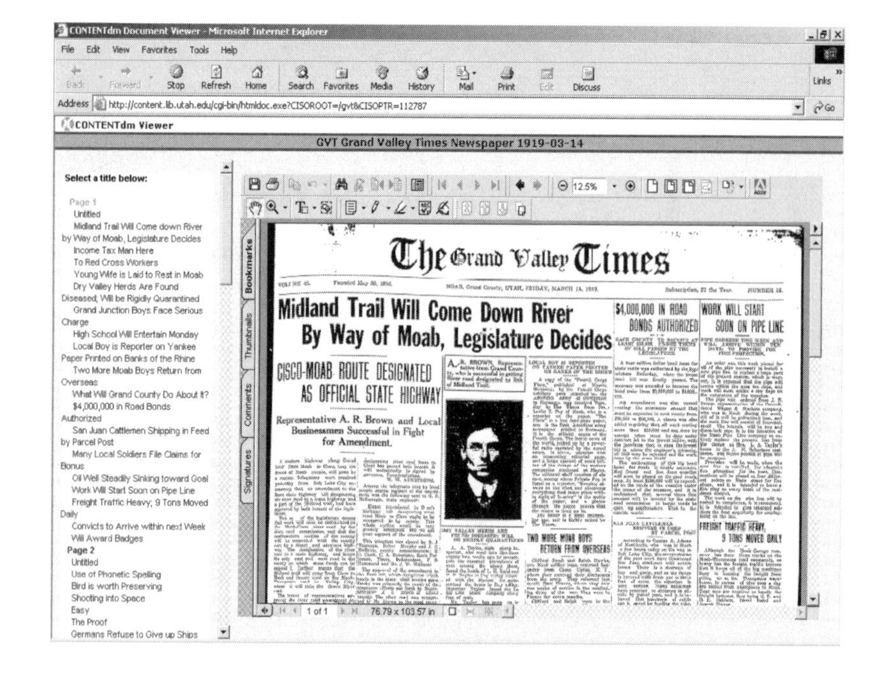
CONTENTdm Document Viewer - Microsoft Internet Explorer
File Edit View Favorites Tools Help
Back Forward Stop Refresh Home Search Favorites Media History Mail Print Edit Discuss
Links
Address http://content.lib.utah.edu/cgi-bin/htmldoc.exe?CISOROOT=/gvt&CISOPTR=112787
Go
CONTENTdm Viewer
GVT Grand Valley Times Newspaper 1919-03-14
Select a title below:
Page 1
Untitled
Midland Trail Will Come down River by Way of Moab, Legislature Decides
Income Tax Man Here
To Red Cross Workers
Young Wife is Laid to Rest in Moab
Dry Valley Herds Are Found Diseased; Will be Rigidly Quarantined
Grand Junction Boys Face Serious Charge
High School Will Entertain Monday
Local Boy is Reporter on Yankee Paper Printed on Banks of the Rhine
Two More Moab Boys Return from Overseas
What Will Grand County Do About It?
$4,000,000 in Road Bonds Authorized
San Juan Cattlemen Shipping in Feed by Parcel Post
Many Local Soldiers File Claims for Bonus
Oil Well Steadily Sinking toward Goal
Work Will Start Soon on Pipe Line
Freight Traffic Heavy; 9 Tons Moved Daily
Convicts to Arrive within next Week
Will Award Badges
Page 2
Untitled
Use of Phonetic Spelling
Bird is worth Preserving
Shooting into Space
Easy
The Proof
Germans Refuse to Give up Ships
125%
Bookmarks
Thumbnails
Comments
Signatures
The Grand Valley Times
Midland Trail Will Come Down River
By Way of Moab, Legislature Decides
CISCO-MOAB ROUTE DESIGNATED AS OFFICIAL STATE HIGHWAY
Representative A. R. Brown and Local Businessmen Successful in Fight for Amendment.
$4,000,000 IN ROAD BONDS AUTHORIZED
WORK WILL START SOON ON PIPE LINE
TWO MORE MOAB BOYS RETURN FROM OVERSEAS
FREIGHT TRAFFIC HEAVY, 9 TONS MOVED DAILY
1 of 1
76.79 x 103.57 in

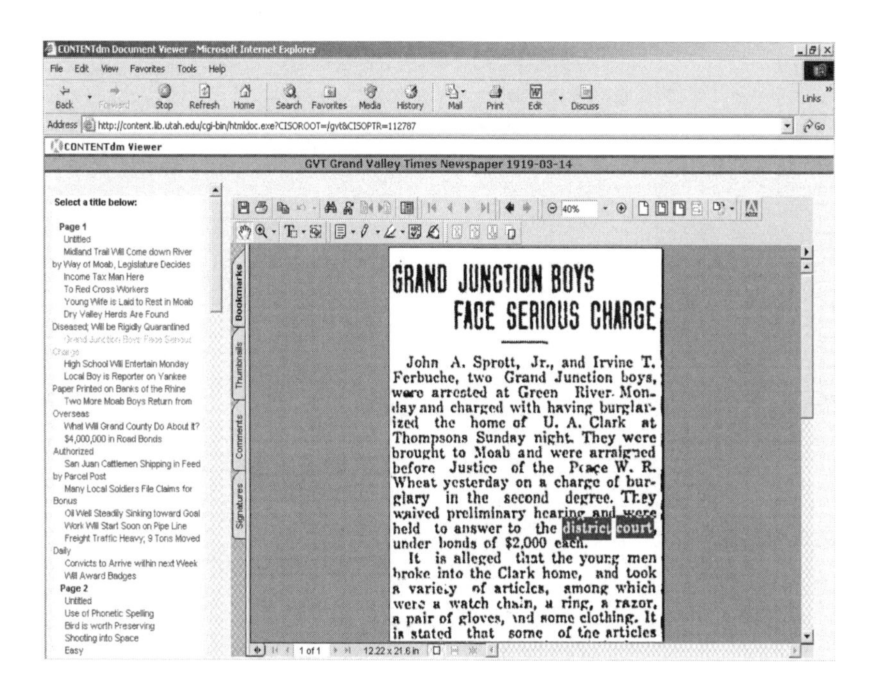

GRAND JUNCTION BOYS FACE SERIOUS CHARGE

John A. Sprott, Jr., and Irvine T. Ferbuche, two Grand Junction boys, were arrested at Green River Monday and charged with having burglarized the home of U. A. Clark at Thompsons Sunday night. They were brought to Moab and were arraigned before Justice of the Peace W. R. Wheat yesterday on a charge of burglary in the second degree. They waived preliminary hearing and were held to answer to the district court under bonds of $2,000 each.

It is alleged that the young men broke into the Clark home, and took a variety of articles, among which were a watch chain, a ring, a razor, a pair of gloves, and some clothing. It is stated that some of the articles

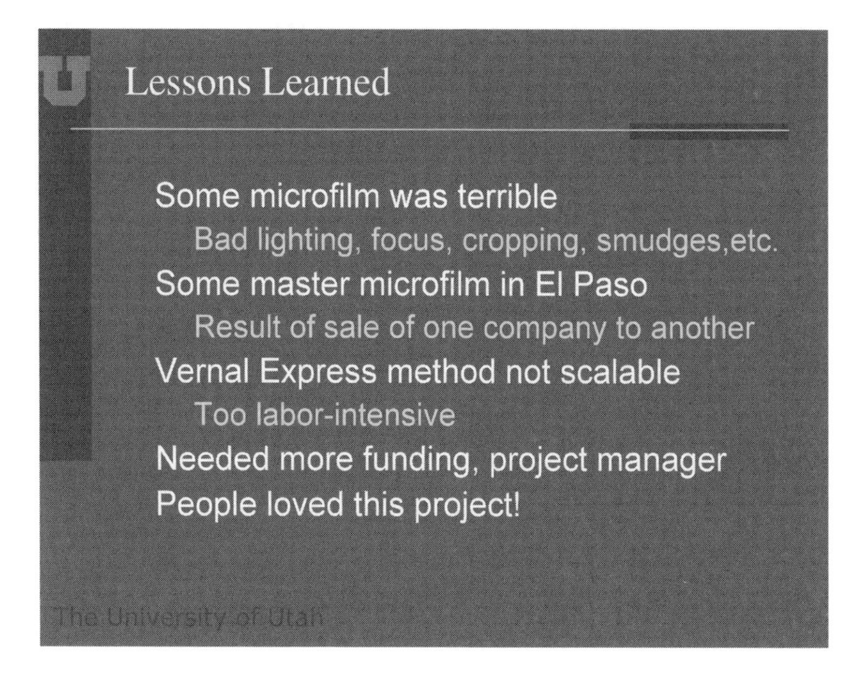

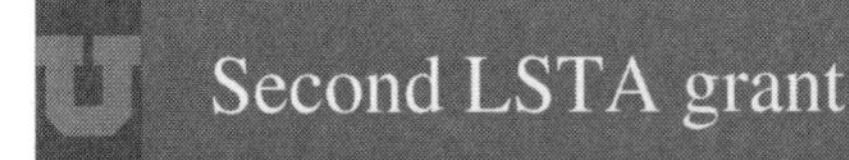
Second LSTA grant

- Proposal
  - Improve digitization process
  - 100,000 more pages
  - Break new ground by scanning from paper
  - Hire full-time project manager
  - Apply for federal funding
  - Begin publicity campaign
- Unprecedented community support
  - $100K matching funds raised:
    - Utah Academic Library Consortium
    - Public libraries
- Awarded $278,000 in November 2002

The University of Utah

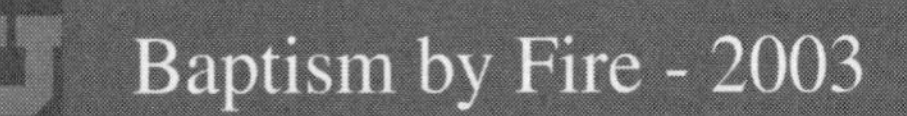
Baptism by Fire - 2003

- January 5 – John Herbert started as PM
- February 1 – IMLS grant proposal
- Website redesigned
- 65% newspapers scanned from paper
- September 23 – IMLS awarded

The University of Utah

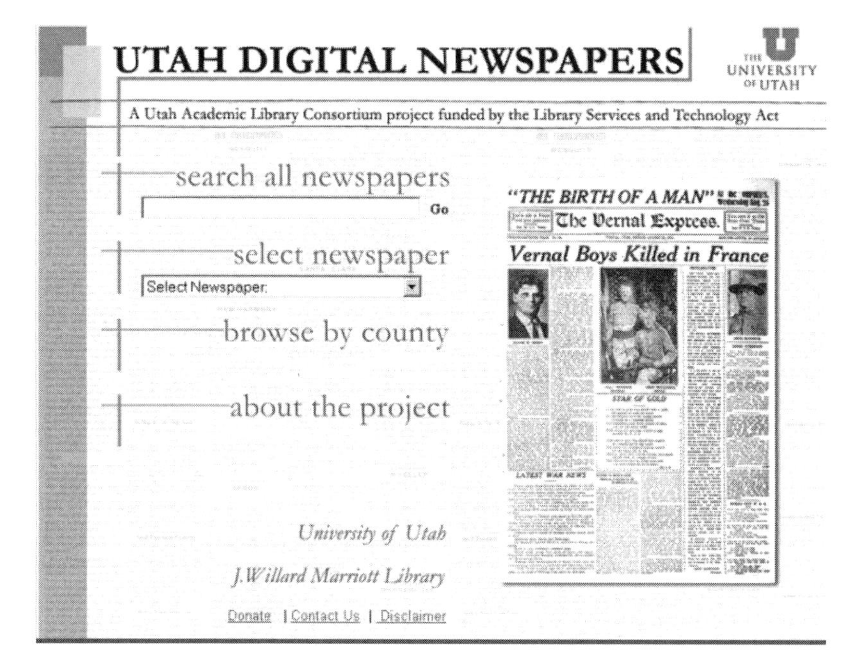
UTAH DIGITAL NEWSPAPERS
THE UNIVERSITY OF UTAH
A Utah Academic Library Consortium project funded by the Library Services and Technology Act
search all newspapers
Go
select newspaper
Select Newspaper:
browse by county
about the project
"THE BIRTH OF A MAN"
The Vernal Express.
Vernal Boys Killed in France
STAR OF GOLD
LATEST WAR NEWS
University of Utah
J.Willard Marriott Library
Donate | Contact Us | Disclaimer

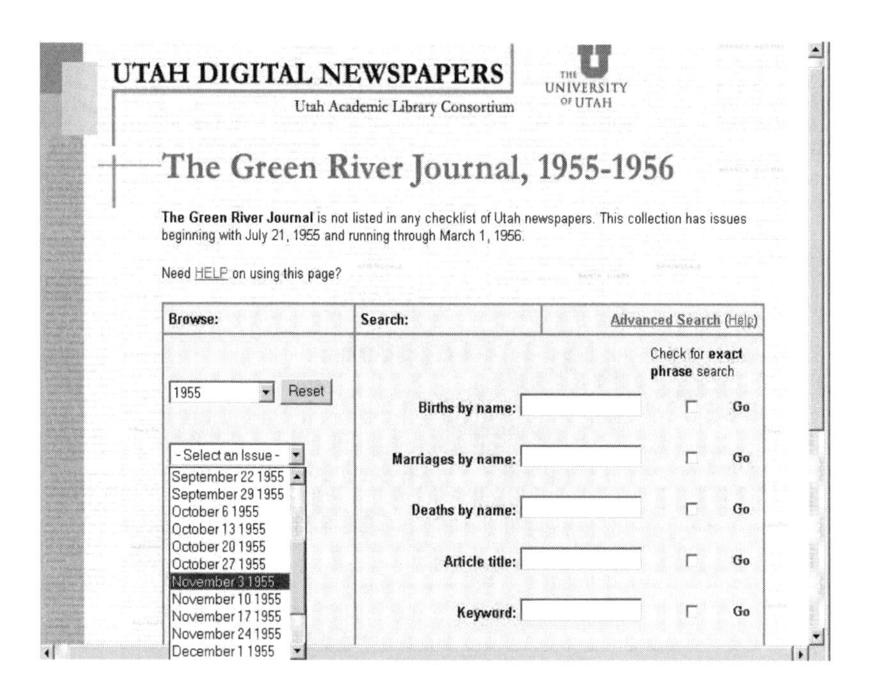
UTAH DIGITAL NEWSPAPERS
THE UNIVERSITY OF UTAH
Utah Academic Library Consortium
The Green River Journal, 1955-1956
The Green River Journal is not listed in any checklist of Utah newspapers. This collection has issues beginning with July 21, 1955 and running through March 1, 1956.
Need HELP on using this page?
Browse:
Search:
Advanced Search (Help)
Check for exact phrase search
1955
Reset
Births by name:
Go
- Select an Issue -
September 22 1955
September 29 1955
October 6 1955
October 13 1955
October 20 1955
October 27 1955
November 3 1955
November 10 1955
November 17 1955
November 24 1955
December 1 1955
Marriages by name:
Go
Deaths by name:
Go
Article title:
Go
Keyword:
Go

THE UNIVERSITY OF UTAH
J. Willard Marriott Library Digitized Collections
home | browse | advanced search | my favorites | about | help
back to search results
View: doc description page description page & text
Search this document:
search terms
search
add doc to favorites
add page to favorites
prev page | next page
Newspaper
Page 1
Articles (page 1)
Untitled
So You Want to Race a Boat! or ... Skippers Sabbath
Geneva Draws Eyes of the World
The Old Prospector Says
Gary King I B M Graduate
Coach McIntosh Announces Plans for Green River High Basketball Season
Green River to Get New Business Firm - Laundry and Dry Cleaning Plant
Elections and Right of Sufferage
Meeting Memos
Churches
Farm Issue up to Congress
Untitled
Page 2
Articles (page 2)
Page 3
Articles (page 3)
Page 4
Articles (page 4)
Bookmarks
Thumbnails
Comments
Signatures
34%
The Green River Journal
So You Want To Race A Boat!
Or... Skippers Sabbath
Coach McIntosh Announces Plans For Green River High Basketball Season
BASKETBALL
Pirates Have Tough Schedule

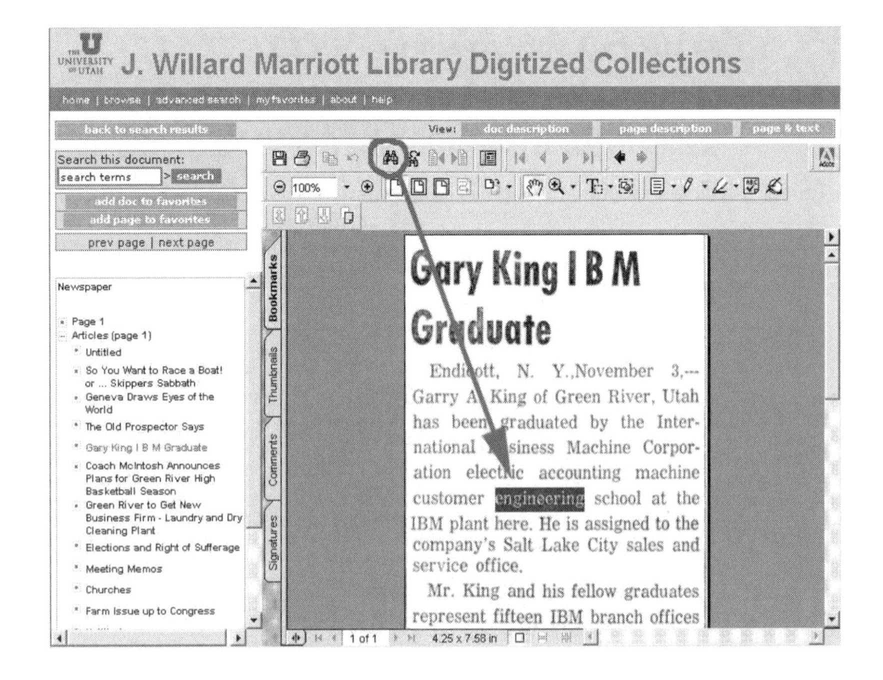
THE UNIVERSITY OF UTAH
J. Willard Marriott Library Digitized Collections
home | browse | advanced search | my favorites | about | help
back to search results
View: doc description page description page & text
Search this document:
search terms
search
add doc to favorites
add page to favorites
prev page | next page
100%
Newspaper
Page 1
Articles (page 1)
Untitled
So You Want to Race a Boat! or ... Skippers Sabbath
Geneva Draws Eyes of the World
The Old Prospector Says
Gary King I B M Graduate
Coach McIntosh Announces Plans for Green River High Basketball Season
Green River to Get New Business Firm - Laundry and Dry Cleaning Plant
Elections and Right of Sufferage
Meeting Memos
Churches
Farm Issue up to Congress
Bookmarks
Thumbnails
Comments
Signatures
Gary King I B M Graduate
Endicott, N. Y.,November 3,---
Garry A. King of Green River, Utah
has been graduated by the Inter-
national Business Machine Corpor-
ation electric accounting machine
customer engineering school at the
IBM plant here. He is assigned to the
company's Salt Lake City sales and
service office.
Mr. King and his fellow graduates
represent fifteen IBM branch offices
1 of 1
4.25 x 7.58 in

Final Thoughts

By far our most popular digital project

Any large-scale project evolves

Not all details need to be decided in advance

Over to John…

The University of Utah

UTAH DIGITAL NEWSPAPERS

John Herbert

University of Utah

UTAH DIGITAL NEWSPAPERS

THE UNIVERSITY OF UTAH

Funded by the Institute of Museum and Library Services and the Library Services and Technology Act

Search All Newspapers:

Search

Exact phrase | Advanced Search

Search/Browse A Single Newspaper:

Select Newspaper

Browse By County:

County Map

Help Us Improve. Please give us your feedback.
Take 2 minutes and fill out our online survey

Recent Additions:
Deseret News
1850-1898
Salt Lake Tribune
19th Century completed

Coming Soon:
Vernal Express
1936-1947

Ogden Standard
1923-1932

Times Independent
1933-1947

- Help: How To Use This Website
- Collections titles and dates
- Website Statistics
- Utah Newspaper Hall of Fame
- Utah Newspapers Project Handbook

Donate | Contact Us | About The Program | Disclaimer
Marriott Library | Adobe Acrobat Reader Required

The Ogden Standard.

SAN FRANCISCO IS A DOOMED CITY

400 DEAD BODIES ARE GATHERED AT ONE PLACE

Click on image to go to this issue

The San Francisco Quake of 1906:
A local view of one hundred years ago in history

http://digitalnewspapers.org

Utah Digital Newspapers

- Online collection of historic Utah newspapers
  - 1850 - 1961
- Keyword searchable
- 48 titles from 27 (of 29) counties
- 450,000 pages / 5 million articles
- Content hosted at three sites
  - U of U, BYU, and Utah State
- $2 million raised
  - State and federal grants
- Nine straight quarters of online growth
  - 14x increase from 1st qtr. 2003 to 1st qtr. 2006

Total Website Visits

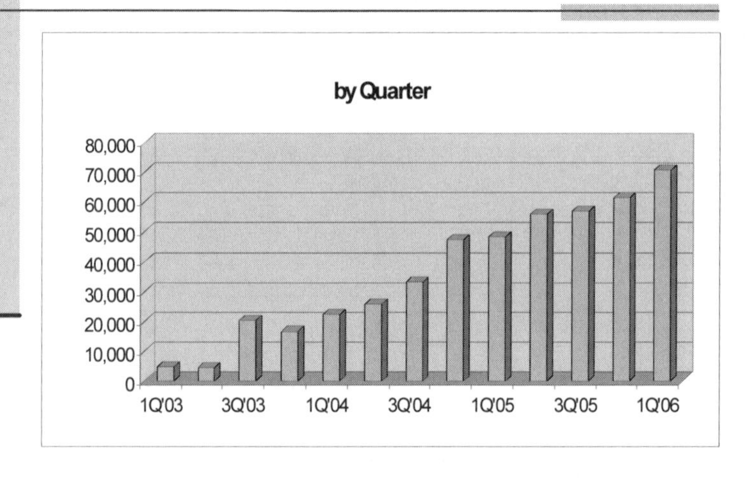

Process Summary

- Major processes are out-sourced
  - Scale and volume require efficiency
  - Even if you have the capability, be sure to understand volumes before you do-it-yourself
- We archive
  - Raw scans to LTO tapes
    - 4-bit tiff's, avg 28 MB's
    - 500K pages require 14 TB's
  - Vendor deliverable files on DVD's
    - PDF images with imbedded text; xml files
  - We can re-work from 2 different points in the process
- "High-tech" data transfer between locations
  - Hard drives and DVD's sent thru the mail
  - ftp not reliable enough given the high volume of data

Scanning from Paper

- PRO's
  - Capture new, high quality digital image
    - Using 21st century technology
  - Image quality more controllable
    - You/your vendor create images according to your spec
  - Cleaner images mean better OCR and higher search accuracy
- CON's
  - Harder to find originals
    - And they may need repairs (avg cost = 20 cents/pg.)
  - More expensive to scan than microfilm
  - Harder to find scanner
    - Need overhead camera; flatbeds won't work
    - Probably has to be local vendor

Scanning from Microfilm

- PRO's
  - Readily available
    - Almost every important title has been filmed
  - Cheaper, faster to scan
  - Scanning can be remote
    - Film boxes are easily transported
- CON's
  - Digital image quality dependent on film quality
    - Varies widely, even within a single reel
    - U.S. standards set in 1980's
      - After a lot of newspaper film had been created
  - Search accuracy lower (generally)
  - Our process: scan up to 3 times to get good image

Article-level Segmentation

- Articles are viewed stand-alone
  - Don't have to zoom/pan
- OCR is more accurate
  - More consistent font
  - Hyphenated words are put together
- Headlines and sub-headings are keyed
  - Nearly 100% accurate
- Articles are classified
  - Aid in searching

OCR Options

- Most OCR provides more than one option for a word
  - Our testing shows optimal number is 2 *for single-word searching*
- However, more word options degrade phrase searching
  - e.g., butch dutch cassidy
  - Proximity searching seems to be the best solution
- Beware of "letter accuracy" numbers
  - 95% letter accuracy equates to 77% accuracy on 5-letter word
  - Best unit measure for accuracy is "word"
- Filter the OCR results
  - English (or other) dictionary
  - Surnames
  - Place names
  - Numbers

Web Images

- Classic trade-off
  - Higher quality images are easier to read, but...
  - Larger files use more disk space and take longer to download
- 15-20% of users on dial-up connections
  - Need fast download times
- We create PDFs from bi-tonal TIFFs
  - Issues:
    - Pictures and photos are "cartoon-like"
    - Very small fonts (size 4) are a problem
  - Full-page images average 300K
  - Using 8-bit jpeg at 40% quality for SL Tribune

Costs and Volumes

Newspapers have low unit costs

Processing (per page)

	paper: $1.85	film: $1.57
Preservation	0.20	0.00
Scanning	0.30	0.22
Processing	1.15	1.15
Hardware	0.20	0.20

Internal staffing costs and general overhead

Approx. another $1/page

But, they are voluminous

8-page weekly	416 pages/year
25 years	10,400 pages
10-page daily (6/wk.)	3120 pages/year
10 years	31,200 pages

User Feedback

- Newspapers have very popular appeal
  - You're bringing history to life for the general public
  - A "populist" project may be a departure from a more traditional academic approach
- Put the interests of users/customers first
  - Do your best to understand their needs
    - Who they are
    - What they're doing
    - What they think of you
  - Stay in touch with them because....
    - The environment is always changing

Our Users

89% give overall rating of good or excellent
81% will return soon
76% will tell others about us
71% rate search accuracy as good or excellent
64% found new sources for their research
60% are more knowledgeable of their family's history
60% visit at least monthly
58% visit for genealogy
43% are outside Utah
18% use dial-up connection
Only 1% are 20 years old or less
Single, most often asked for improvement is to add more content

THE CALIFORNIA NEWSPAPER PROJECT

Andrea Vanek

Center for Bibliographical Studies and Research
University of California, Berkeley

I'd first like to acknowledge my colleagues who are with me today: Mary Elings, Archivist for Digital Collections at The Bancroft Library, University of California, Berkeley (UCB), and Henry Snyder, Director of the Center for Bibliographical Studies and Research and the California Newspaper Project at the University of California, Riverside (UCR).

As part of this National Digital Newspaper Program (NDNP) panel, the Library of Congress (LC) asked awardees to address what participation in the program has meant to them. Our NDNP grant has been a catalyst for implementing a digital newspaper program in California. There has been a lot of interest for several years in providing online access to historical California newspapers both at the State and local levels. The California Newspaper Project (CNP) has received numerous queries on digitizing newspapers, as has the California State Library (CSL). Three years ago the CSL asked the CNP to investigate newspaper digitization for a state program. Two years ago we participated in a Library Services and Technology Act (LSTA) grant to the California Preservation Program to conduct a newspaper digitization feasibility study. The results were positive, but we were not able to get any kind of commitment to store and host the digital files. We were at a standstill until we received our NDNP award in May 2005.

The California Newspaper Project is one of several projects of the Center for Bibliographical Studies and Research (CBSR) at UCR. The CBSR is a research center in the College of Humanities, Arts, and Social Sciences (CHASS). The newspaper project also has offices at UCB and has always had close ties to the CSL. The CNP is entering its final year of a United States Newspaper Program grant to catalog and microfilm newspapers, and had no experience managing a digital project. There was, however, a lot of expertise to draw on in the University of California (UC) system. Although the CBSR functioned quite independently in the past, we realized we needed help with the NDNP. We consulted the UC California Digital Library, UCB Digital Publishing Group, UCR Computing and Communications (C&C), CHASS College Computing, and the UCR Library. Our NDNP award was considered very prestigious at UCR and everyone was very enthusiastic about helping. C&C agreed to help with storage and hardware needs and purchased a new server for us. Fortunately, Mary Elings, who has managed many digital projects and is a metadata specialist, agreed to devote a percentage of her time to the NDNP project.

On the strength of our NDNP award and the UCR storage commitment, we applied for and received a LSTA award from the CSL to create the California Digital Newspaper Collection at UCR. The award for July 2005–June 2006 encompasses digitizing 44,000 pages of the Alta California, our most important early newspaper, and its predecessors, selecting a content management system, and creating an online collection at UCR. All pages contributed to the NDNP will also be mounted at UCR, but with article-level access. (See http://cdnc.ucr.edu.) This month, we applied for a second LSTA grant to continue developing the UCR collection by digitizing 74,000 pages and improving the user interface, searching and browsing functions. With this second LSTA grant, the CDNC would provide access to California newspapers from 1846-1910 by June 2007.

Last fall we issued an RFP for digital services based on LC NDNP specifications plus a request for an article-level solution. OCLC Preservation Service Centers, partnered with CCS-GmbH, won the contract. Working with vendors with expertise in metadata and scanning newspaper microfilm especially when it's problematic, has been an enormous help. We've been in production the last several months. Our master negatives are duplicated at UCB. The duplicate negatives are sent to Pennsylvania for scanning. The TIFFs are sent to Germany and Romania for processing and metadata creation. The NDNP digital files are sent to UCB for quality review, and then on to UCR where they are mounted on our server. A copy of the files is then sent to LC. The LSTA files go directly to UCR from Europe.

We met with advisors, historians and librarians, last year to consider titles for digitization. As was mentioned, NDNP awardees are to contribute 100,000 pages of newspapers published from 1900–1910. The San Francisco Call was selected as our primary paper; the Los Angeles Herald and several regional papers that cover agriculture, water rights, mining, fishing, and the oil industry are under consideration.

Most of California's important historical newspapers were filmed in the 1950's through the 1980's by the CSL, UCB, and three commercial agencies in California. The CSL and UCB negatives are available to us for digitization. Since storing newspaper negatives when orders for duplication are low was no longer viable for the commercial agencies, we were able to acquire the negatives for the University of California. We therefore have a large pool of titles to select from for the NDNP and CDNC.

We've spent a great deal of time inventorying and inspecting the master negatives of titles under consideration. Much of the film is problematic. The head of UCB Microfilming Services made several versions of duplicate negatives for scanning and OCR testing. A low contrast version on low contrast film tested best for the Call.

This past year has been difficult; there's been a lot to learn. But, we're all very excited about these projects and love working on them. The NDNP has given us a solid footing on which to build our state program. It's led us to collaborate with other departments and individuals, both within the University of California and beyond. We hope to eventually expand the CDNC, following a model such as Utah's, and provide best practice for newspaper digitization to libraries and museums throughout the state, preservation, hosting and cross-searching among future digital newspaper collections.

THE U.S. NATIONAL DIGITAL NEWSPAPER PROGRAM: UNIVERSITY OF KENTUCKY LIBRARIES

J. Wendel Cox

Special Collections and Digital Programs
University of Kentucky Libraries

Ludwig Wittgenstein, the Anglo-Austrian philosopher of such profound influence on modern philosophy, has something of a reputation as a difficult and even elusive thinker. Certainly, many have been vexed by, and attracted to, not only Wittgenstein's ideas, but also the allusive nature of his aphoristic writing. Nevertheless, Wittgenstein could also be thunderously direct, as when he frequently admonished Rush Rhees, his student, friend, and fellow philosopher, to «Go the hard way; go the bloody hard way!» Wittgenstein's admonition was not encouragement to make every undertaking a demonstration of endurance or fortitude. Rather, he urged Rhees to see work as an effort to do the best with what we have, to be true to our abilities and to the circumstances at hand, and to act with an honest understanding of both possibility and limitation. Behind Wittgenstein's charge is an additional imperative to treat work as an obligation not only to ourselves but also to others, and one it would be best to remember as we go about our tasks.

Wittgenstein's charge to Rhees has often been with me during my short tenure with the University of Kentucky's National Digital Newspaper Program (NDNP) project. To date, our effort as part of NDNP's two-year test phase has been hard work, and it has sometimes seemed as if we had not only gone the bloody hard way, but actually lost our way and traveled down a dark, doomed path. More recently, however, as our command of how to digitize newspapers has grown sure, and the value of our hard-won insights has become evident to us and to others, the encouragement, and even the joy, in Wittgenstein's admonition has returned to me. And Wittgenstein's advice to his friend has served to remind me that our efforts are best if they are true to obligations to ourselves and to others.

In fact, as NDNP participants, we have several obligations, some of which are profound. Most importantly – and most obviously – we have an obligation to make available the wealth of information in America's historic newspapers, and to make it available, without charge, as part of a patrimony that belongs to a nation and to the world. We also have obligations that arise from the preliminary nature of our efforts, from the difficulty of film-to-digital conversion and the inherent problems of newspaper digitization, and from the enormity and collective nature of a national effort to digitize 30 million U.S. newspaper pages, circa 1836 to 1923, from each of the fifty states and the several territories. With our effort, as with so many other undertakings at what remains but the beginning of a digital age, we have much to learn. And with so much to learn, we have an obligation to share, and to do so with humility and courage.

If the necessity of brevity requires me to simplify, to offer more conclusion than description of our experience, let me say ours is neither a simple nor entirely happy story, although I am already confident it has a happy ending. Where five of the six current NDNP awardees have decided to work with a vendor for the film-to-digital conversion of their newspapers, we alone are responsible for all aspects of our project. We do it all – title selection, film evaluation, and content collation; scanning, image manipulation, and generation of deliverables; configuration of a dedicated production server, creation and support of a local area network, and troubleshooting specifications and software; research of newspapers, composition of title histories, and creation of a history of Kentucky newspapers, circa 1900–1910 – and we have learned a great deal as a result. That we have just now begun to find our feet, and grow in confidence, further convinces me of the imperative to share our experiences, to communicate, and to build a basis for collaboration to sustain the National Digital Newspaper Program as it grows and expands. Open, honest, and generous communication can be difficult, not the least of all because it requires one to share what has worked, but also what has failed; to describe not only what one has done well, but also where one has erred, encountered obstacles, or learned difficult lessons. We have not always known how to proceed, we have made mistakes, and we will doubtless lose our way again in the months and years to come. In many ways, we have «done it good» – the phrase so often used, sometimes disparagingly, to describe reports like this one – in no small measure because we have also 'done it bad, and learned to do it better.'

In many respects, the University of Kentucky's participation in the National Digital Newspaper Program involved no wrenching decision or new direction in our efforts. Instead, it continued long-standing efforts to preserve and provide access to the wealth of Kentucky's newspapers, and marked a natural progression based on our experience, our expertise, and the resources available to us at our institution. Participation afforded us a host of opportunities. It presented an opportunity to enrich our already extensive digital collections, which have come to include archival finding aids, photographic images, audio and transcript of oral history interviews, and other resources serving both the state of Kentucky and the nation. It presented an opportunity to participate in a national digital library initiative from its inception, and it presented an opportunity to take a prominent role in shaping an invaluable national resource. And, not least of all, our participation also allowed us to finally answer a question so often put to us: When will you digitize newspapers?

It was also clear that many of these same circumstances afforded us extraordinary advantages in doing the work of Kentucky's NDNP project, and left us able to undertake every facet of film-to-digital conversion. We have also discovered these circumstances provide a familiarity, an intimacy, with what appears before us on a microfilm and an insight into how best to convert it to a usable digital object, which may not be available to other projects. Many microfilms of historic newspapers, as we know from experience, do not reflect our current best practices for preservation. In fact, there is likely something of a paradox in work with historic newspapers, one where the most intellectually compelling titles, as perhaps first to have been microfilmed, may also be the least likely to have been captured in a manner even remotely resembling best practices. We find a host of anomalies in our film, even our best or most recent film, including poor or uneven lighting, out-of-order pages, out-of-order issues, blurry pages, and blank pages not filmed. Who could have anticipated a microfilm made with pages placed on a grey background, with little to contrast camera bed from newsprint, would make it nearly impossible to detect the beginning or end of a page, or to capture the entire contents of a roll of film? Likewise, when a page is missing, where is it missing? In the digital? On film? In the original? How should we order a newspaper without page numbers? How do we recognize when an issue without page numbers has out-of-order pages? The list might continue. It grows with most every new title or reel of film we process. With skill, experience, and intimate knowledge of microfilm and digitization, we have the ability to address such unexpected circumstances.

Likewise, when an intriguing title, overlooked in initial selection, appears with a closer look at our master database of negatives, we can pull the title, examine it, and quickly make a decision to include or exclude it. When a film of significant intellectual merit proves to have images of some pages reduced to mere fragments, we have found ways to deal with such difficulties; indeed, we have sometimes sought such challenges precisely to test the limits

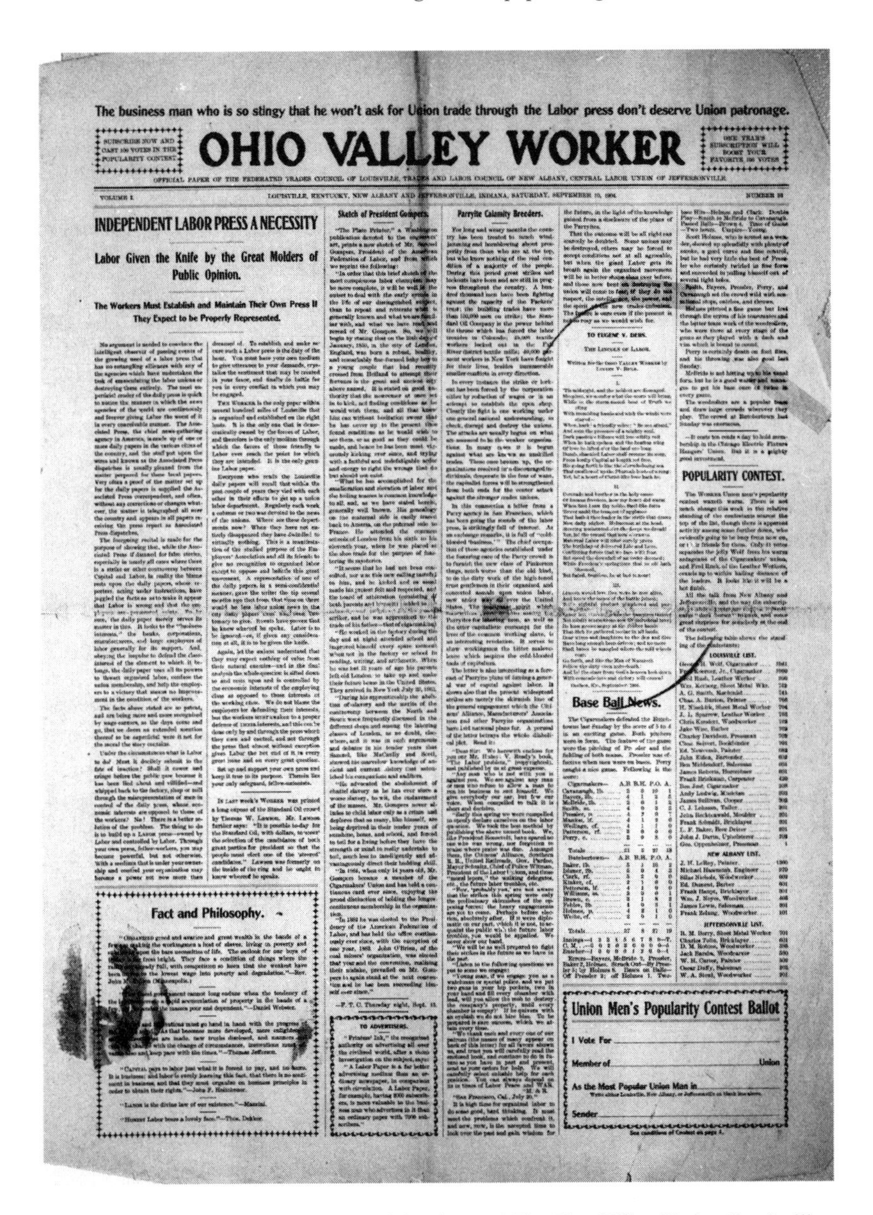

The business man who is so stingy that he won't ask for Union trade through the Labor press don't deserve Union patronage.

OHIO VALLEY WORKER

INDEPENDENT LABOR PRESS A NECESSITY

Labor Given the Knife by the Great Molders of Public Opinion.

The Workers Must Establish and Maintain Their Own Press If They Expect to be Properly Represented.

Sketch of President Gompers.

Parryite Calamity Breeders.

POPULARITY CONTEST.

Base Ball News.

Fact and Philosophy.

Union Men's Popularity Contest Ballot

I Vote For

Member of Union

As the Most Popular Union Man in

Sender

Fig. 1. The front page of the only surviving issue of *The Ohio Valley Worker* (Louisville, Kentucky), dated September 11, 1904. *The Ohio Valley Worker* was one of several labor newspapers, and one of almost four dozen newspapers and periodicals, then published in Louisville.

of what is possible. In making a decision to choose newspapers that were intellectually compelling, rather than available on microfilm that necessarily met technical standards, we have bent initial recommendations for selection, especially when to do otherwise seemed contrary to the long-term interests of the program. To suffer selection to present technological limitations, even as our ongoing creation of durable master images provides the basis for subsequent reprocessing with improved technology, seems to us a mistake. With our knowledge and experience, we can make such judgments with confidence, materially improve our deliverables, and facilitate and enrich the experience of our users.

Moreover, the small size of our project team, and our proximity to each other, make it possible to consult whenever the need arises. I might walk one direction through our office and consult Kopana Terry on a microfilm mystery, discuss a metadata puzzle with Margie Plarr, pose a question about our storage, network, or software to Kathryn Lybarger, or puzzle over online presentation with Eric Weig. Or I might turn in the other direction to answer questions from our student operators – Sommer, Patrick, Soham, Andrew, Lisa, Nicole, Jeremy, Sara, Rachel, and Damon – who manually alter raw images and describe reading order of individual newspaper pages. If I open a half door to an adjoining office, I can ask Mary Molinaro about the direction of the project, our budget, or sundry other issues. Or I can walk out of my office, through one door and then another, and talk to Rebecca Ryder, Shell Dunn, or Marie Dale about our microfilm. In a matter of steps, we have ready access to almost everyone immediately concerned with our project, and each of us to the other. Conversations, collaboration, and learning occur constantly in our environment. We can thrash through a vexing question while sitting around a table, exchanging e-mail, talking over an office divider, or walking to get coffee. Moreover, we have documented our decisions, our discussions, and our processes as a reference for ourselves and as a record to share with others, as an e-mail archive, on our wiki, in our required reports, and even in diaries of daily developments.

The benefits of our hard work are already evident to us. We have established a productive process for newspaper digitization, one readily repurposed to the digitization of magazines and journals, books, typescript and manuscript documents, and other sources for the creation of digital objects. We have extended our understanding of our microfilm and newspaper holdings. We have traded our expertise in newspaper preservation, microfilm, and digitization for access to previously unknown issues of one of Kentucky's turn-of-the-century African-American newspapers held at a distant repository. We have contributed our understanding of the software we use to improve its performance, and suggested changes to the technical specifications for deliverables. And we have become a still more desirable partner for other digital collaborations, and a resource for other institutions interested in applying for their own National Digital Newspaper Program grant or undertaking their own newspaper digitization effort.

Gathered here in Salt Lake City for these past few days, we have discussed newspapers, their preservation, and how we might make these marvels of the printed past available and accessible to others. Our love for this work has been evident in our presentations, in our conversations, and in our efforts to share what we know with each other. Such passion is admirable, even as it often has a price. Passion can lead us to strive for perfection or believe that we must be perfect. The counterproductive nature of the desire for perfection, of course, is readily apparent to everyone who encounters it, except when we are in the throes of our own obsession to achieve it. Our experiences during the first year of the National Digital Newspaper Program suggest the need for a flexibility and creativity in the face of almost constant challenges we will encounter in digitizing America's historic newspapers. In many respects, the current incarnation of the National Digital Newspaper Program is a point of departure. Experience with the entire process of conversion, with the different paths to it, has already suggested, and likely will continue to suggest, where change needs to be made. To be productive, we must accept we will make imperfect things, and work from there. If this vast effort to digitize historic newspapers is to succeed, it will not be because we have been perfect, but because we have erred, made mistakes, undertaken what may have seemed ill-advised, and then learned from our struggles and helped each other. We must go the bloody hard way.

A METS APPLICATION PROFILE FOR HISTORICAL NEWSPAPERS

Morgan Cundiff

Network Development and MARC Standards Office
Library of Congress

XML

«XML has become the de-facto standard for representing metadata descriptions of resources on the Internet.»

Jane Hunter. *Working Towards MetaUtopia – A Survey of Current Metadata Research*

The Importance of Standards

«In moving from dispersed digital collections to interoperable digital libraries, the most important activity we need to focus on is standards … most important is the wide variety of metadata standards [including] descriptive metadata … administrative metadata …, structural metadata, and terms and conditions metadata …»

Howard Besser. *The Next Stage: Moving from Isolated Digital Collections to Interoperable Digital Libraries*

What is METS?

METS is an XML Schema designed for the purpose of creating XML document instances that express the hierarchical structure of digital library objects, the names and locations of the files that comprise those objects, and the associated metadata. METS can, therefore, be used as a tool for modeling real world objects, such as particular document types.

```
<mets>
  <metsHdr/>
  <dmdSec/>
  <amdSec/>
  <fileSec/>
  <structMap/>
  <structLink/>
  <behaviorSec/>
</mets>
```

Fig. 1. The 7 Sections of a METS Document

```
<mets>
 <dmdSec>
  <mdWrap>
   <xmlData>
    <!-- insert data from different namespace here -->
   </xmlData>
  </mdWrap>
 </dmdSec>
 <fileSec></fileSec>
 <structMap></structMap>
</mets>
```

Fig. 2. The Descriptive Metadata Section with mdWrap

```
<mets:mets>
 <mets:dmdSec>
  <mets:mdWrap>
   <mets:xmlData>
    <mods:mods></mods:mods>
   </mets:xmlData>
  </mets:mdWrap>
 </mets:dmdSec>
 <mets:fileSec></mets:fileSec>
 <mets:structMap></mets:structMap>
</mets:mets>
```

Fig. 3.The Descriptive Metadata Section with MODS as extension schema

```
<mets:mets>
 <mets:dmdSec>
  <mets:mdWrap>
   <mets:xmlData>
    <mods:mods>
     <mods:relatedItem type="constituent">
      <mods:relatedItem type="constituent"></mods:relatedItem>
     </mods:relatedItem>
    </mods:mods>
   </mets:xmlData>
  </mets:mdWrap>
 </mets:dmdSec>
 <mets:fileSec></mets:fileSec>
 <mets:structMap></mets:structMap>
</mets:mets>
```

Fig. 4. The Descriptive Metadata Section with MODS and relatedItem elements

MODS relatedItem element

1. Child element to MODS.
2. The relatedItem element has same content model as mods (titleInfo, name, subject, physicalDescription, note, etc.).
3. The relatedItem element makes it possible to create very rich analytic descriptions for contained works within a MODS records.

4. The relatedItem element is repeatable and it can be nested recursively (thus making it possible to build a hierarchical tree structure).
5. The relatedItem elements make it possible to associate descriptive data with any structural element.

```
<mods:mods>
 <mods:titleInfo>
  <mods:title>Baltimore Sun</mods:title>
 </mods:titleInfo>
 <mods:relatedItem type="constituent">
  <mods:titleInfo>
   <mods:title>Sports</mods:title>
  </mods:titleInfo>
  <mods:relatedItem  type="constituent">
   <mods:titleInfo>
    <mods:title>O's Split Beantown Twi-niter</mods:title>
   </mods:titleInfo>
  </mods:relatedItem>
  <mods:relatedItem type="constituent">
   <mods:titleInfo>
    <mods:title>Chisox Nip Tribe</mods:title>
   </mods:titleInfo>
  </mods:relatedItem>
 </mods:relatedItem>
</mods:mods>
```

Fig. 5. Use of MODS relatedItem element to express logical structure

```
<mets:mets>
 <mets:dmdSec>
  <mets:mdWrap>
   <mets:xmlData>
    <mods:mods>
     <mods:relatedItem>
      <mods:relatedItem></mods:relatedItem>
     </mods:relatedItem>
    </mods:mods>
   </mets:xmlData>
  </mets:mdWrap>
 </mets:dmdSec>
 <mets:fileSec></mets:fileSec>
 <mets:structMap>
  <mets:div>
   <mets:div></mets:div>
  </mets:div>
 </mets:structMap>
</mets:mets>
```

Fig. 6. METS document with two hierarchies (logical and physical)

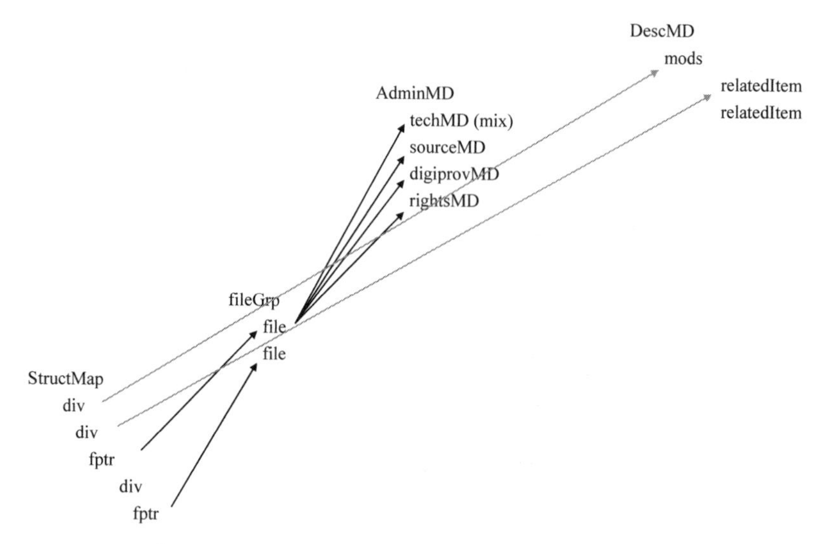

Fig. 7. Linking in METS Documents (XML ID/IDREF links)

What is a METS Application Profile?

«METS Profiles are intended to describe a class of METS documents in sufficient detail to provide both document authors and programmers the guidance they require to create and process METS documents conforming with a particular profile.»

A profile is expressed as an XML document. There is a schema for this purpose. The profile expresses the requirements that a METS document must satisfy. A sufficiently explicit METS Profile may be considered a «data standard».

A METS Profile is a human-readable prose document and is not intended to be «machine actionable».

METS Profile for Historical Newspapers [draft]

The METS Profile for Historical Newspapers specifies how METS documents representing digitized historical newspapers should be encoded. Note that the profile is to be used to represent a single issue of a newspaper. The profile uses MODS to express the logical structure of a newspaper issue, and uses the METS structMap to express the physical structure of the newspaper issue. [draft abstract]

URL to find Profile and related documents:
http://www.loc.gov/standards/mets/test/ndnp/profile_notes.html / mcundiff@loc.gov

METS Profile (features)

A METS Profile represents one issue of a newspaper. The Profile presumes the use of alto files (or some equivalent) where the zones on the corresponding digital image (expressed as coordinates) are correlated to the corresponding logical entity (e.g., article or paragraph) and also to the corresponding OCR text.

The Profile maintains a strict separation between logical entities and physical entities. The primary logical entities are issue, issue section, article, article section, illustration, and advertisement.

The top-level MODS record describes the issue. The other primary logical entities (issue section, article, article section, illustration, and advertisement) are described in a heirarchy of MODS relatedItem elements.

Logical structure is represented using MODS in the METS dmdSec. It is necessary to use the latest version (version 3.2) of MODS.

- **issue**
    - **issue section**
        - **article** (or article-like entity)
            - **paragraph**
            - **illustration** (photograph, drawing, map, table)
            - **article section**
                - **paragraph**
                - **illustration**
        - **illustration**
        - **advertisements**
    - **article**
        - **paragraph**
        - **illustration**
        - **article section**
            - **paragraph**
            - **illustration**
    - **illustration**
    - **advertisements**

Fig. 8. Hierarchy of Logical Entities

The primary logical entities are expressed as values of the MODS genre element.

The allowable genre values (for Profile compliance) are listed in Newspaper Genre Terms [draft]. It is also possible to tag subparts of the primary logical entities. The typical example of this is tagging the paragraph. This is accomplished using the MODS part element.

There are only three physical entities. They are: issue, page, and pageRegion. The physical entities are represented in the structMap section of the METS document as div types (div type="news:page"). There is only one structMap.

Page regions are correlated to the corresponding logical entity by means of an IDREF link. Note that one or more page regions may correspond to a single logical entity. This makes it possible to make the necessary associations when the logical entity is split into more than

```
<mods:mods>
 <mods:titleInfo>
  <mods:title>Baltimore Sun</mods:title>
  <mods:genre>newspaper</genre>
 </mods:titleInfo>
 <mods:relatedItem type="constituent">
  <mods:titleInfo>
   <mods:title>Sports</mods:title>
  </mods:titleInfo>
  <mods:genre>section</genre>
  <mods:relatedItem  type="constituent">
   <mods:titleInfo>
    <mods:title>O's Split Beantown Twi-niter</mods:title>
   </mods:titleInfo>
   <mods:genre>article</mods:genre>
   <mods:relatedItem type="constituent">
    <mods:titleInfo>
     <mods:title>Aparicio puts tag on Jensen to end 7th</mods:title>
    </mods:titleInfo>
    <mods:genre>photograph</genre>
   </mods:relatedItem>
  </mods:relatedItem>
 </mods:relatedItem>
</mods:mods>
```

Fig. 9. Use of MODS relatedItem element to express logical structure

one physical entity, e.g. when a paragraph is continued on the next column or an article is continued on a different page.

An example document can be found at
http://memory.loc.gov/cocoon/diglib/loc.news.sr.1002/default.html

Parting Thoughts

Agreement on a data standard (such as a METS profile) will facilitate interoperability. Interoperability can be between any two agents (digital library applications, preservation repositories, search and retrieval systems, etc.).

Newspaper community has a «quality vs. quantity» dilemma. Large volume of material to be digitized necessitates automatic processing. Automatic processing produces dirty data and less satisfying results. High quality processing (requiring more human intervention) is more expensive but produces far better results and pays dividends far into the future (the data will be used over and over without additional cost).

RE-ENGINEERING DIGITAL LIBRARY SOFTWARE FOR NEWSPAPERS

Perry Willet

Digital Library Production Service
University of Michigan

Where we started

- DLXS software
- Basic data models: books/journals, finding aids, images
- XML/XSLT/CSS processing of UTF-8 data, with an XML-aware search engine (XPAT)

DLXS Book Model

- One image per page
- 100K–200K per image on average
- Uncorrected OCR in the background:
- 1K–3K per page on average
- Generally 1–2 columns on a page
- Simple navigation/sequence
- Browsing by author/title
- Limit searching by year

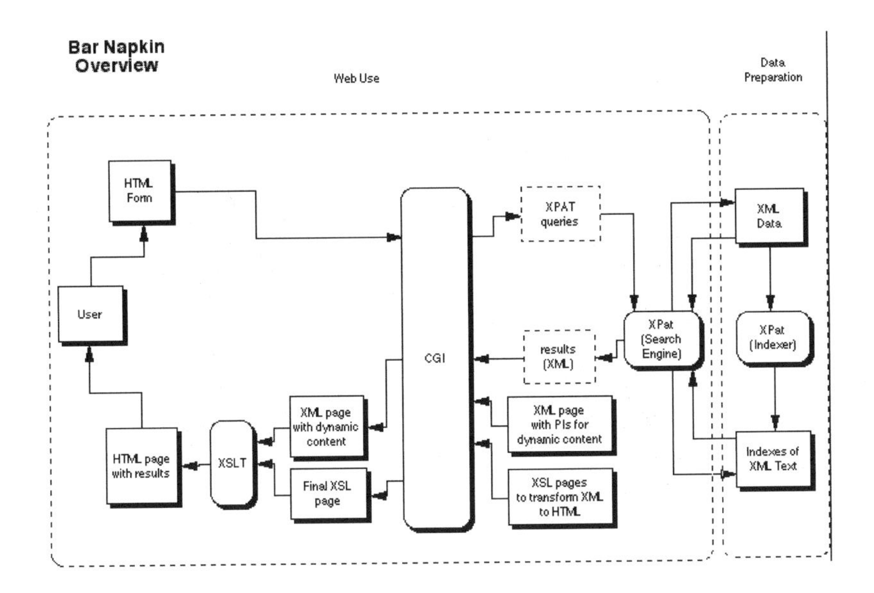

The Projects, I

- British Library newspapers
  - 19th newspapers
  - 2 million pages initially
  - Apex handling digital conversion

The Projects, II

- Michigan Daily (student newspaper)
  - 1890-
  - Spotty paper source
    - bound, with very narrow margins
  - Poor quality microfilm
    - From the 1950s on
    - Some done locally

The Newspaper Difference, I

- Full page images
  - Much larger physically (3-6 Mg)
  - Much larger file sizes than we normally process
  - Multiple, irregular columns
  - Poorer quality print
- As a result, more difficult to display on screen

The Newspaper Difference, II

- Cropped articles
- Jump continuations
- Generally no authors
- Titles less important
- Browsing by full date
- Complicated rights issues (?)

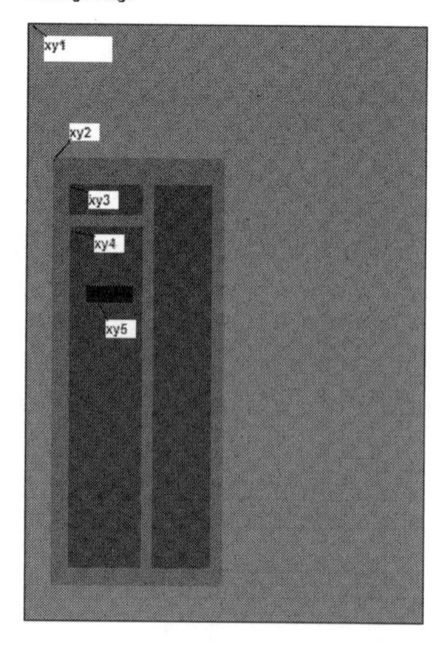

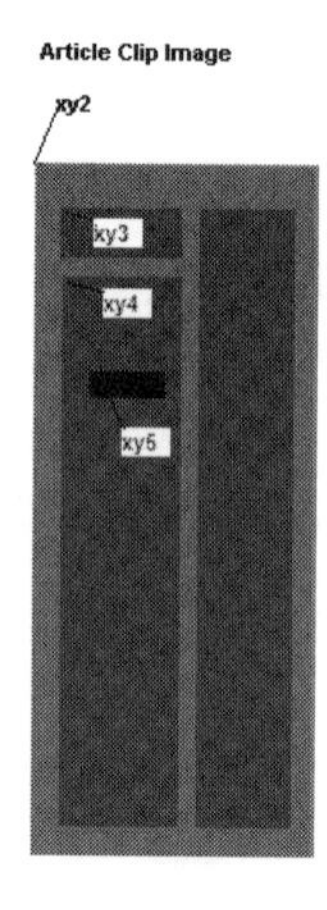

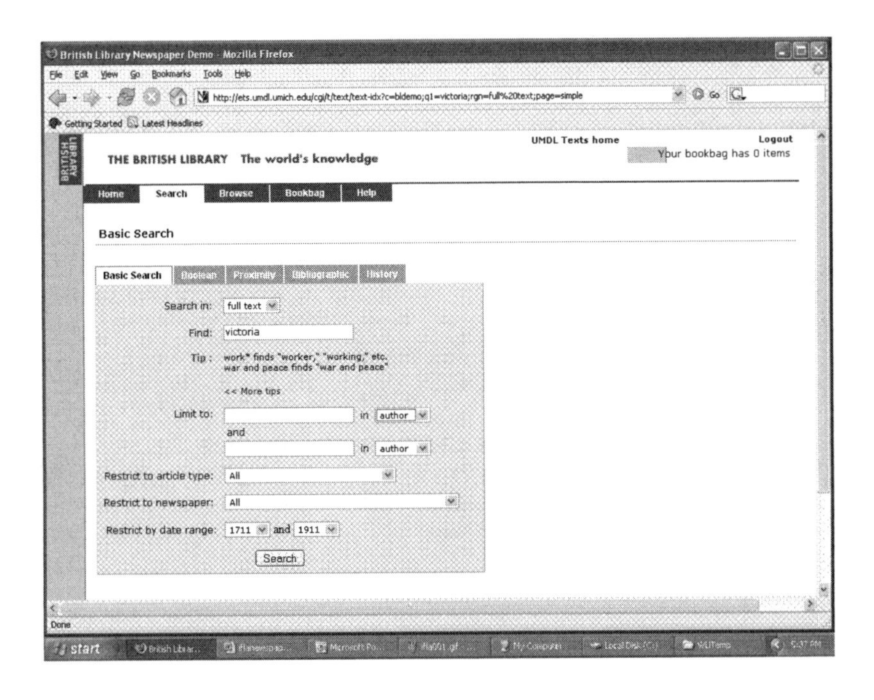
British Library Newspaper Demo - Mozilla Firefox
File Edit View Go Bookmarks Tools Help
http://ets.umdl.umich.edu/cgi/t/text/text-idx?c=bldemo;q1=victoria;rgn=full%20text;page=simple
Getting Started Latest Headlines
UMDL Texts home
Logout
THE BRITISH LIBRARY The world's knowledge
Your bookbag has 0 items
Home Search Browse Bookbag Help
Basic Search
Basic Search Boolean Proximity Bibliographic History
Search in: full text
Find: victoria
Tip: work* finds "worker," "working," etc.
war and peace finds "war and peace"
<< More tips
Limit to: in author
and
in author
Restrict to article type: All
Restrict to newspaper: All
Restrict by date range: 1711 and 1911
Search
Done
start

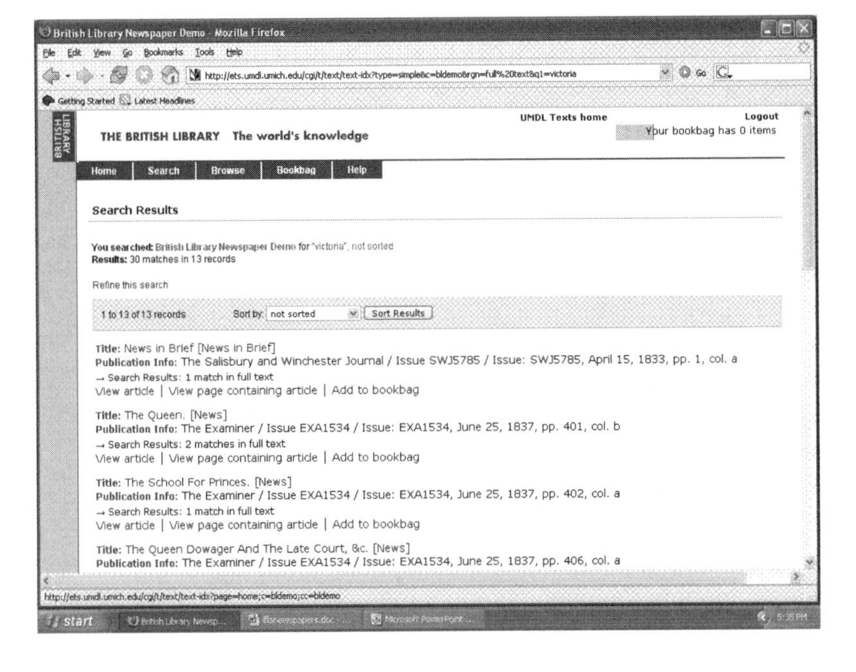
British Library Newspaper Demo - Mozilla Firefox
File Edit View Go Bookmarks Tools Help
http://ets.umdl.umich.edu/cgi/t/text/text-idx?type=simple&c=bldemo&rgn=full%20text&q1=victoria
Getting Started Latest Headlines
UMDL Texts home
Logout
THE BRITISH LIBRARY The world's knowledge
Your bookbag has 0 items
Home Search Browse Bookbag Help
Search Results
You searched: British Library Newspaper Demo for "victoria", not sorted
Results: 30 matches in 13 records
Refine this search
1 to 13 of 13 records
Sort by: not sorted
Sort Results
Title: News in Brief [News in Brief]
Publication Info: The Salisbury and Winchester Journal / Issue SWJ5785 / Issue: SWJ5785, April 15, 1833, pp. 1, col. a
→ Search Results: 1 match in full text
View article | View page containing article | Add to bookbag
Title: The Queen. [News]
Publication Info: The Examiner / Issue EXA1534 / Issue: EXA1534, June 25, 1837, pp. 401, col. b
→ Search Results: 2 matches in full text
View article | View page containing article | Add to bookbag
Title: The School For Princes. [News]
Publication Info: The Examiner / Issue EXA1534 / Issue: EXA1534, June 25, 1837, pp. 402, col. a
→ Search Results: 1 match in full text
View article | View page containing article | Add to bookbag
Title: The Queen Dowager And The Late Court, &c. [News]
Publication Info: The Examiner / Issue EXA1534 / Issue: EXA1534, June 25, 1837, pp. 406, col. a
http://ets.umdl.umich.edu/cgi/t/text/text-idx?page=home;c=bldemo;cc=bldemo
start

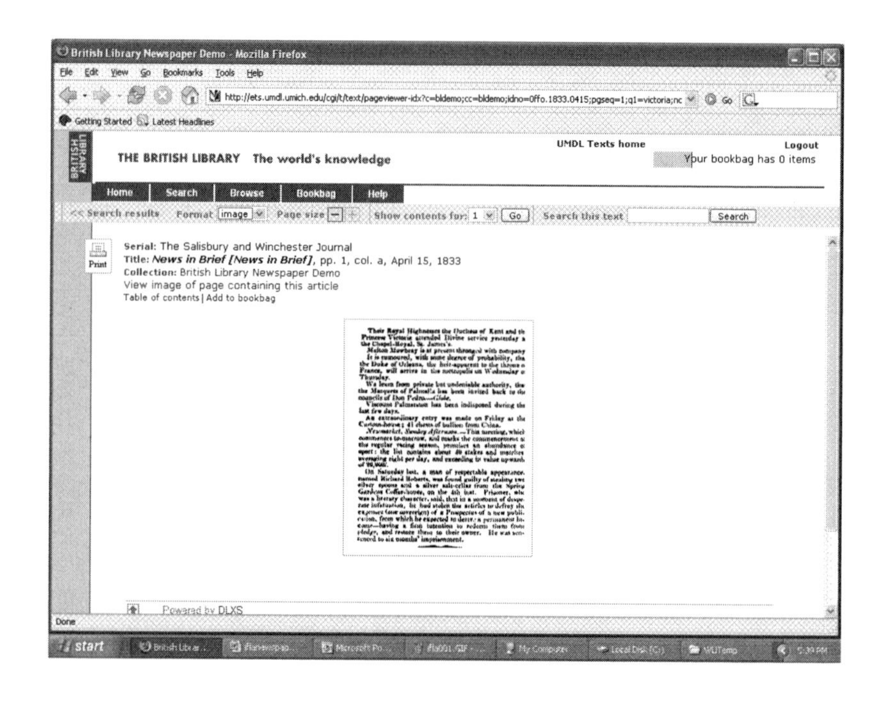
British Library Newspaper Demo - Mozilla Firefox
File Edit View Go Bookmarks Tools Help
http://ets.umdl.umich.edu/cgi/t/text/pageviewer-idx?c=bldemo;cc=bldemo;idno=0ffo.1833.0415;pgseq=1;q1=victoria;nc
Getting Started Latest Headlines
BRITISH LIBRARY
THE BRITISH LIBRARY The world's knowledge
UMDL Texts home
Logout
Your bookbag has 0 items
Home Search Browse Bookbag Help
<< Search results Format image Page size Show contents for: 1 Go Search this text Search
Print
Serial: The Salisbury and Winchester Journal
Title: News in Brief [News in Brief], pp. 1, col. a, April 15, 1833
Collection: British Library Newspaper Demo
View image of page containing this article
Table of contents | Add to bookbag
Powered by DLXS
Done
start

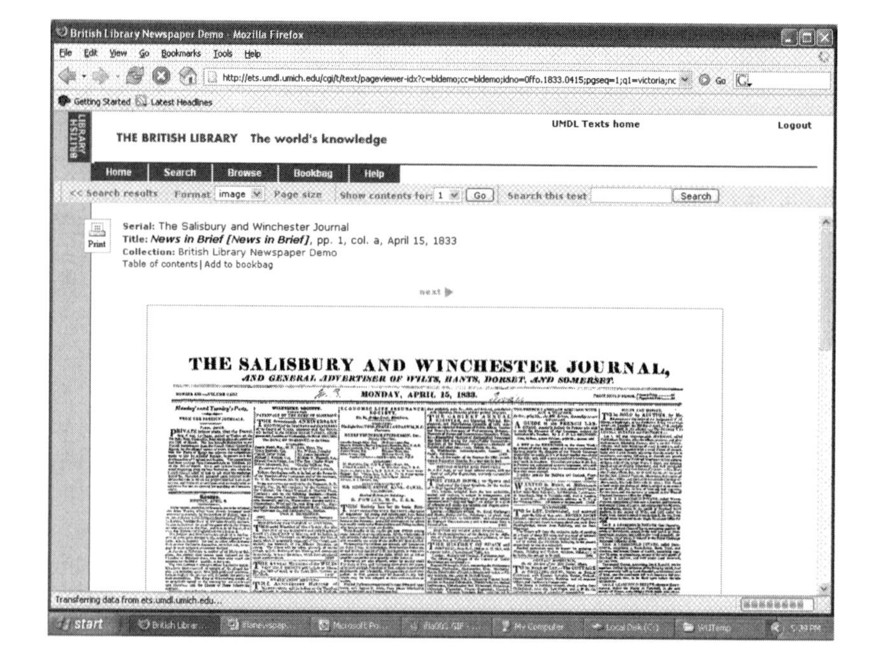
British Library Newspaper Demo - Mozilla Firefox
File Edit View Go Bookmarks Tools Help
http://ets.umdl.umich.edu/cgi/t/text/pageviewer-idx?c=bldemo;cc=bldemo;idno=0ffo.1833.0415;pgseq=1;q1=victoria;nc
Getting Started Latest Headlines
BRITISH LIBRARY
THE BRITISH LIBRARY The world's knowledge
UMDL Texts home
Logout
Home Search Browse Bookbag Help
<< Search results Format image Page size Show contents for: 1 Go Search this text Search
Print
Serial: The Salisbury and Winchester Journal
Title: News in Brief [News in Brief], pp. 1, col. a, April 15, 1833
Collection: British Library Newspaper Demo
Table of contents | Add to bookbag
next
THE SALISBURY AND WINCHESTER JOURNAL,
AND GENERAL ADVERTISER OF WILTS, HANTS, DORSET, AND SOMERSET.
MONDAY, APRIL 15, 1833.
Transferring data from ets.umdl.umich.edu...
start

Left to Do

- Highlighting terms on page image
- Date searching/browsing

Other Issues

- Column / article based approach
- Best practice for coordinates, relationships between parts?
- Vendor practices differ from digital libraries. Are we even talking?
- Rights issues with wire services

TOPIC MAP PRESENTATION FRAMEWORK: AN APPROACH TO DELIVERING NEWSPAPER CONTENT OVER THE WEB

Alison Stevenson, Elizabeth Styron

New Zealand Electronic Text Centre (NZETC)

Introduction

This paper will discuss some of the requirements for the successful online delivery of newspaper archive content to users and examine an innovative approach taken to fulfil those requirements by using a semantic framework.

There are currently numerous large projects going on around the world which aim to create online newspaper archives. So far, much of the public, technical discussion around these projects has focused on the digitisation process – the use of microfilm for scanning, OCR requirements and techniques, file naming conventions, image format choices, storage strategies, and so on. Since the imperative for digitisation is often as much about preservation as it is about access, this is not surprising. However the delivery of content from the newspaper archive to users is a similarly important process which requires a similar level of commitment to technical research and development if it is to be successful. Of course the successful delivery of newspaper content over the web is predicated on the existence of a high quality, well-structured digital collection which to deliver. No amount of sophisticated search algorithms, novel browsing functionality or intuitive interface design can compensate for inaccurately transcribed text, poor quality images or inaccurate metadata. But it is equally true that the impact and usefulness of even the most interesting, high-quality content will be diminished if that content is not discoverable, navigable and presented in a way that meets user needs.

The use of a semantic framework to meets these needs is an approach is based on the digital library delivery system configured by the New Zealand Electronic Text Centre (NZETC). The working name of the system is the Topic Map Presentation Framework (TMPF). It has been developed as a production system at the NZETC since 2002 and is currently used to deliver the Centre's own growing collection of digital resources, a nationally important website containing more than 40,000 pages and over half-a-million hyperlinks. Since 2005 the NZETC has been working with APEX to further develop the TMPF as means of providing sophisticated access to digitised newspaper archives wherein the semantic navigation of online resources greatly enhances the user experience in digital libraries. Using this approach, an ontology codifies an analysis of the structure and relationships in the domain of newspaper publishing and archiving, including publishers, issues, articles, pages, clippings, places, and dates. Metadata is automatically harvested from the source materials into this conceptual framework, producing a map of the content. This map is then used to present the content online in a meaningful structure.

This paper will also briefly cover some of the open technologies used, including Topic Maps, the CIDOC Conceptual Reference Model, Apache Cocoon, and Apache Lucene.

Delivering Newspaper Content Over the Web

Delivering newspaper content over the web presents many challenges and requires a delivery system that is technically sophisticated on the inside and intuitive to use on the outside. There are challenges to be met in several areas: the forms of content to be delivered, the granularity of access provided, modes of access enabled, extensibility, customization, and usability. This section will look briefly at each of these areas in turn to provide a context for the subsequent discussion of the TMPF.

As regards the forms of content to be delivered over the web from a newspaper archive, a key question is whether to provide user access to the transcribed text of the newspaper, to images of the original printed newspaper, or to both? Delivering both forms of content has several advantages. The images enable access to content which cannot be transcribed such as photographs, illustrations and complex diagrams. They also provide information through visual details such as the size of headline, the style of font, or design of page layout which is not conveyed by the transcribed text. Providing full page images allows illustrations such as photographs or cartoons to be seen alongside the article to which they relate. The transcribed text itself can be usefully provided to users because, in addition to providing the raw material for full text searches, in most cases it will be more legible than the original. As text it is also more malleable than an image in that the presentation can be altered to fit user needs by altering font sizes, page layout and other variables. In some projects there may be an additional requirement to provide user access to source images as distinct from access images. Consideration is also needed of what tools and mechanisms will be provided to enable users to engage with and use the content. Tools, for example, to view access images in close detail; to provide printable versions of newspaper pages and articles; to move from content in the archive to related content in other online collections; to link to the content from external systems; or to download metadata records for inclusion in bibliographic systems such as ProCite, WriteNote or EndNote. Where content is missing from an archive, whether it is a missing issue or a missing page from a particular issue, a method should be found to communicate this to the user to create a coherent user experience.

The granularity of access provided is an interesting question. Should users be able to navigate or search to the level of a newspaper page, or to the individual articles on those pages? This is an area in which the delivery system is almost wholly dependant on decisions made during the digitisation process. If article-level access images and mark-up have not been created the delivery system can only operate at the page level. In general, it is more challenging to define articles within newspapers than to define structural sub-units of journals and monographs. In most journals, the articles are easily identified as distinct units within the whole. Chapters serve that function for books. Smaller pamphlets are typically treated as a whole, without sub-units. When both commercial publishers of historic newspapers, as well as institutions such as the British Library, poll user groups to find out whether users prefer working with page-level or article-level files, the overwhelming response is that the preference is for article level access. Users certainly want the ability to view an entire page, but most users seem to find that navigating from a hit list of relevant article citations directly to the article itself makes for a more efficient and satisfying user experience. The USA's Library of Congress (LOC) is currently in the midst of a project to create a test bed of digitized newspapers for its National Digital Newspaper Program (NDNP), the specifications for which are page-level files. Nevertheless, many of the US State Libraries which are doing the digitization of the issues coming from their own collections are creating two sets of digitized objects: issue-level files for delivery to the LOC and also a set of article-level files for themselves, since the state level editorial boards selecting the titles for conversion requested them. While it remains to be seen what the LOC will ultimately specify once the test bed is created and users have weighed-in on the results, the vast majority of other institutions involved with digitizing significant quantities of newspaper content are adopting article-based models over page-based models.

When we consider the modes of access to be provided, we are asking what search facilities will be presented to the user, what browsing methods will be enabled? Where an article-based model has been adopted during the digitisation process then the delivery system should make the most of this source material and allow navigation straight to a given article as well as between articles on the same page or in the same issue, and from page to page and issue to issue. Browsing by newspaper or article title, by date, by author, by subject or by any other item of metadata may be appropriate. Simple full text searching of all newspapers should be available as well as an advanced search interface. This should provide common advanced search functionality including phrase queries, searching of selected metadata fields, and use of standard Boolean operators. It might also be appropriate to provide other functionality such as wildcard queries, stemming, proximity operators and thesaurus support. Limiting the search to particular sort of content e.g. editorials, adverts, images should also be supported if the underlying metadata to identify these items is available. Finally, as regards modes of access, there is a need to develop support for access by other systems through interoperability tools and protocols such as OpenURL[1], OAI-PMH[2] and SRU / SRW[3]. At the NZETC we feel strongly that, where possible, systems should conform to relevant public guidelines, specifications and standards to achieve a high level of modularity of the system architecture and to facilitate broad interoperability.

Extensibility is the degree to which the system will enable the inclusion, not only of other resources and data types, but also of metadata from other sources so as to enhance existing content. Customization is the extent to which the interface is configurable, both by the institution maintaining the archive (e.g. to meet branding guidelines) and by the user. For a user this might mean a «MyNewspaperArchive» approach which could allow users to set personal preferences for the display of content and to create a temporary collection of newspaper pages and articles of interest to them. Finally, usability covers a range of issues around user satisfaction, task efficiency and how easy it is to learn to use the system.

The NZETC Topic Map Presentation Framework

These were the challenges facing the NZETC when we started develop the Topic Map Presentation Framework (TMPF) for newspaper delivery. The work was prompted by the actions of the National Library of New Zealand and the National Library of Australia, both of whom issued, in 2005, public requests for proposals to provide online access to their existing newspaper archives. In response to these requests the NZETC starting working with APEX CoVantage to explore what could be achieved by combining experience in developing semantic navigation frameworks at the NZETC with the newspaper digitisation expertise at APEX. This section will describe some of salient features of the TMPF before describing the example newspaper delivery system built using the TMPF.

The TMPF in production at the NZETC is a dynamically-generated semantic framework – a metadata repository implemented using the ISO Topic Map standard instead of the more usual implementation based directly on a relational database. The topic map metadata repository provides the system with an unusually flexible and open-ended conceptual structure. This has a number of benefits, including greatly simplifying the integration of disparate information systems and facilitating the presentation of contextually rich web pages.

1 OpenURL is ANSI/NISO Standard Z39.88-2004.

2 The Open Archives Initiative Protocol for Metadata Harvesting.

3 Library of Congress standard for web services for search and retrieval based on Z39.50 semantics.

Users are able to move around the resources on the site tracking topics of interest rather than merely browsing the material linearly or through text searching. In a topic map, web-based resources are grouped around items called «topics», each of which represents some subject of interest. In the NZETC topic map, the topics represent books, chapters, and illustrations, and also people and places mentioned in those books.

Topics in a topic map are linked together with hyperlinks called «associations». There can be different types of association in a topic map, representing the different kinds of relationship in the real world. For instance, in the NZETC topic map, the topic which represents a particular person may be linked to a topic which represents a chapter of a book which mentions that person. This association would be labelled to indicate that it represents a «mention». Similarly, the same person's topic might be linked to a particular photograph topic, via a «depiction» association. This identification and codification of topics and associations is essentially the act of creating an ontology. Modelling domain relationships requires a sophisticated analysis of real work entities, a difficult and time consuming task. We have therefore taken advantage of the seven year effort by the CIDOC Conceptual Reference Model group to create a high-level ontology known as the CIDOC CRM[4]. This ontology was designed to enable information integration for cultural heritage data and their correlation with library and archive information. The NZETC has based the semantics of the TMPF on the event-based model of the CIDOC CRM as illustrated below (Fig. 1).

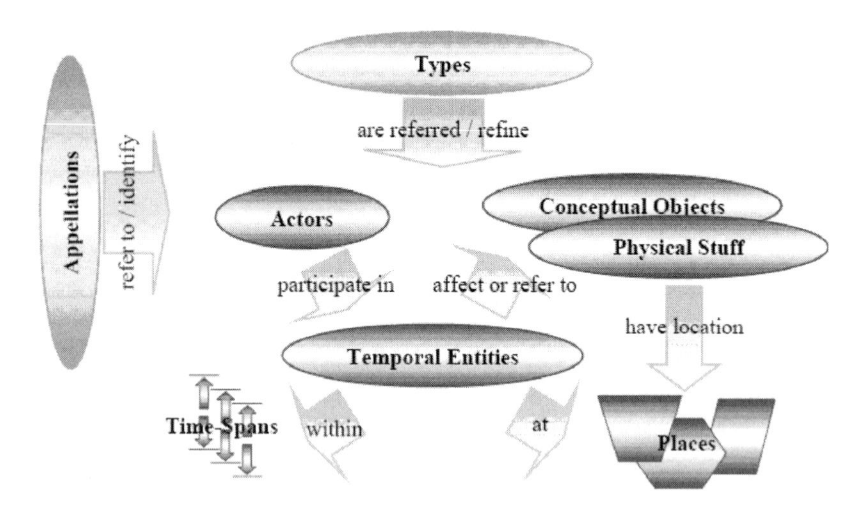

Fig. 1. A qualitative metaschema of the CIDOC CRM taken from Martin Doerr «The CIDOC CRM – An Ontological Approach to Semantic Interoperability of metadata» AI Magazine, Volume 24, Number 3 (2003)

This allows us to express relationships such as those illustrated in Fig. 2.

The central topic, Te Rangihaeata, was a chief of the Ngati Toa tribe. In the topic map, the topic which represents him is associated with three other topics, each of which has an occurrence. The association on the left represents a depiction of Te Rangihaeata. The picture

4 CIDOC CRM http://cidoc.ics.forth.gr/.

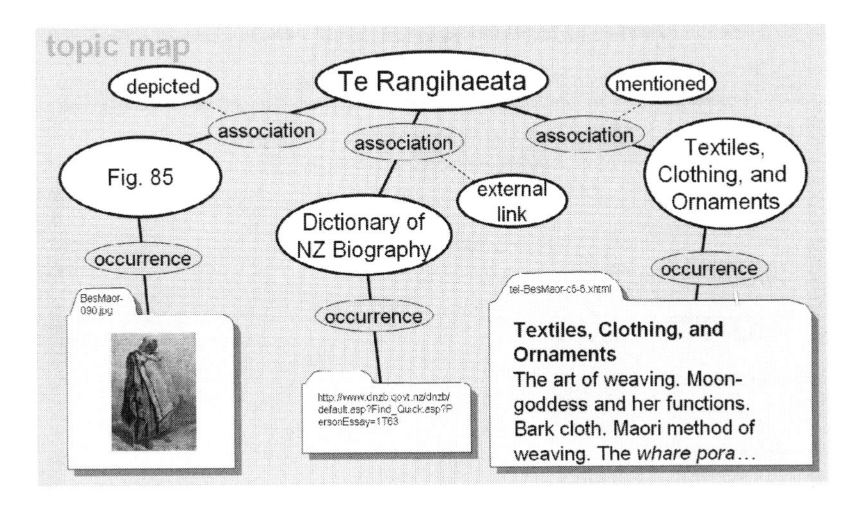

Fig. 2. Illustration of relationships encoded in NZETC TMPF

which depicts him is «Figure 85» from a book by Elsdon Best called *The Maori As He Was*. On the right, «Textiles, Clothing and Ornaments» is a chapter from the same text, which mentions him. Both of these associations were of course harvested from the XML file containing the Elsdon Best book. In the centre, Te Rangihaeata is associated with a web page on the website of the Dictionary of New Zealand Biography. This last piece of information was harvested from our name list. Note that the central topic «Te Rangihaeata» was harvested twice – once from the Elsdon Best book, and once from the names list. But these two topics merged together automatically, leaving us with just one topic with 3 associations.

To construct our topic map, we use XSLT[5] stylesheets to extract metadata from each of our XML text files, and express it in the XTM[6] format. In this way we automatically create hundreds of topic maps, each of which describes one of our texts. We also harvest information about people, places and organisations from a MADS[7] authority file which we construct from what is mentioned in our collection. Finally we merge the harvested topic maps together to create a unified topic map which describes our entire website.

By harvesting not only bibliographic metadata but also references to people, organisations and places, the site provides individual pages for topics of interest, linked automatically to those places they are mentioned or illustrated. Being automatically generated from the source XML files, maintenance is simple and the number and types of topics linked to can be increased simply by adding extra mark-up to the texts.

Each page on the website represents one of these topics, along with any associated topics. Fig. 3, a screenshot, is the page for Te Rangihaeata.

---

5 W3C specification for the syntax and semantics of a language for transforming XML documents into other XML documents http://www.w3.org/TR/xslt.

6 XML Topic Maps http://www.topicmaps.org/xtm/.

7 Metadata Authority Description Schema. A Library of Congress standard for a MARC21-compatible XML format for the type of data carried in records in the MARC Authorities format. http://www.loc.gov/standards/mads/mads.xsd.

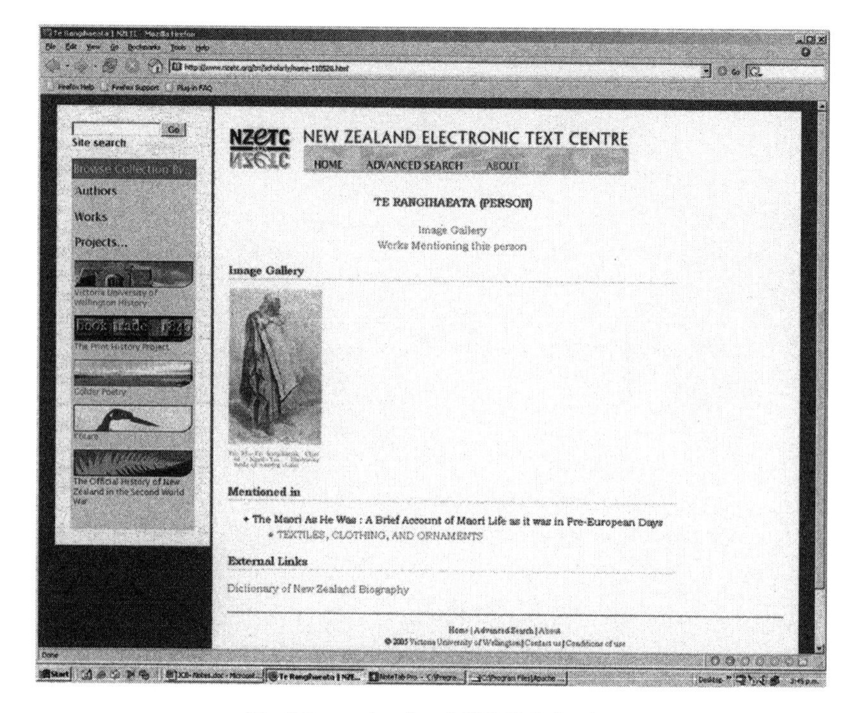

Fig. 3 Screenshot from NZETC Collection

The topic map manages all the hyperlinks, bibliographic metadata, structural metadata, annotations, classifications, name authorities and glossaries for the entire website. By extracting all the metadata needed from every resource available and merging it all together in the topic map, it is ensured that all relevant information is prepared and readily available to the presentation system, so that the presentation of every web page can include as much contextual information as is desired.

When TMPF generates a web page about a particular topic (whether a newspaper series, article, page, or any other type of topic), it queries the topic map to find all the information resources related to that topic. This would include the name of the topic, including aliases and names it might have in different languages, background articles, links to external websites, photos, etc. TMPF would then display those resources appropriately, either by generating hyperlinks to those resources or by simply including the content of other resources. For an example of how a page can be enriched by including related content from the topic map, see the hyperlink reference to Governor Grey in the pamphlet «One of England's Little Wars,» on the NZETC website (Fig. 4).

The hyperlink pointing to the page about Grey has a tool tip (an HTML title attribute) saying «Sir George Grey. Soldier, explorer, colonial governor, premier, scholar.» This tool tip was drawn not from the encoded text of the pamphlet but from a record about George Grey in an authority file. When the authority file was imported into the topic map, a topic was created to represent George Grey, and this topic was merged with all the references to George Grey in the encoded texts, so that every hyperlink on the website which points to the George Grey page now has the same «authoritative» tool tip.

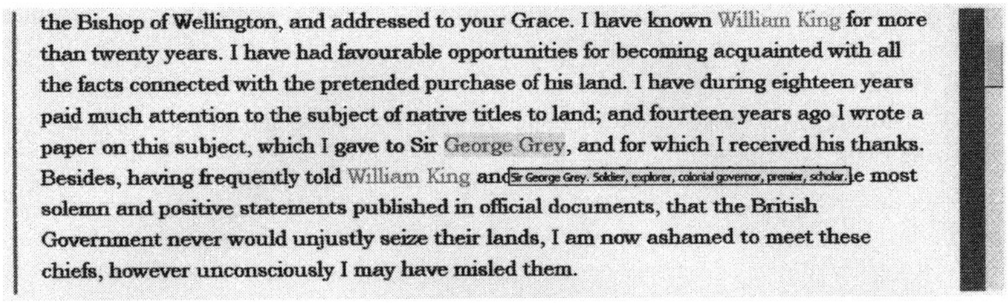

the Bishop of Wellington, and addressed to your Grace. I have known William King for more than twenty years. I have had favourable opportunities for becoming acquainted with all the facts connected with the pretended purchase of his land. I have during eighteen years paid much attention to the subject of native titles to land; and fourteen years ago I wrote a paper on this subject, which I gave to Sir George Grey, and for which I received his thanks. Besides, having frequently told William King and Sir George Grey. Soldier, explorer, colonial governor, premier, scholar. e most solemn and positive statements published in official documents, that the British Government never would unjustly seize their lands, I am now ashamed to meet these chiefs, however unconsciously I may have misled them.

Figure 4 Screenshot from NZETC website. http://www.nzetc.org/tm/scholarly/tei-HadOneO-t1-body.html#name-208095-1

At the system level TMPF makes use of a number of public guidelines, specifications and standards, as listed in the table below. Adopting relevant standards encourages a high level of modularity of the system architecture and facilitates broad interoperability. Thus, for example, TMPF can be customised to handle any XML-based source materials and is not limited in the file formats is can deliver. Common internet formats, Flash, Java applets, PDF or other derivatives can be included.

PURPOSE	SPECIFICATION	REFERENCE
Encoding (general)	XML	http://www.w3.org/TR/REC-xml/
Addressing	URI	http://www.w3.org/Addressing/
Text encoding	TEI	http://www.tei-c.org/Guidelines2/
OCR encoding (under development)	ALTO	http://www.loc.gov/ndnp/techspecs.html
Authority control	MADS	http://www.loc.gov/standards/mads/
Transformation of XML source materials into presentation formats. Extraction of metadata from XML source materials	XSLT	http://www.w3.org/TR/xslt
Presentation	HTML	http://www.w3.org/MarkUp/
Page formatting	CSS	http://www.w3.org/Style/CSS/
Image processing	SVG	http://www.w3.org/Graphics/SVG/
Information mapping	ISO Topic Maps	http://www.isotopicmaps.org/
Conceptual reference model	CIDOC CRM	http://cidoc.ics.forth.gr/

Tab. 1

Using the TMPF for Newspaper Delivery

When the NZETC started to work with APEX to use the TMPF as a newspaper delivery system we created two small demonstration sites for the National Library of Australia and the National Library of New Zealand using content from their newspaper archives. The Australian site has 7413 web pages, including 204 issues, consisting of 847 newspaper pages and 6362 articles. The New Zealand site is about half that size. The creation of these demonstration sites was work undertaken by the NZETC and APEX to explore how well the Topic Map system worked with newspaper content and does not represent any decision by either National Library to use this technology. The NZETC is just one of many respondents to the RFPs issues by the libraries. The use of the TMPF to deliver example content from the two libraries on these demonstration sites is not indicative of any technology or vendor choices or decisions made by either library. The two demonstration sites are not available to the public.

The APEX Intelligent Zoning and Algorithmic Conversion (IZAAC) was used to convert digital images of the newspapers into XML encoded text.[8] In Apex's process, an Article is defined as a «complete newspaper story.» This concept is extended to a number of newspaper elements, including small, continuous units of like content, such as news briefs and classified advertisements, and stand-alone features, such as photographs, illustrations, and crossword puzzles. The IZAAC process relies on human cognition to identify and zone articles, rather than relying on an automated process.

Automated approaches are adequate for extremely simple layouts and standardized formats; but when applied to newspapers, the results are usually unacceptable. Logical analysis alone cannot recognize discontinuous portions of an Article even on the same page, let alone across pages. Perhaps for this reason, many commercial software packages that rely on automated article definition use proxy terms for Articles, such as «chunks». Chunks can miss portions of an Article or may overlap across Articles. Neither is acceptable from a user-experience perspective.

Illustrations that are part of an Article are included with the Article. Illustrations that do not have associated text are treated as separate Articles. Captions are included with the illustrations and are tagged as such, supporting searches by caption. Articles are always associated with the page on which they appear.

The availability of article-level metadata and more accurate OCR text output exponentially increases the points of access into the collection which the TMPF can provide to users. The newspaper demonstration sites provide access to both the access images and to the transcribed text. They also give users the option to hide the transcribed text if they are only interested in viewing the images.

The TMPF for newspaper delivery supports browsing of the full list of newspaper titles by title and by date. Users can browse within a selected newspaper issue and navigate from page to page, and article to article. While viewing a particular article they have the option to move directly to the page on which that article appears, directly to the front page of the issue of which the article is a part or to the web page for the particular newspaper title. Users can also browse from article to article on a given page or in a given issue. This is enabled through a topic map which includes topics for a newspaper series (e.g. «The Times»), a newspaper issues (e.g. «The Times 18th June 1942»), pages, articles, article images, publishers and dates. As with the TMPF used in production for the NZETC collection this very simple ontology for the newspaper domain is encoded as an extension of the more complex and sophisticated CIDOC CRM.

Neither support for browsing by date through an interface similar to calendar pages, nor browsing by geographic region was implemented for the TMPF newspaper delivery demonstration sites. However TMPF already harvests publication date information in its topic map, including relating the dates to a calendar of years, decades, and centuries. Exposing these date topics for browsing will require only minor additions to the user interface layer. Although TMPF already includes publication place information in its topic map, this is not quite the same as geographic coverage. However, only minor development work would be

---

8 Although the TMPF used to deliver the NZETC collection.

required to harvest geographic coverage from newspaper source files and present a browsable user interface, including using, for example, a clickable map. In fact, because TMPF uses a topic map to define browse points, any and all metadata harvested into the topic map (whether from the newspaper source materials or from external data sources) can be used as the basis for browsing the newspaper collection. The TMPF does not currently include any personalisation features such as allowing users to save pages or search results, although these are of course bookmarkable and therefore can be saved and returned to by the user through their browser.

To enable users to view the access images of the newspaper pages and articles we used «Zoomify» technology to provide zooming and panning functionality. The free Zoomify EZ encoder creates multiple copies of an image at many resolutions tiers, from the original source resolution down to a thumbnail (Fig. 5). Each tier is then cut into many small tiles. All the tiles from all the tiers are combined into a folder of JPEG files with an index of the exact location of every tile. Tile organization is pyramidal in that tiles are stacked from a thumbnail down to the highest resolution, tier upon tier. When the converted image is viewed, the Zoomify Flash Viewer requests tiles from the appropriate tier to fill the display area. Each zoom and pan requests only a small additional number of tiles: those at the level of zoom desired or for the part of the image panned to. These additional tiles are streamed on-demand, to the viewer. No tiles are ever delivered unless required for the current display, or for a display that is anticipated to immediately follow (intelligent pre-fetching).

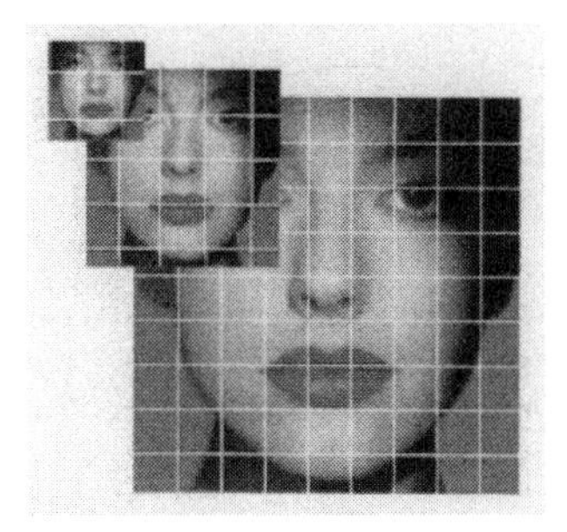

Fig. 5. Pyramidal Tiled Multi-Resolution Image from Zoomification Process. Taken from http://www.zoomify.com

The user has the ability to zoom in and out of the image, and to pan left, right, up and down around a page or an article. A thumbnail image in the top left hand corner is a further navigational aid as a red rectangle shows the current location of the zoomed in view.

To enable searching over the newspaper archive we used the Apache Lucene[9] search engine, again as we do for the TMPF in production at the NZETC. It provides all the search functionality discussed in the «Delivering Newspaper Content» section above, including an optional module for synonym expansion in search queries using the WordNet thesaurus. Users can limit their search to a particular newspaper title and / or by a date range.

Search results are displayed as a list of links to relevant resources with large result sets split across several pages. The user can set the number of results displayed on each query result

9 Apache Lucene http://lucene.apache.org/java/docs/index.html.

screen, and navigate easily between result screens. Result pages are also bookmarkable. Results are sorted by the Apache Lucene search engine which employs a sophisticated relevance ranking algorithm. Article titles and other important or quality-assured metadata can be boosted in importance when building the Lucene search index, so that Lucene accords hits on these fields a greater weight. Lucene's query syntax also allows users to boost the priority of individual words or phrases in their queries, so that documents containing those terms are regarded as more relevant than unboosted terms.

If contextual or background information exists about a newspaper title, issue, page or article then this information can be delivered along with the newspaper content. For example if a historian had written an essay on the publication history of «The Manawatu Herald» this history could be included on the web page listing all available issues of the «The Manawatu Herald». Such a background article can be written either directly in HTML or in XML and is linked to the newspaper it describes by using the persistent identifier of the newspaper as the subject of the article, in the article's metadata header.

When missing pages or printing irregularities are encountered in the source material the TMPF system handles different types of omissions in different ways. If there is a story behind the omission, this story can be encoded as another text and linked to an appropriate part of the collection: the newspaper series, individual issue, article or page. TMPF would then include and display this explanatory material in the appropriate context. Alternatively, where content is missing from inside a document, the omission may be encoded using appropriate XML mark-up in the source material (such as the <gap> element in the TEI mark-up language) to describe the missing content or explain the omission. Where entire issues are missing, XML files empty of content can be used as placeholders for the missing material. Errors and irregularities in the newspaper source material such as inconsistent page numbering or incorrect dates can be explicitly marked as anomalies using appropriate XML mark-up, such as the <sic> and <corr> elements in the TEI mark-up language.

The TMPF approach means a wide range of textual materials can be included in the delivery system. As discussed above, the TMPF is currently used by the NZETC to present its digital collection which includes books, journals, letters, and pamphlets. TMPF is fully extensible to handle a potentially infinite variety of materials. Different document types can be presented in distinct ways, or, to the extent that they can be interpreted in terms of a common conceptual model, they can then be presented in an identical fashion, to provide a consistent user experience regardless of the different document formats, encoding practices, and storage technologies. TMPF is designed to be easily extensible to other data types, metadata schemas, and knowledge domains. The use of a topic map for the central metadata repository in TMPF provides an open-ended framework for importing, mapping and meaningfully presenting information from a number of distinct information systems.

TMPF can import and merge pre-existing metadata from other sources. The NZETC has used TMPF to import metadata records from other sources and merge them with metadata describing TMPF's own collection. To import and merge metadata from external sources, the metadata should be exported in some XML format, and an XSLT transformation is used to extract metadata in the common XML Topic Map (XTM) format, which is then imported and merged. Merging of metadata records in general requires only that items of interest can be identified by a URI. For newspapers this might be an ISSN, DOI, URN, or simply an HTTP URL. The topic map metadata repository in TMPF can record mappings between different name authorities and perform cross-walks between sets of metadata using those authorities. All metadata records for resources with a particular identifier are automatically merged. Merging behaviour is a key part of the specification of the Topic Map standard and is a built-in feature of the topic map metadata repository component of TMPF.

In general ease of use is the result of a well thought-out and robust system architecture that lies beneath the interface. This is a characteristic of TMPF which provides a 100% customisable interface providing complete control over the delivery system's look and feel. Thus the interface can be designed to be both satisfying and efficient to use. For example to minimise the amount of time it takes to accomplish a particular task, the interface does not involved the repeated opening of new windows. Though TMPF does not prevent the use of client-side JavaScript for linking and the use of frames and pop-up windows these techniques have not been used in the newspaper delivery system since they are obstacles to regular navigation. Regular browser features such as the «Back» button and bookmarking are supported. TMPF does not encode session identifiers in URLs, which is a common obstacle to bookmarking. To support the user TMPF accommodates context sensitive help by assigning help documentation to any topic in the system. Help can be authored as one or more XML documents and linked to the relevant part of the system by adding subject classification metadata (i.e. the help document is itself tagged as being «about» a class of topic, such as monthly publication histories, newspaper issues, articles, pages, etc.)

The TMPF interface is completely customisable and supports integration of links to other services. Such links may also be classified into different types (e.g. «further reading,» «discussion forums,» «annotations,» etc.), and each type of link presented independently.

These links may be further classified in various ways:

- by access/visibility (e.g. «public,» «internal,» «QA»);
- by perspective (e.g. «historical,» «geographical»);
- by provenance («scholarly,» «user-contributed,» «Te Puna,» «Te Papa,» «Ministry of Culture and Heritage»); and
- by natural language (e.g. «English,» «Maori»).

Multiple user interfaces can present filtered views of these links appropriate for particular audiences.

TMPF is built out of XML-based components; hence it is based entirely on Unicode. This provides the ability to represent all characters in Maori and other Polynesian languages.

As for our TMPF production system at the NZETC, we used Apache Cocoon to transform the XML texts created by APEX into readable documents using XSLT stylesheets. Cocoon can deliver documents in a variety of formats, including HTML, PDF, RTF, SVG, JPEG, PNG, and any other XML-based format. We can also integrate software to produce Microsoft's eBook Reader format.

Cocoon can perform these transformations on demand, i.e. when a request is received from a web browser. Each request is handled by reading the appropriate XML document or documents, and processing the XML data in a succession of stages, first applying logical, then presentational transformations. Each stage is distinct and can be effectively managed by different people. Our web designer can edit the look of the site, the web developer can edit the structure of the site, and the text-editors can edit the content of the site (the e-texts), all independently of each other. To install a new text, the editors can simply upload the XML document and associated image files into the webserver via FTP. The document will then be automatically converted to HTML and divided into separate pages for each chapter, and scaled-down thumbnail versions of the JPEG graphics will be created using the XML graphics format SVG. To change the overall look of the site, the web-designer can upload new design elements such as CSS stylesheets, new versions of the logo, navigation menu, etc, in the same way. When a document is displayed to the reader, the content will be automatically inserted into this new design.

Apache Cocoon is a Java servlet and hence it can be deployed on a wide variety of systems. At the NZETC we run Cocoon inside the Apache Tomcat servlet container (the official reference Implementation for the Java Servlet specification), using JVM version 1.4 from Sun Microsystems.

Conclusion

This paper has highlighted the many challenges required to successfully deliver online newspaper archives. The TMPF has been developed within academic communities and has not enjoyed the benefits of high-level marketing and promotional efforts. It has not been tested in a large scale projects delivering online newspaper archives. However in the work that the NZETC and APEX have done so far it does seem that the sort of semantic framework created by the TMPF provides a means to fulfil many of the very complex requirements which must be met when delivering of a newspaper archives on the web. Further work is required both in the areas of system development and user testing but we believe the ontological approach to be a valid and interesting one.

THE EARLY EAST ASIAN PRESS IN THE EYES OF THE WEST. SOME BIBLIOGRAPHICAL NOTES

Hartmut Walravens

Staatsbibliothek zu Berlin Preußischer Kulturbesitz

The East Asian press was studied relatively late in the West. One of the reasons is that newspapers did not exist in China, Japan, and Korea until these countries opened to Western influences. There were certainly forerunners of newsprint also in the indigenous tradition, like the famous *Peking Gazette* (*Jingpao*) which is often claimed to be oldest newspaper of the world. We find numerous little articles in Western papers on the *Jingbao*, usually from secondary or tertiary sources; they do not take into account that this gazette had limited circulation and that it just contained edicts and decrees – thus it does not fit the modern definition of newspaper. But it definitely was a forerunner of newsprint.

In China a number of missionary periodicals are counted among the forerunners of newspapers but even such non-religious items like Karl Friedrich Gützlaff's *Dongxiyangkao meiyuetongjizhuan* – were usually monthlies, or irregularly published serials. Some Western language items do qualify as newspapers, like *A Abelha da China* (1822–1824), Macao's first (Portuguese language) newspaper, but Chinese press history really starts only with the Hong Kong and Shanghai Chinese papers. The *Shenbao*, founded by the British businessman Ernest Major in 1872, became very successful and was probably the best known paper before 1949.

The history of Chinese newspapers and their forerunners is sketched very well by Roswell S. Britton in his pioneer work: *The Chinese Periodical Press 1800–1912*. In a number of chapters: «Indigenous newspapers and gazettes,» «Introduction of Western Journalism,» «Chinese Reactions to the Alien Press,» «Wang T'ao and the Hongkong Newspapers,» «Alien Periodicals in the Treaty Ports,» «The Shun Pao and other Shanghai Papers,» «General Newspaper Developments,» «Liang Ch'i-ch'ao and the Reform Press,» «Authority and the New Press,» «The Revolutionary Press,» «The New and the Old,» especially the prehistory of Chinese newspapers is well shown. Also the rapid and successful launching of Chinese language papers is thoroughly documented. A bibliography of no less than 140 titles, 24 illustrations as well as the use of Chinese characters throughout the book make it attractive. Britton lists an earlier, careful study by A. S. Polevoj[1], but apparently did not use it to its full potential: *Periodičeskaja pečat' v Kitae* was the first full length book on the Chinese press, giving a sketch of its historical development and focusing on the characteristic features of the major Chinese papers, giving ample samples from their contents. In an appendix the author provides a listing of 476 papers (with Chinese characters) by place of publication. He also adds facsimiles of caricatures from Chinese papers – this seems the first attempt to make such drawings available to the Western reader. A later treatment of the subject is by E. Krebs: *Die politische Karikatur in China*, where 18 samples, with explanations, are given from Peking dailies.

A short introduction to the Chinese press, with listing of titles, was provided by Carl Fink[2], formerly editor of *Der Ostasiatische Lloyd in Shanghai*, in a booklet *Die Presse des Fernen*

1 1886–1971; Polevoj studied at the Oriental Institute in Vladivostok and then lived in China from 1917 to 1939 when he emigrated into the United States.

2 1861–1943. See P. W.: Carl Fink† *Ostasiatische Rundschau* 1943, 108; ibid., 18.1937,331–332.

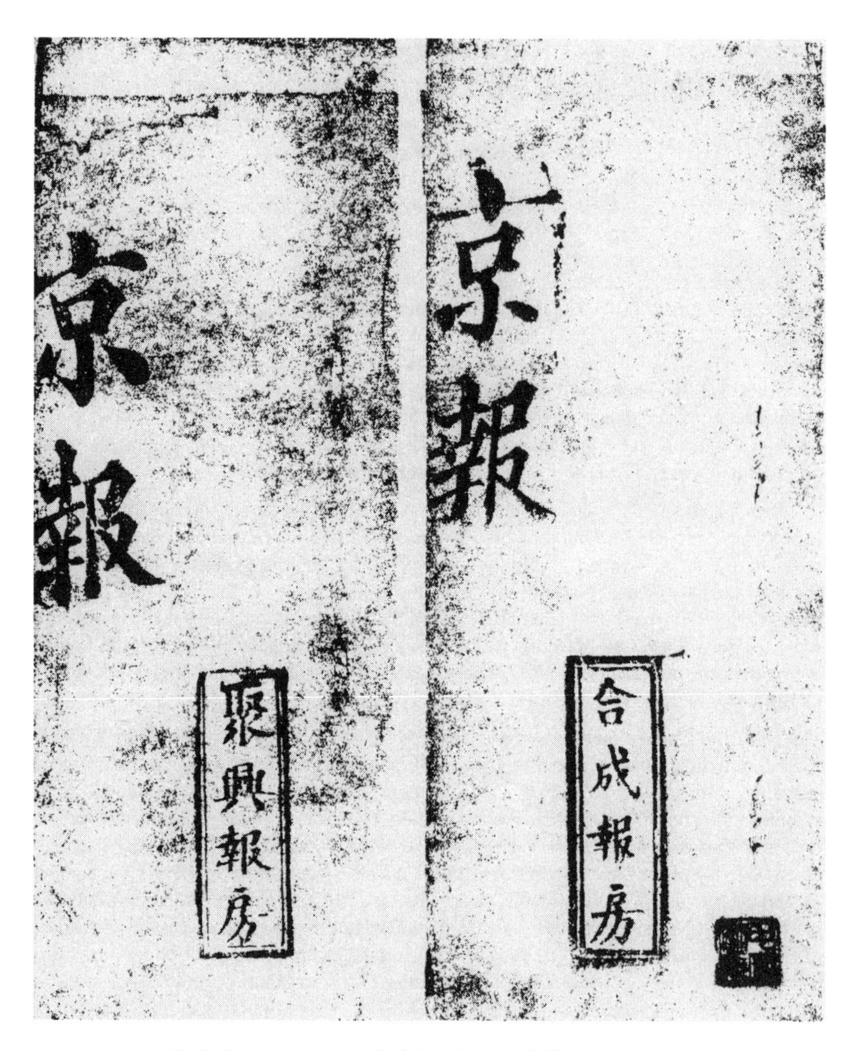

Ill. 1. *Jingbao*, covers of editions by two different publishers

Ostens (1926). Particularly valuable is the Ph.D. dissertation by Kim Heun-Chun: *Die Aufmachung der modernen Zeitung in Ostasien* [«The Get-Up of the Modern Newspaper in East Asia»], Leipzig 1928. He analyses the distribution and presentation of contents within the papers. While he finds that the foreign forms of mass communication were quickly and easily adapted by Japanese journalists, owing to their aesthetic sense, he considers the Koreans fact-oriented and mainly interested in the political lead articles which certainly influenced the form of presentation. In China at that time he notices too many divergent developments and considers the Chinese press still in a process of formation.

Thomas Ming-heng Chao analyzed *The Foreign Press in China* in a preliminary paper for a conference of the Institute of Pacific Relations in 1931. He presented many details on the

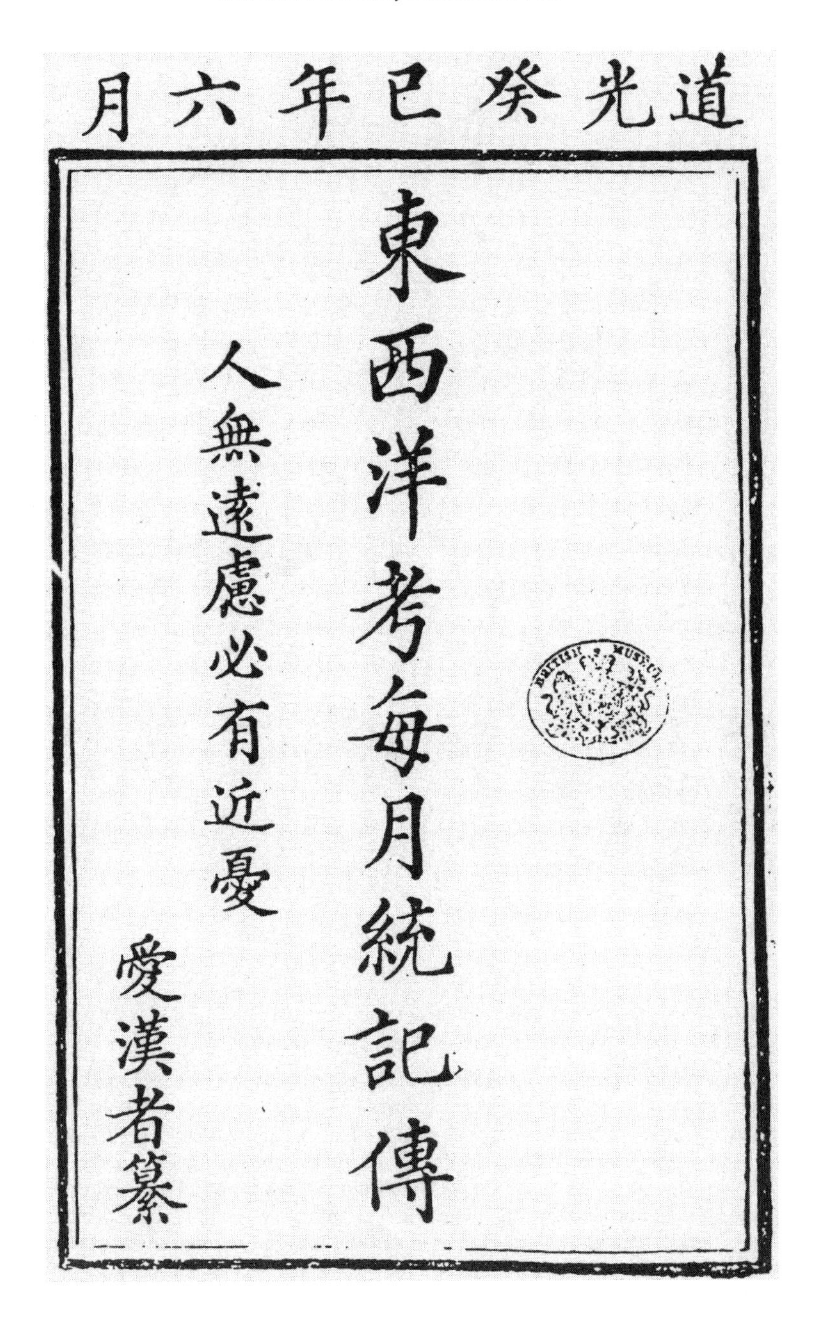

道光癸巳年六月

東西洋考每月統記傳

人無遠慮必有近憂

愛漢者纂

Ill. 2. *Dongxiyangkao meiyuetongjizhuan,* by Karl Gützlaff, Pomeranian missionary. 1833

大清同治

壬申三月二十三日

申報

英四月三十日

本館告白

本館條例

一本新報議價于上海各店零賣每張取錢八文各遠處發賣每張取錢十文本館躉賣每張取錢六文

一如有騷人韻士有願以短什長篇惠教者如天下各名區竹枝詞及長歌紀事之類概不取值

一如有名言讜論實有係乎國計民生地利水源之類者上關皇朝經濟之需下知小民稼穡之苦附登新報概不取酬

Ill. 3. *Shenbao* 1872–1949, Shanghai

editorial policy, contents, and staff from the point of view of a contemporary. A nice feature is the addition of caricatures of some of the leading journalists.

Rudolf Löwenthal[3] (1909–1996) studied *Zeitungswissenschaft* («newspaper science») in Berlin before he went to China as an *emigré*. In a series of articles and one book he studied especially the newspapers in languages other than Chinese, like the Russian and German as well as the religious press in China. He also dealt with the paper supply for Chinese newspaper publishing,[4] and with the bibliography of Chinese press history. The religious press comprises mainly periodicals as the author also indicates in the title of his book, a pioneering work that for the first time assembled a wealth of information on the Catholic, Protestant, Buddhist, Taoist, Confucian, Islamic, Jewish and Russian Orthodox periodical publications in China. Löwenthal extended his studies even to other countries, e.g. the

3 H. Walravens: Schriftenverzeichnis von Rudolf Löwenthal (Loewenthal). *Monumenta Serica* 45.1997, 417–437; Michael Pollak: Rudolf Loewenthal (1909–1996). Ibid., 425–417.

4 Printing paper: its supply and demand in China. *Yenching Journal of Social Studies* 1.1938, 108–121.

Ill. 4. *Polevoj: Periodičeskaja pečat' v Kitae*

Chinese press in Australia. Löwenthal's methodical approach shows him as a trained newspaper researcher. He is factual, data-oriented and refrains from lofty interpretations.

In 1942 a Ph.D. thesis on the paper production and trade in China, Japan and Manchukuo was defended by Ingeborg Rühl.[5] This is an economic study, taking into account the war situation, but not going into any detail regarding the newspaper industry.

Wolfgang Mohr[6] (1903–1979) was a real newspaper professional not a journalist but an engineer who specialized in printing technology; he knew Chinese and spent the years 1932–1956 in China. His three volume work on the development of the Chinese press is more of a documentation than a press history. The centre piece of the work is a collection of facsimiles from Chinese papers, arranged in systematic order. It starts with a description of the early press, until 1911, the end of the Chinese empire, and deals with the government and the private press separately. The following main section covers the newspapers under the Peking government (1912–1927) and the Nanking government (1928–1949) with detailed treatment of the press during the war, and then continues to show the development in the People's Republic of China until 1954. Newspapers in Taiwan, the People's Republic and Chinese language papers around the globe are treated in a relatively short way. The conclusion comprises presentations of special groups of papers, like the party press, and individual papers. All these documents are commented upon in volume 1 which also features

---

5 Ingeborg Rühl: *Die Papierwirtschaft in China, Japan und Mandschukuo*. Erlangen 1942. VI, 185 p.

6 See Herbert Franke: Wolfgang Mohr† 1903–1979. *Oriens extremus* 27.1980, 151–154; Wolfgang Bauer: Wolfgang Mohr† *Nachrichten der Gesellschaft für Natur- und Völkerkunde Ostasiens* 127/128.1980, 11–13, Portr.

94 THE FOREIGN PRESS IN CHINA

MR. J. PLAUT

of the Trans-Ocean Kuo Min News Service.

Ill. 5. *The Foreign Press in China*, portrait of J. Plaut

chronological listings, including Chinese characters, as well as a bibliography. Volume 2 provides numerous lists, statistics and maps illustrating the development of the Chinese press. All in all, this is more of a catalogue than a press history but the careful documentation and its down to earth approach make it an extremely valuable reference tool which may serve as the basis of further analytical research.

The *Shanghai Pictorial Dianshizhai huabao* found special interest in Germany. It was first made known by Max von Brandt who had been the German minister to both Tokyo and Peking until he retired after 33 years of service and devoted himself to writing. He considered the *Pictorial* a mirror of Chinese life and published 82 of its illustrations / episodes with commentary while the translations were prepared by Wang Yintai (1888–1961) who at that point in time studied in Berlin but was to become a politician in China later on.[7] The author commented:

> The last decades have produced already a large, perhaps too large number of books on China and the Chinese, but we always received a picture seen by foreign eyes, described by a foreign pen, lacking the originally which alone would be able to catch the sympathetic interest of the general reader – in spite of the care of the authors to observe this world strange to them and us, and despite the detail in which the described it.

The author divided his selection in ten sections according to subjects like «Imperial Court,» «Family Life,» «Death and Burial,» «Pastimes,» «Law Enforcement,» etc. and provided ample commentaries on the respective scenes, drawing heavily on his own experience from his China years.

---

7 See. Howard L. Boorman: *Biographical Dictionary of Republican China*. 3. New York: Columbia Univ. Press 1970, 399–400.

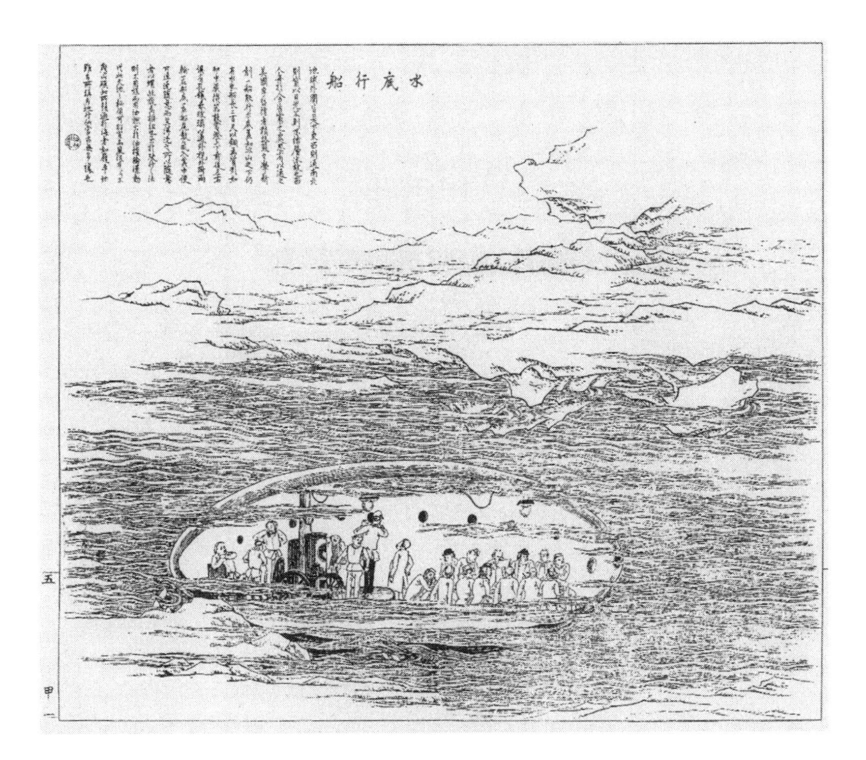

Ill. 6. *Dianshizhai huabao* – submarine

Bodo Wiethoff focused on the description of Europe and the Europeans in the *Shanghai Pictorial*, while Fritz van Briessen who stayed as a journalist in China in the early 1940s selected another 52 scenes from the paper on different subjects, like «Examinations,» the «War in Vietnam,» the «Strange Customs of the Western Barbarians,» etc. Again translations and comments accompany the pictures, this time in order to look at the situation in China from a distance and analyse its perception of current events, and foreign impact.

A lot of the material in the *Shanghai Pictorial* was taken from foreign sources, and this fact was documented in a paper by Julia Henningsmeier. A thorough introduction to the subject for English speakers was only given recently in an Ann Arbor dissertation by Ye Xiaoqing.

The *Dianshizhai huabao* was published from 1884 to 1898 in Shanghai by the well-known daily *Shenbao* owned by the British businessmen Ernest and Frederick Major, and became popular. This was partly due to the publisher's business acumen but to a large degree by the well executed large illustrations which contain descriptive text in the same way as traditional Chinese paintings. The illustrations were printed lithographically; they were executed by different artists the best known of which is Wu Youru who also published a pictorial newspaper by himself.

Korea

Korea's press has been little studied as a separate subject. Because of the political development it was sometimes covered by investigations into Japanese newspaper history. We may

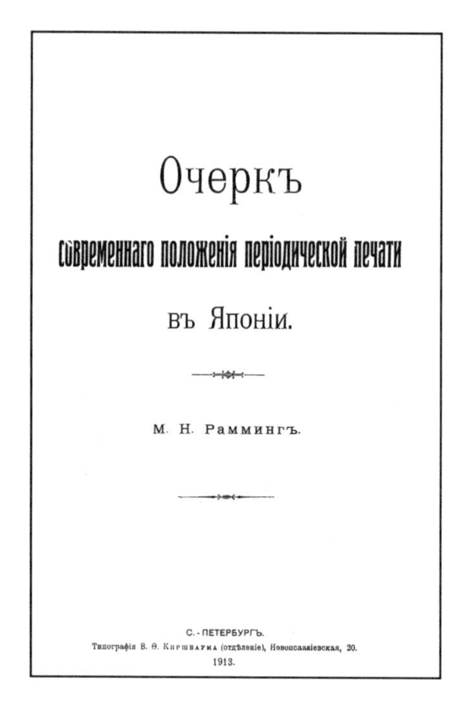

Очеркъ

современнаго положенія періодической печати

въ Японіи.

М. Н. Раммингъ.

С.-ПЕТЕРБУРГЪ.

Типографія В. Ѳ. Киршбаума (отдѣленіе), Новоисаакіевская, 20.

1913.

Ill. 7. Ramming: *Očerk sovremennago položenija periodičeskoj pečati v Japonii*. 1913

point out here Altman's study on Korea's first newspaper which was published in Pusan as of Dec. 1881: The Japanese *Chôsen shimpô*.

Japan

Pioneer in the field of Japanese press history was Martin Ramming[8] who investigated Japanese newspapers during his stay in Japan in 1911 and 1912, following his term of study at St. Petersburg University. He published the results of his trip as *Očerk sovremennago položenija periodičeskoj pečati v Japonii* in 1913. He gave a history of the Japanese press, characterized the main papers, described the juridical situation of the press, informed about the news agencies, outlined the contents of the papers and the role of advertisements and dwelled on Japanese journalism.

Ramming returned to the subject in 1934 when he was director of the Japan Institute in Berlin: *Die japanische Zeitung in Vergangenheit und Gegenwart*. This is an update of the previous paper, with the added advantage that Kanji (Japanese characters) are given throughout. There is also a listing of the more important Japanese newspapers.

Also Ramming's renowned *Japan-Handbuch*[9] has an article on the Japanese press (p. 664–666), not, however, from Ramming's pen but by Werner Wosseng. Like the whole

8 H. Walravens: Ramming, Martin. *Neue Deutsche Biographie* 21.2003, 133.

9 Berlin. Steiniger 1941. 740 p.

Das Werden
der Japanischen Zeitungen

Vom Flugblatt zur Weltpresse

Von Jiro Hayasaka

übersetzt und ergänzt von
Karl Ferdinand Reichel

1943

Konrad Triltsch Verlag Würzburg

Ill. 8. Hayasaka: *Das Werden der japanischen Zeitungen.* 1943

Handbuch, also this article is completely free from ideology and gives a sober and factual account of the genesis of newspapers in Japan and their situation in 1940.

It is hardly surprising that another contribution was published in Germany before the end of WW II, considering the political connections between Japan and Germany during those years. Hayasaka Jiro's *Outline of the Japanese Press* was offered in German translation as *Das Werden der japanischen Zeitungen*, with notes and additions by the translator. It is only for the latter that this title is mentioned here – as an originally Japanese publication it would be out of the focus of the present survey.

Albert A. Altman, of the Hebrew University of Jerusalem, researched the early history of modern newspapers in Japan in several articles: In *The Press and Social Cohesion During a Period of Change: the Case of Early Meiji Japan* he gave a survey of the development of Japanese papers during the first years of the Meiji reform, while in *Shinbunshi: The Early Meiji Adaption of the Western-Style Newspaper* he investigated the adaptation of the Western newspaper by the Japanese in the historical and political context. He started with the first (English language) paper *Nagasaki Shipping List and Advertiser* (1861) and went on to the *shinbunshi* («news booklets»), a forerunner of newspapers, and to well-developed dailies as a tool to influence the masses, as for example in 1905 when a protest against negotiations with Russia was organised. Fukuzawa Yukichi had described the role of European newspapers in his *Seiyô jijô* (The Situation in the West, 1866); and in 1868 already no less than 17 *shinbunshi* were published. The government was quick in recognizing the potential of the new media and using it for its own goals as described with regard

90108
Leifer, Walter: Die Presse in China. In: DDZ. Jg. 3. 1949, H. 11, S. 25-28: Histor. Abriß.

90109
Löffler, Klemens: Der Buchdruck der Ostasiaten und Gutenberg. In: Echo der Gegenwart. Jg. 77. Aachen 1925, Nr 201 MiA v. 27. Aug., Bl. 2r.

90110
Löwinger, Eugen: Die Presse in China. In: Z. [Jg. 1.] 1919, Nr 23 v. 30. Okt., S. 3-5.

90111
Lübke, Anton: Die chinesische Presse. In: ZV. Jg. 36. 1935, Nr 26 v. 29. Juni, S. 461-462 (Auslandspresse/Weltpresse. XII).

90112
(Mackenzie:) Chinesische Zeitungen. In: ÖUBZ. Jg. 36. 1908, Nr 49 v. 3. Dez., S. 629-630: Aus: „The Daily Telegraph". London 1908.

90113
Mayer, Norbert: Die Presse in China. In: ZW. Jg. 10. 1935, Nr 12 v. 1. Dez., S. 589-606.

90114
Menz, G[erhard]: Das chinesische Zeitungswesen. In: DP. Jg. 16. 1926, Nr 12 v. 24. März, S. 2-4.

90115
(Mergenthaler, Andreas:) China. In: HdW. 3., völlig neubearb. Aufl. 1937, S. 119-128.

90116
Mewius, F.: Presse und Papier in China. In: Prometheus. Jg. 30. Nr 1555. Leipzig 1919, Nr 46 v. 16. Aug., S. 364-365.

90117
„Moskito-Presse". In: ZV. Jg. 36. 1935, Nr 36 v. 7. Sept., S. 631 (Auslandspresse/China).

90118
Navarra, Bruno R. A.: Graphisches aus China. In: 1400-1900. Deutscher Buch- u[nd] Steindrucker. Gutenberg-Jubiläums-Ausg. Berlin 1900, S. 803-804.

90119
Otte, Friedrich: Die chinesische Presse. In: Vossische Zeitung. Berlin 1920, Nr 331 v. 4. Juli, Bl. 9r; Nr 355 v. 18. Juli, Bl. 5r (Literarische Umschau).

90120
Otte, Friedrich: Presse und Zeitung in China mit einem Ausblick auf Sprache und Literatur. In: Mitteilungen der Auslands-Hochschule an der Universität Berlin. Jg. 42. Berlin 1939, S. 21-56: Auch als S.A.

90121
Otte, Friedrich: Zeitungen in Ostasien. In: KDA. Jg. 69. 1942, Nr 7, S. 74: China.

90122
Patera, Herbert B.: Zeitung und Zeitungswesen in China. In: Neue Freie Presse. Wien 1938, Nr 26477 MA v. 27. Mai, S. 9.

90123
Patzig, Hans-Günther: Die Propaganda im ostasiatischen Konflikt. In: ZW. Jg. 15. 1940, H. 1, S. 23-29 (Propaganda): Betr. China u. Japan.

90124
Die Presse des Fernen Ostens. In: P/S. Jg. 9. 1934, Nr 10, S. 1-2: Betr. China u. Japan.

90125
Presse und Regierung in China. In: Der Ostasiatische Lloyd. Jg. 28. Shanghai 1914, Nr 14 v. 10. Apr., S. 313-315.

90126
Rochlin, R[aphael]: Aus dem erwachenden China. In: ZV. Jg. 33. 1932, Nr 31 v. 30. Juli, S. 534.

90127
Schwedler, W[ilhelm]: Zeitung und Nachrichtenwesen im alten China. In: ZW. Jg. 10. 1935, Nr 3 v. 1. März, S. 110-112 (Internationale Pressestatistik/China).

90128
Sofer, L.: Orientalische Zeitungen. In: Illustrirte Zeitung. Bd 130. Nr 3371. Leipzig 1908, 6. Febr., S. 202.

90129
Tao, Pung Fai: Die Volksführung im heutigen China. (Berlin 1941.) 141 gez. Bl. 4° [Maschinenschr.]
- Berlin, Phil. Fak., Diss. v. 11. Juli 1941
- Darin über d. Pressewesen.

90130
Tyau, Cimon T. Z.: Das chinesische Zeitungswesen. In: Blätter für die gesamten Sozialwissenschaften. Jg. 5. Berlin 1909, H. 5, S. 83-86.

90131
Vom chinesischen Zeitungsstil. In: Generalanzeiger. Jg. 23. Oberhausen 1926, Nr 99 v. 9. Apr., S. 10.

90132
Vom Zeitungswesen in China. [Von] E.W.M. In: SBZ. Jg. 52. 1927, Nr 17 v. 29. Apr., S. 137-138.

90133
Wassiljewsky, A.: Die Zeitungen in China. In: BDB. Jg. 67. 1900, Nr 242 v. 17. Okt., S. 7923-7924.

90134
Wickson, Henry: Zeitung im alten und neuen China. In: Essener Volkszeitung. Jg. 62. Essen 1929, Nr 215 v. 4. Aug., S. 2.

90135
Yui, Chien-hsuin: Das alte chinesische Nachrichtenwesen und die chinesische Staatspresse. Berlin: Fährmannverl. 1934. 86, 4 S. 8°

90136
Das Zeitungswesen in China. In: Deutsche Roman-Zeitung. Jg. 13. Berlin 1876, Nr 38, Sp. 154-155 (Feuilleton d. Deutschen Roman-Zeitung).

90137
Das Zeitungswesen in China. [Von] WV. In: Hamburger Fremdenblatt. Jg. 101. Hamburg 1929, Nr 359 AA v. 28. Dez., S. 2.

90138
Zeitungswesen und Reklame in China. In: Der Neue Orient. Jg. 2, Bd 3. Berlin 1918, H. 1, S. 43-44 (China).

1.2. 1949–1970

90139
Chi-ching, Chang: Die chinesischen Zeitungen und die Reform der chinesischen Schrift. In: DJ. Jg. [4.] 1956, Nr 7, S. 8-10.

90140
China. In: HdA. [4. Aufl.] 1960, S. 752-757 (Ferner Osten); HdW. (5. Aufl.) Bd 1. 1970, S. 72-76.

90141
China <Kontinent>. In: HdA. [4. Aufl.] 1960, S. 757-762 (Ferner Osten).

90142
Chinas „Unterwanderungspresse" im Vormarsch. In: ZV/ZV. Jg. 61. 1964, Nr 10 v. 6. März, S. 296 (Die Presse im Ausland/Ostblock).

Ill. 9. Hagelweide: Literatur zur deutschsprachigen Presse: Eine Bibliographie. Band 9: Länder außerhalb des deutschen Sprachraums. München: Saur 1998 to the *Shinbun zasshi* (1871). The crisis of 1873 and the citizen rights movement (*jiyû minken*), however, supported a critical and polemical press, unhampered by government influence.

In a further paper, *Proprietor Versus Editor: The Case of the Osaka Asahi shimbun in the Late Nineteenth Century* Altman focused on the early history of the *Asahi shinbun* which was founded in 1879. He described the tendency of the proprietors of newspapers to exert a major influence on the papers' lines.

Western literature on the East Asian press has been numerous but most contributions if we compare e.g. the listing of the German Language material by Gert Hagelweide[10], consist of journalistic treatment of the subject on two or three pages but lack depth. Only very recently there has been a revived interest in press history in Europe as documented by Rudolf Wagner's essay on early Chinese newspapers and the public sphere, Natascha Vittinghoff's thesis on Chinese journalism[11], and Barbara Mittler's book on the *Shen-pao*.

The selected references surveyed here show a high level of expertise and gave readers a reliable picture of the newspapers in the respective countries.

Bibliography

China

1 Chinesisches Zeitungswesen.
Das Ausland 1834, 328

2 Cordier, Henri
La presse européenne en Chine.
Revue de l'Extrême-Orient 1. 1882, 121–128
Abridged version: Mémoires de la Société des études japonaise, chinoises, tartares, indo-chinoises et océaniennes 4. 1885, 156–158 (P. de Lucy-Fossarieu)
Condensed version: The European press in China. The London & China Express 24. 1882, Nr 965, S. 118–120

3 Die Presse und das Verlagsrecht in China.
Archiv für Post und Telegraphie 18. 1890, 81–85

4 Polevoj, A. S.
Periodičeskaja pečat' v Kitae. S illjustracijami.
Vladivostok: Vostoc]nyj Institut 1913. X, 165 p. , ill.
(Izvestija Vostočnago Instituta 47)

5 Krebs, E.
Die politische Karikatur in China.
Ostasiatische Zeitschrift 8. 1919/20, 268–274

6 Chinesische Presse.
In: Die Presse des Fernen Ostens.
(Berlin: ALA 1926.) p. 49–63

7 Kim, Heun-Chun
Die Aufmachung der modernen Zeitung in Ostasien (Japan, China und Korea)
Leipzig: A. Twietmeyer in Komm. 1928. 61 p.

10 Hagelweide: *Literatur zur deutschsprachigen Presse. Eine Bibliographie.* Band 9: Länder außerhalb des deutschen Sprachraums. München: Saur 1998. (Dortmunder Beiträge zur Zeitungsforschung.35)

11 Vittinghoff: *Die Anfänge des Journalismus in China (1860–1911)*. Wiesbaden: Harrassowitz 2002. XI, 507 p. (Opera sinologica.9)

8 Chao, Thomas Ming-heng
The foreign press in China. Preliminary paper prepared for the Fourth Biennial Conference of the Institute of Pacific Relations to be held in Hangchow, from October 21st to November 4th, 1931.
Shanghai: China Institute of Pacific Relations 1931. 114 p.

9 Britton, Roswell S.
Zhongguo baozhi 中國報紙 The Chinese periodical press, 1800–1912.
Shanghai: Kelly & Walsh 1933. VI, 151 p., 24 ill.
Reprint: Taipei: Ch'eng-wen 1966.

10 Yui, Chien Hsuin
Das alte chinesische Nachrichtenwesen und die chinesische Staatspresse.
Berlin: Fährmann Verlag 1934. 86 p., 4 p. Chinese characters

11 Moorad, G. L.
When China goes to press.
China Journal 27. 1937, 22-28, 5 p. ill.

12 Löwenthal, Rudolf 羅文達
Western literature on Chinese journalism: a bibliography.
(Tientsin: Nankai Institute of Economics 1937.) IV, 1007–1066, VI p.
Reprinted from Nankai Social & Economic Quarterly, vol. IX, no. 4, January 1937.

13 Löwenthal, Rudolf 羅文達
The Chinese press in Australia.
Collectanea Commissionis Synodalis 10. 1937, 427–430
Offprint [Peking? 1937.] 4 p.

14 Löwenthal, Rudolf 羅文達
The Russian daily press in China.
The Chinese Social and Political Science Review 21. 1937/38, 330–340, 1 folded table

15 Löwenthal, Rudolf
The religious periodical press in China. With 7 maps and 16 charts [as separate supplement]. By Rudolf Löwenthal, Ph.D. 羅文達, Yenching University, with the assistance of Ch'en Hung-shun 陳鴻舜, Ku T'ing-ch'ang, 古廷昌, William W. Y. Liang, B.A. 梁允彝.
Peking: The Synodal Commission in China 1940. VI, 294 p. 4°
Parallel title: Zhongguo zongjiao qikan 中國宗教期刊 [written by William Hung].

16 Hsiao, Ch'ien
The Chinese press.
Asian Review - The Asiatic Quarterly Review Ser. IV, 38. 1942, 192–204

17 Hummel, Arthur W.
Posters and news bulletins in wartime China.
Quarterly Journal of Current Acquisitions, Library of Congress 1. 1943:2, p. 58–59

18 Mohr, Wolfgang
Die moderne chinesische Tagespresse. Ihre Entwicklung in Tafeln und Dokumenten. Teil 1–3.
Wiesbaden: Steiner 1976. 209; XIII, 178; XXVII, 263 p. 4°
(Münchener Ostasiatische Studien. Sonderreihe 2)

19 Wagner, Rudolf G.
The early Chinese newspapers and the Chinese public sphere.
European Journal of East Asian Studies 1. 2001, 1–34

20 Mittler, Barbara
A newspaper for China? Power, identity, and change. Shanghai's news media, 1872-1912.
Cambridge, Mass.: Harvard Univ. Press 2004. XVI, 504 p.
(Harvard East Asian studies monographs 226)

Dianshizhai huabao

21 Dianshizhai huabao 點石齋畫報 Ill. by Wu You-ru et al.
Shanghai: Wenyi chubanshe (1998). 2734 p.
(Zhongguo gudian jingpin yingyin jicheng)

22 Der Chinese in der Öffentlichkeit und der Familie wie er sich selbst sieht und schildert, in 82 Zeichnungen nach chinesischen Originalen. Erläutert von M. von Brandt.
Berlin: D. Reimer (Ernst Vohsen) (1911). VIII, 165 p. 22,5 x 27 cm
Printed by J. J. Augustin in Glückstadt

23 Bodo Wiethoff
Berichte über Europa und Europäer in einem frühen chinesischen Bildermagazin.
Nachrichten der Gesellschaft für Natur- und Völkerkunde Ostasiens 95/96. 1964, 113–125, 2 ill.

24 Fritz van Briessen
Shanghai-Bildzeitung 1884–1898. Eine Illustrierte aus dem China des ausgehenden 19. Jahrhunderts.
(Zürich:) Atlantis (1977). 157 p.
«Die chinesischen Texte wurden von Dr. Yen I-chang, Köln, ins Deutsche übertragen.»

25 Henningsmeier, Julia
The foreign sources of Dianshizhai huabao, a nineteenth century Shanghai illustrated magazine.
Ming Qing yanjiu 1998, 59–91

26 Ye Xiaoqing
The Dianshizhai Pictorial. Shanghai urban life, 1884–1898.
Ann Arbor: Center for Chinese Studies, The University of Michigan 2003. 249 p.
(Michigan monographs in Chinese studies 98)

Korea

27 Altman, Albert A.
Korea's first newspaper: The Japanese Chôsen shinpô.
Journal of Asian Studies 43. 1984, 685–696

Japan

28 Ramming, Martin
Očerk sovremennago položenija periodičeskoj pečati v Japonii.
S.-Peterburg : Kirs]baum 1913. 81 p.

29 Ramming, Martin
Die japanische Zeitung in Vergangenheit und Gegenwart.
Mitteilungen des Seminars für Orientalische Sprachen an der Universität Berlin. 1. Abt. 37. 1934, 105–132

30 Noma, Seiji
Kodansha. Die Autobiographie des japanischen Zeitungskönigs.
Berlin: Holle [1935]. 333 p.
Translation by F. Marquardsen.

31 Hayasaka, Jiro
Das Werden der japanischen Zeitungen. Vom Flugblatt zur Weltpresse. Übersetzt und ergänzt von Karl Ferdinand Reichel.
Würzburg: Konrad Triltsch 1943. 71 p., 18 ill.
Original title: Outline of the Japanese Press. 1938.

32 Altman, Albert A.
Shinbunshi: The early Meiji adaption of the Western-style newspaper.

William G. Beasley (Hrsg.): Modern Japan: Aspects of history, literature and society. Berkeley: University of California Press 1975, 52–66

33 Altman, Albert A.
Proprietor versus editor: The case of the Osaka Asahi shimbun in the late nineteenth century.
Asian and African Studies 14. 1980, 241–253

34 Altman, Albert A.
The press and social cohesion during a period of change: the case of early Meiji Japan.
Modern Asian Studies 15. 1981:4, p. 865–876

循環日報

百八十壹年十一月八號 光緒七年歲次辛巳九月十七日 禮拜二 第二千

Ill. 10. Xunhuan ribao, Tsun Wat Yat Po, Hong Kong,
established by Wang Tao. 1973–1941

MICROFILMING AND CATALOGING THE NEWSPAPERS IN THE NATIONAL DIET LIBRARY (NDL)

Keiyu Horikoshi

Newspapers Division
National Diet Library

1. Outline of newspapers held by the NDL

Newspapers are a medium which reflects the trend of the times most acutely. They have unique value and carry information which cannot be provided by other forms of publications. On the other hand, when we look at their physical characteristics, newspapers are made of low quality paper, and thus present librarians with the problem of how to make them available to users while preserving them intact for as long as possible.

The Newspaper collection of the National Diet Library (NDL) started with newspapers inherited from its predecessor, the former Ueno Library, and those held by the former House of Representatives and the House of Peers. The NDL has added to its collection newly acquired newspapers since its foundation in 1948. The NDL has been helped by the legal deposit system to collect domestic newspapers comprehensively and it also tried to collect foreign newspapers from countries important to Japan. The oldest newspaper in the NDL holdings is *Batahiya Shimbun* published in 1862. The NDL hold 8,707 titles of Japanese newspapers which are kept in bound volumes, reduced editions, photo-reproduced editions, or as microfilm reels or microfiches. Including the foreign newspaper collection of 1,756 titles, the NDL newspaper collection amounts to 10,463 titles as of May 2006.

The domestic newspaper collection includes national papers, regional papers, trade papers, political party papers, and sports papers. One of the most characteristic features of NDL's newspaper collection is the collection of newspaper clippings from major domestic papers, that is, articles filed by classification from 1948 to 1992 (about 2 million articles).

Most of the newspaper collection is available in the Newspaper Reading Room in the Tokyo Main Library while the major Asian language newspaper collection is available in the Kansai-kan. Most NDL stacks are closed to users, but 123 titles of major national and regional newspapers, their reduced editions, and three foreign newspapers are freely available on open shelves in the Newspaper Reading Room. FY2005 statistics shows that about 167,693 users visited the Newspaper Reading Room and that 199,250 items were requested and 61,609 items photocopied. The Room is one of the most heavily used special materials room in the NDL.

To preserve newspapers, we bind original newspapers and make microforms of them at the same time. This is also to prevent deterioration of materials and to provide users with efficient access to frequently used materials. For this purpose, the NDL launched a cooperative project, still ongoing, with the Japan Newspaper Publishers and Editors Association (from1998 with the Japan Newspaper Foundation for Education and Culture, a project unit of the former organization) to make microfilms of the newspapers published by the members of the Association. The Association members provide and entrust the NDL with original newspapers and their master negatives. The NDL's role is to preserve original papers and negatives.

Apart from this project, the NDL has also been working on projects to microfilm old newspapers in its holdings for the purpose of preventing the materials' deterioration.

Another pillar of the NDL's projects to promote access to the newspaper collection is the Union Catalog of Newspapers in Japan Database. This is a nationwide database which provides bibliographic information and holding data of newspapers held by libraries in Japan. The Union Catalog aims to promote information-sharing among libraries in the country on their activities of microfilming, photo-reproducing and reprinting newspapers for the purpose of preservation. The database has been available to the public since February 2003 on the Internet.

Today I would like to talk about our microfilming projects which aim at the long-term preservation of the newspaper collection and also about the Union Catalog of Newspapers in Japan to promote access to the collection.

2. NDL's Project to Make Microfilms of Newspapers

2.1. Newspapers Microfilming Cooperative Project

2.1.1. Outline

As I mentioned earlier, in 1953, the NDL launched a cooperative project still ongoing with the Japan Newspaper Publishers and Editors Association (Nihon Shimbun Kyokai; NSK) to make microfilms of the current newspapers. The project has been operated since 1998 with the NSK's project unit, the Japan Newspaper Foundation for Education and Culture. At the beginning, the number of filmed newspapers was 37 and some 136,000 frames were made per year. Now the foundation annually films 54 titles of national and local newspapers and deposits 700,000 frames of master negative films with the NDL. The number of reels of master negative films is some 1,250 per year and the total number of reels made through this project reached 43,261 as of March 2006.

2.1.2. Japan Newspaper Publishers and Editors Association (Nihon Shimbun Kyokai)

The Japan Newspaper Publishers and Editors Association (NSK) is an entirely independent and voluntary organization funded and operated by newspaper publishers of Japan. The NSK was established in 1946 to raise ethical standards in reporting and protect and promote the Japanese newspapers' common interests. The NSK is a member of the World Association of Newspapers.

2.1.3 Japan Newspaper Foundation for Education and Culture

The Japan Newspaper Foundation for Education and Culture was established in 1998, founded by the NSK and authorized by the Minister of Education. The foundation is a non-profit organization with an endowment fund of 8.3 billion yen. Its main purposes are to preserve and develop newspaper culture and to contribute to education.

2.1.4 Roles of the Japan Newspaper Foundation for Education and Culture and the NDL

Both parties share the cost of this project. The original newspapers are provided by member newspaper companies of the NSK and the foundation makes master negative films and deposits them with the NDL. The NDL also holds the original papers. It makes positive films from the negatives and provides them to the public.

2.1.5 Problems

(1) Deterioration of films

Because the master films made at the beginning of the project used TAC (cellulose triacetate) as film base that deteriorates over time emitting an acetic acid odor, we duplicated the master films from 1993 to 2001. The positive films that we are providing to the public also show deterioration and we need to duplicate them.

(2) Use of color films

Recent newspapers have a lot of color pages. Microfilms made in this project are black-and-white and users often ask for photocopies in color. Some newspaper companies have also been asking us to use color films. Color microfilms are available commercially, but they need to be kept at sub-zero temperatures. That makes it difficult for us to use color films in this project and other microfilming projects of the NDL.

(3) Withdrawal from the contract

While there are new participants, some newspaper companies withdraw from the contract of this project for reasons such as shortage of money. We should maintain stability of the contract and call for new participants in consideration of the importance of this project in the long-term preservation and availability of newspapers.

2.2. Microfilming Projects Carried Out Independently by the NDL

2.2.1. Outline

Besides this project, since 1965 we have been microfilming newspapers published in the Meiji and Taisho eras (1868–1926) which the NDL took over from its predecessors, for the preservation of all the original materials. This is also because they are important as materials for research on Japanese modern history. We started from microfilming newspapers published in the 19th century and have completed microfilming those of before around 1955. We also purchase microfilms of frequently used foreign newspapers and those produced and distributed by newspaper companies.

2.2.2. Plan for Digitization

Some say that we should digitize newspapers directly by scanning them without making microfilms. Several newspaper companies publish CD-ROMs of reduced-size editions and provide PDF image data as a pay service on the Internet. In 2004 and 2005 the NDL carried out an experimental project of making image data samples from the existing microfilms. However, we do not have a positive plan to digitize newspapers because the digitization policy of the library gives relatively low priority to newspapers as compared with books.

3. The Union Catalog of Newspapers in Japan Database

3.1. Outline

The NDL provides a database named the «Union Catalog of Newspapers in Japan Database.» By using this database people can search locations of newspapers including reprints, reduced editions and microfilms held by 13,000 libraries, universities, newspaper publishers and other institutions in Japan as well as the NDL. The database is available to anyone through the NDL website. It consists of three files different in format – «member institution master», «bibliography master» and «holding master» – which are linked by institution ID and bibliography ID in order to facilitate the update of data and online search. As of November 30, 2005, the database includes information on 1,253 institutions, 37,081 bibliographic data and 71,525 holding data.

3.2 History

The NDL published the *Union List of Reduced, Microfilmed and Reprinted Newspapers in Japan*, the catalog of microfilm of newspapers held by libraries and other institutions in Japan, in book form every 5 years from 1970 to 1994. In 1997 we started to develop a system inputting the data of the catalog as the *Union Catalog of Newspapers in Japan Database*. After completion of the development in 1998, we started inputting data into the database. The range of the data covered was extended to the original paper form. The data inputting ended in 2000 and we made it available to the limited institutions providing the data for the NDL, followed by the opening to the public in 2003.

3.3 Functions

3.3.1 Search by Bibliographic Information

As with the NDL-OPAC, the online catalog of the NDL, users can search newspapers by title, place of publication, publisher, year of publication, country, text language and so on. Users can also search by selecting forms such as original, reduced and microforms corresponding to the characteristics of newspapers.

The search result shows bibliographic information with a link to the full listing of institutions holding the newspaper. The name of the institution is linked to the page containing its contact information such as the address and the phone number, and the collection details indicating the periods of holdings and volume numbers.

3.3.2 Search by Locations

Users also can search a holding institution by specifying its name or address. The detailed page of the search result has a list of newspapers held by the institution. This page also has links to the bibliographic data of each newspaper.

3.4. Future Tasks

3.4.1. Review of the Method of Updating Data

In cases data need be updated, each institution informs us by e-mail, phone, fax or letter what should be renewed. Then the staffers of the Newspaper Information Section of the Newspapers Division upload the data on a web page specially made for the purpose. The current system is not a suitable method for updating a large quantity of data all at once because we need to update page by page just for one institution, one title or one location. It is preferable to add a function which will enable us to update all the data at once by preparing the text files in CSV form. Moreover, holding institutions have requested that they do not want to inform the NDL about updating each time but wish to connect remotely to the web so that they can upload the data by themselves. These are the considerations including technical capability.

3.4.2. Integration with the NDL-OPAC

Update of the NDL's holding information should be reflected on the Union Catalog Database as well. When the data of the NDL-OPAC are updated, the department concerned sends a printout of the data to the Newspapers Division. Referring to the printout, the staffers of the Newspaper Information Section update the Union Catalog Database. This procedure creates duplication of work inside the NDL. There are also more or less time lags. Even worse, users are obliged to do double work in many cases: search by both the NDL-OPAC and the Union Catalog Database. Integration of system and implementation of seamless interfaces needs to be achieved in the future.

3.4.3. Correspondence to Newspapers in Asian Languages

With increasing frequency, users ask us about the institutions holding newspapers in Korean, Chinese and other Asian languages. At present, since the database system does not correspond to Unicode, newspapers whose bibliographic data is written in languages other than Japanese and ASCII code cannot be registered. We are aiming to change the specifications when the system will be replaced next time.

4. Conclusion

The newspaper microfilming cooperative project based on the agreement with the Japan Newspaper Foundation for Education founded by the NSK bore fruit and significantly accomplished its mission to preserve newspapers in Japan. As the national library of Japan, we consider that this project should be carried on in the future, though under the conflicting proposition of whether it is for use or preservation. Now the technologies for digitalizing materials are progressing, more efforts for further cooperative relations between the Japan Newspaper Publishers and Editors Association and the NDL are required in order to utilize and preserve newspapers effectively.

In addition, as the Union Catalog of Newspapers in Japan Database, it is difficult to construct and maintain a genuine union catalog of newspapers unless the NDL cooperates with other libraries and newspaper publishers. A close cooperative relationship with each institution is essential.

Television and radio broadcasts, the media whose characteristic is quick reporting, as with Newspapers, are not conserved institutionally, at least in Japan. As for the Internet, which has been developed as a huge information transmission system in the past 10 years, automatic collection is technically possible to some extent. However, comprehensive collection has not yet been conducted due to the unresolved rights issues. We consider that the value of newspapers as a source material is invariable even though the information and social environment has been changing.

THE INTERNET AGE – JOURNALIST'S INFORMATION POWER IS CHANGING

Seonhwa Jang

Seoul Economic Daily

1. Introduction

We are at the turn of the century where the Internet has been growing rapidly and influences virtually everybody's life. The Internet is the largest group of computers ever linked together in the world such as network of networks. The Internet has become a gigantic information warehouse. Networked communication tools like Internet remove physical barriers to communicate, which is explained by time-space compression. It is not limited to remove geological barriers based on the speed of communication. More broadly, the Internet influences people's way of thinking. Much wider communication area makes people to share information with anybody if he or she is connected to the network and even make it possible to start a new business in the cyber space. It has made new social trends. In journalistic point of view, the Internet made a new media that gives a chance to public to participate in social issues more positively and aggressively than before. The Internet has various aspects. It is not easy to define only one great feature of the Internet conclusively though. In general, we can point out three major characteristics of the Internet. Firstly, it is interactivity. Interactivity involves two-way communication. Internet users click on linked pages to get additional information. The information itself is not interactive unless it does something in response to what users want. It gives a chance to people to express their interest and also it is a new tool to collect public opinion. Secondly, it is hypertext connected with other channels via web. The word hyper in hypertext means "extension into other dimensions". In that sense, hypertext consists of nodes of information and links each other in a multidimensional space. Hypermedia is conceptually and structurally same as hypertext except that hypermedia contains not only text but also sound and image information. (Chu, 2003) It makes easy to transit one dimension to another on the web. Thirdly, it is the open space. The Internet is a huge open-network free from network protocol or complicated communicational regulations. Therefore, any Internet users not only could suggest new standards or agenda for better communication but also participate in building requests for comments. It gives netizens equality in the cyberspace. If a user is connected in the Internet then he or she can communicate with anybody who log on to the web. Sharing information becomes much easier.

2. Status of Korean Internet

Korea was ranked top in ITU (International Telecommunication Uion)'s digital opportunity index (DOI) which is disclosed in the World Summit on the Information Society (WSIS) under the aegis of the United Nations.

The DOI is the first e-index based on internationally agreed ICT indicators. The index, which measures countries' adoption and access to information and communication technologies (ICTs), was developed with an aim to utilize it as a gauge in bridging the digital divide and promoting the broad development goals included in the United Nations Millennium Declaration through increased access and use of ICTs. As regards the DOI rankings, Korea scored the top with 0.76 points while Hong Kong and Japan scored 0.67

country	ranking	Country	ranking
Korea	1	United States	11
Hong Kong	2	Austria	12
Japan	3	United Kingdom	13
Denmark	4	Israel	14
Sweden	5	Australia	15
Canada	6	Germany	16
Singapore	7	Belgium	17
Taiwan	8	Spain	18
Netherlands	9	Italy	19
Switzerland	10	France	20

Tab. 1. DOI Ranking

and 0.66 points respectively, taking the second and third places followed by Denmark, Sweden and Canada. In the case of the ratios of broadband Internet subscribers to both the fixed and mobile Internet subscribers, in particular, Korea showed conspicuous results. All the fixed Internet subscribers in Korea are connected to the broadband Internet whereas only 52.6% of fixed Internet subscribers in Hong Kong, and 40.6% in Japan, were shown to be using the broadband network. Also Korea ranked 8th in IDC (International Data Center)'s evaluation for ISI (Information Society Index) readiness among 53 countries in 2004. Korea is the only Asian country which included in top 10 countries. IDC is the global market intelligence and advisory firm in the information technology and telecommunications industries. ISI is one of IDC's annual project groups 4 indicators, such as computer, Internet, Telecom, Social. As a national economic status measuring by GDP, ISI gauge a national information power.

	ITU's DOI(2005)	UN's e-government index	IDC's ISI(2004)
Sweden	5	3	2
Denmark	4	2	1
Canada	6	8	-
Korea	1	5	8
US	11	1	3*
Japan	3	14	18
Singapore	7	7	13

Tab. 2. Ranking International Index

It groups eight ICT indicators, such as the percentage of population covered by cellular telephony, into the five categories(Infrastructure, Affordability, Knowledge, Quality, and Usage). About Internet index of Korea is not ended here. In 2005, Korea also ranked fifth in United Nations' evaluation for e-Government readiness among 191 countries, thanks to its advanced information technology and nationwide broadband network. Korea's e-participation index which assesses government efforts to reflect public opinion in its decision-making process, ranked fourth up from sixth in 2004 and 12th in 2003.

According to the «Survey on the computer and Internet usage 2005» from MIC (Ministry of Information and Communication) in Korea, Internet users are estimated to be 33.01 million of persons, which have increased by 1.43 million persons, and the Internet use rate is 72.8% increased by 2.6% point since December 2004. Since year 2000, Korean Internet users have grown steadily. Thanks to the government supporting broadband high speed Internet network, we made world best information society infrastructure in a short time.

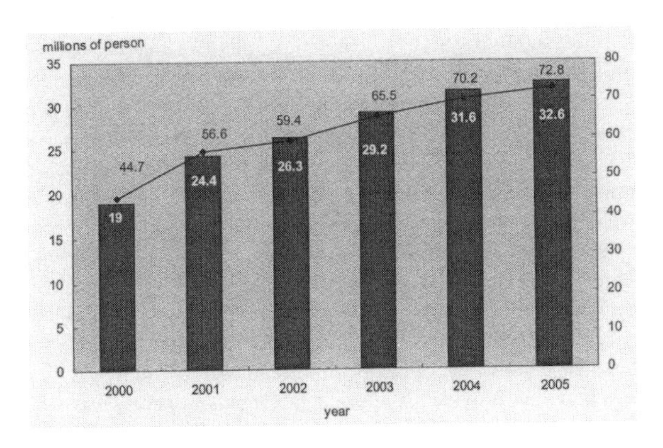

Fig. 1. Annual Internet users and trend of usage (unit:millions of person, %)

Those figures show roughly that how much Korean society is Internet-oriented. It can be possible to people more intended to information into Internet. The first tool for gathering information in Korea is Internet. Therefore news consumer in young generation read articles not by paper but by accessing Internet.

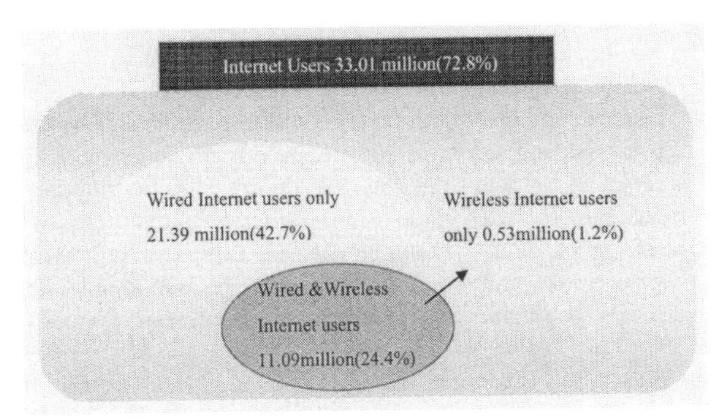

Fig.2. Korean Internet usage by access type (unit:%, million presons)2005

2.1 Status of Korean Newspapers

Strictly speaking, Korea has 123 years old modern newspaper history. In terms of the true meaning of private newspaper, in the history of modern Korean newspapers begins with the appearance of the Independence Daily on April 7, 1896 published by Dr. Suh, Jaepil. However 13 years before the Independence Daily published, there contained modern style articles newspaper in Korea. It was Hansung Sunbo which was published its first edition on October 1, 1883. Hansung Sunbo was published for enlightening public by reformists. At that time Yi Dynasty that is the last emperor of whole Korean history adopt an open-door policy against Japan's modern political and social machinery for domestic reform. Hansung Sunbo was an official gazette, and its importance lies in not so much in the achievement of its primary mission of publicizing news as in marking the establishment of modern newspaper.

The history of the Korean newspapers is broadly categorized into three periods. The first period ranged from 1892 through 1953. It is defined the dark age of modern Korean history because of Japanese annexation, liberation, and Korean war. The second period was from 1953 through 1986 that military dictatorship governed people. The third period was from 1986 to the present that democratic government has been settled down. The aforementioned three periods of the Korean newspaper show different characteristics in each period. A summary of the newspapers' characteristics in each period follows. The first period marked the first appearance of the independent daily newspaper, and is highlighted by the current mass-circulation dailies *Dong-A Ilbo* and *The Chosun Ilbo*. During the first period, the efforts of newspapers were centered on enlightening people and on struggling against the Japanese colonial policy, while setting up the democratic political system and developing the newspaper business. In the second period, military dictatorship had controlled newspaper by oppressive measures, and the gist of the government's speech policy was the adoption of a two-pronged strategy that provided capital for the organs of expression while mobilizing them for the country's development. The government took the reins of the press by dismissing journalists, controlling the freedom of speech and reshuffling the organization of the press. The government inspected the organs of expression and exercised its influence over them by sending its agents to them. The military dictatorial government that had secured sovereignty in 1961 began to control the press, detaining 960 journalists. At that time, 152 newspapers disappeared from publication. The important change that was in the press in 1960s was the appearance of financial newspapers. *The Seoul Economic Daily* was published 1960 as the first financial newspaper in Korea.

A type of report permit system was started, and was put into use with the issue of press cards on Dec. 17, 1971, designed to control the press and a pressroom system for governmental bureaus had been introduced. Also, related laws and regulations had been strengthened. Clauses restricting the freedom of speech, such as the Registration of Publishing Companies and Printing Offices Act and the Import and Distribution of Foreign Publications Act, had been included under the extraordinary martial law provisions. There had been also the mergers and abolitions of newspapers. In November 1980, the new military authorities conducted the merger and abolition of the press to exercise control over it. The government issued report guidelines to keep it under observation, too. The third period was of the democratic regime. As the people's resistance against the military dictatorship reached its peak in 1987, the administration adopted gradual democratization measures. Journalists fought to realize the democratization of the press organizing labor unions in each entity. Moreover, newspaper publication became unrestricted. The *Hankyoreh* was published, and some newspapers of religious organizations such as *Kukminilbo* (Dec. 10, 1988), *Segyeilbo* (Feb. 1, 1989) and *Pyunghwa Shinmun* (1988) were launched. There was a sudden growth in the publication of local newspapers as well.

If we look back on past history, we can say that the freedom of speech has been secured only about for 15 years in Korea. although the first modern newspaper had appeared more than 120 years before. Two to three years of the Yi Sung-man administration, one year of the Jang Myun government and the period after the 6.29 Declaration in 1987 can account for the aforementioned years of freedom of speech. When we consider these historical experiences, it can be premature for us to say that the freedom of speech has planted its roots in Korea. Nevertheless, the level of the freedom of speech that we are enjoying today, though not enough, has been the fruits of journalists' unceasing fights for the freedom of speech, people's support and civil struggles for democratization right up to the present.

2.2 The Korean newspapers in the world and their situation

Traditionally, the newspapers published in Asian countries have had very strong circulations. The 62% of the top 100 world newspapers are of Korea, China and Japan. The *Chosunilbo*, *Dongailbo* and *JoongAng Daily of Korea* were among the top 100 world newspapers.

Ranking	Country	No.top dailies
1	Japan	20
2	China	19
3	USA	18
4	India	17
5	United Kingdom	7
6	Germany	3
7	Korea, Republic	3
8	Thailand	3
9	Italy	2
10	Australia	1

Tab. 3. Dailies: countries of top 100 dailies

However the recent situation of newspapers has reached a critical situation. The overall media environment turned less favorable for the print media sector. The rapid rise of other media outlets, including the Internet has served to diminish the credibility and popularity of newspapers, resulting in a state of crisis for the print media. According to a biennial consumer survey in 2004 by the Korea Press Foundation found that only 48.3 percent of Korean entire household subscribed to newspapers, making the first time the rate drop below the 50 percent level. Responsible for the decreasing popularity of newspapers are the rise of the Internet as a new form of media outlet, which has caused more young people to distance from newspaper. In adopting the internet era, newspaper companies are digitizing news content and providing news bundles to the Internet portal service companies.

One of the known digital news contents service is KINDS (Korean Integrated News Database System) which is served by Korea Press Foundation since 1991. It connects from 181 media organizations and 10,883,357articles up to April 2, 2006. KINDS is the largest service of news articles. KINDS provides full texts from 14 major national dailies, 7 financial dailies, 8 English 19 internet news. It also provides articles from television network news programs, news bulletins, local dailies, magazines and professional newspapers. KINDS service contributes to the quality of reporting with its vast quantity of articles on many specific topics. Magazine articles provided by major weekly and monthly news magazines and professional newspapers articles are included in our online services.

Special features of KINDS are followed:

1. The Largest News Database System in Korea: KINDS has more than 10 million articles from 181 companies that composed of national dailies, economic dailies, TV news, English language dailies, Internet medias, local dailies, professional newspapers, and news magazines; especially articles from 10 major national dailies that were begun after January 1, 1990.
2. Convenient and Accurate Search Service: Users may search articles from 181 medias by typing key words and operators (see chart below), the specific name of newspaper, date of publication, name of writer, column title and/or subjects. For 10 major national dailies, there is an advanced search service available, which utilizes published section, and/or just articles from the front page.
3. Diverse News Contents: KINDS covers articles from a wide range of media covering a period of several decades. Our database covers articles not only from national dailies

but also from TV news programs, news magazines, and professional newspapers. Articles produced between 1960 and 1989 are provided in the form of PDF files. PDF files of the *Dongnip Shinmun* (the Independent) and *Daehan Maeil Shinbo* are also available.

4. Function of Scrap and Saving Search Conditions: Users may save searched articles in a personal categorized scrap folder, along with any search methods that will be used repeatedly, thereby skipping the need to use the same search process in the future.

2.3 Homepage Management of the Press Organs

As the Internet homepages are used largely, also the newspapers began to offer not only the news directly produced by themselves but various contents like information on real estate and on education, etc. managing homepages of themselves.

Ranking	Country	No.top dailies
1	Japan	20
2	China	19
3	USA	18
4	India	17
5	United Kingdom	7
6	Germany	3
7	Korea, Republic	3
8	Thailand	3
9	Italy	2
10	Australia	1

Tab. 4. Number of daily newspaper websites (World Newspaper Trend 2005)

According World Newspaper Trend's survey, Korea is 4th ranked in the number of daily newspaper websites. In Korea most of newspaper publishers run their own homepages. The produced news is offered via the Internet. Information specialists including librarians constitute the management body. In the past, the main work of the information specialists that served newspapers were paper clipping and data arrangement. But, since the 1990s when newspapers began to introduce computer systems, digital contents production became their main task. Now, news is offered in HTML and PDF formats on the homepages of the press organs. To use the organs' homepages one need to become a member of the websites, and then news contents are basically offered for free. The paid information services are offered linking to various contents like information on real estate, on education and on persons, etc., and they offer the functions of Internet portals.

With the Dot-com business booming in Korea, one of the most winning businesses was the Internet portal business. The earning models of this business are Internet advertisments. If we consider the fact that also the main earning sources of newspapers are the advertisements, we can say that the portals and newspapers are in competition with one another. The difference depends on whether they produce news contents or not. The representative Korean Internet portals are NAVER, DAUM, NATE, etc., and the average number of daily users exceeds 25 million. The contents that the Internet portals needed to increase the number of users were news reports, and since 2000, press publishers began to competitively sell news articles to the portals as much as they could sell the one-source multi-use articles. Today, 5 years after the article contents sale to the portal began for the first time, many of young readers don't read the papers any more. All of them do read daily news on the Internet portals. Likewise, as the feedback culture spread widely, they are actively expressing their own opinions.

3. Press is Requested Change of Research Methods for the Internet Era

3.1 Past Methods of Research by Reporters

In this historical background, the peculiarities of the news gathering in the Korean press circle have included contact-oriented off the record methods. Writing reports based on the school ties and personal connections were one of the important ways of working, instead of searching for unreported news through gathering and analysis of the existing published information. Also the type of «announcing journalism» was pointed out as a problem in gathering news. The phrase: «announcing journalism» means a type of report that faithfully uses the information, the analysis and interpretation on this information and the definition of reality offered by the news source – abandoning the method of verification, analysis and interpretation of the facts. A survey revealed that about 93% of the news sources have offered reporters so-called canned news. Canned news offers reporters the utmost convenience, especially because the news sources offer reporters news more perfect than that of the reporters themselves, increasing a tendency toward concentrating more on public relations. As a result, there is every possibility that reporting without examining what the truthfulness of reports will mislead readers.

The «announcing journalism» has been a custom owing to various structural factors in the press. It was a complicated result coming from lack of expertise of reporters, problems in coverage system, manpower shortage, the relaxed professional sense of reporters and the strengthened publicity of the established power group, etc. This phenomenon was also a legacy of the institutional press that had been domesticated under the authoritarian regimes during the long-lasted military dictatorships.

The coverage system constituted by the beat systems i.e. a closed access system) and press corps built up an exclusive news coverage system. Only the state approved reporters could gather news from the allotted news sources. It had a character of a generalized custom established for the convenience of news gathering rather than an official system. The press corps system came from an intended agreement in the sense that it led journalists to collaboration rather than competition for news gathering. The system secured, through the agreement on the reports, that no reporter of specific newspaper could get scoops by gathering information exclusively, so the risk of an unprinted report could be removed in advance. This press corps system featured pre-intended agreement, as this restrained the competition for news gathering in advance; additionally, this made the improvement in the quality of reports through journalistic competition unlikely. The problems and opposite functions of the beat system and press corps system:

1. The news gathering and report through the beat system and press corps system was apt to lead to biased information. The phenomenon of the so-called «announcing journalism» that showed uniform and indistinctive news articles on most of the papers that could be attributed to the dependence on the beat and press corps systems.
2. The possibility of corruption, represented by bribes, can be prevalent among these systems. Receiving bribes decisively restricts the right to free access to information of people by weakening the function of independent thought and action of the press, which limited the free and open circulation of information.
3. These systems can wholly block the public's right to know that can be satisfied only through fair competitions. Limited information is offered to readers by the beat system, with news being necessarily censored and controlled, and therefore could not be viewed by the public.

3.2 Changes in the Environment for the Freedom of Press Information

The fast appearance of the changing environment since the 1990s was a change to the world press. It was caused by the technical revolution in computer and IT (information and telecommunication) areas. Digital technologies were the main engine which drove changes. The Internet built the circulatory system of information by compressing time and space, and as a result of it, a large part of the information covered by the already existing papers and broadcast media has become to be supplied through the Internet. In addition, since everybody able to have their won Internet homepages, the dispatching capacity of information that has been exclusively possessed by the mass media like papers and broadcasters before the appearance of the Internet is passing now into all people's hands. It became for everyone to have ways to express opinions freely and exchange and discuss these opinions with others through the Internet. This change means a new restoration of the right to freedom of speech that has been restricted till now by the mass media like papers and broadcasters. According to the Fourth Annual World Press Freedom Index released by Reporters Without Borders (RWB) in November, 2005, Korea ranked 34th among the 167 countries, the 1st in Asia. Korea surpassed the U.S. that ranked 44th by 10 grades. The free environment for communication using the Internet in Korea is considered to have attributed much to the high valuation on the country's current situation. The Internet and computer telecommunication have allowed everyone the freedom of speech. Consequently, a new enforcing power has been constituted and the expectation that there will be a democratic development through it emerged.

The digital revolution has brought changes also to the media receivers such as social members. Owing to the development of computer and telecommunication technologies, big changes are now being caused to the standardization, concentration, synchronization, specialization, maximization and centralization which had been the specific characters of the industrial society. There are changes from standardization to non-standardization, from concentration to dispersion, from synchronization to non-synchronization, from specialization to integration, from maximization to reduction and from centralization to decentralization. These conceptual changes are weakening the unified norms with which the state has bound individuals in every matter with a certain compelling force.

Because of the Internet, the individualization is happening in the demand and supply of information. Each person selects and collects information according to their own wishes. And, the reception of information shows active aspects too. The usage of information and the attitude to the contacts with information change into more independent, selective and active channels, throwing away the passive position from which information has been simply received in unilateral way. The press is introducing fresh coverage systems following these external changes. The team system, specialized reporter system and expert reporter system are these new methods. The systems that appeared to complement the contradiction of the beat system are the news gathering in teams, specialized reporter system and expert reporter system. The team system is the way a few reporters form a small group to gather news in classified subjects or issues of society. News gathering centering on the emerging social issues and subjects such as reunification, environment, health and leisure, etc. is a peculiarity of the team system differentiating itself from the usual news gathering way centered on the departments of politics, economy, society, culture and the editorial department, etc. News gathering systems that are sensitive to the current, ongoing changes of reality are being introduced, with existing systems being abandoned. The *Joong Ang Daily* employed 15 specialized reporters with doctorate degrees and attempted to adopt a full-scale specialized reporter system. But, this system has not yet become well established. The report-the Korean Press Situation-of the 2000 Committee on the Korean Press proposed 14 things to the press for the improvement of the Korean press. Among these proposals, they underscored that the standardization of the press that is caused by the alignment phenomenon between the newspaper publishers should be discarded. It was pointed out that the private censorship adopted for survival under the press suppression during the past military dictatorship had become a custom. Changes were necessary to survive under the fast changing press environment. Changes must be attempted according to the tendency that the readers' taste becomes diversified following the changes in their values and moral sense. Specially, in case of the papers with a low market share, if they make papers that satisfy the taste of a certain class of readers after having targeted the class, they will be able to secure their independent market under keen market competitions.

3.3 Changes in the Environment for Press Coverage

During the military regimes since the 1960s, the Korean press had reported filtering information being unable to report the facts as it had been in a mutually favourable alliance with the political regime of the day, adopting a suppression and appeasement policy. Readers received news through the press that was engaged in a unilateral reporting way that the government announced news and reporters transmitted it. In this period, the authority of the papers and the trust in them reached its uppermost peak. There were limitations for reporters to objectively report the facts because of the suppression and appeasement policy of the government. The governmental bureaus restricted coverage using only the reporters selected under the name of the press corps. As the flow of information, then, was conducted through a certain route, reporters could not help but depend on the customary and closed-door coverage based on their personal relationships. This closed way of searching for information of the Korean reporters developed into the press corps whose reporters are limited by the government and powerful companies. The problem that has been pointed out regarding the beat system was that it was liable to mislead the circumstantial judgment as the coverage was done by the same reporters. In particular, the executives made use of this system as a means of coexistence keeping deep relations with the reporters that mainly worked with high-ranking government officials.

News can be compared to buildings or products. In the press, the expertise based on decision-making can be appreciated greatly in value. With the introduction of the Internet, the environment for news gathering is changing rapidly in Korea. Since 2000, there have been higher appreciations over the planning and inquiry reports rather than over the customary coverage inside of the Korean press. According to the comparison between the coverage reports and planning reports that have won the Korean Reporter Prize, since 2000 the planning reports and inquiry reports came to the center surpassing the coverage reports. This reflects a real shift in emphasis. With the appearance of the Internet, there are many changes in the coverage custom and search for information of the young generation reporters. As information technologies become to be fully applied to the coverage, the CAR (Computer-Assisted Reporting) appeared as a new coverage skill. Jang (2005), compared and analyzed in classified career grades the ways of searching for information of reporters that are results of the changes in the environment for coverage which have been opened up. The subjects of the study were composed of 9 executive reporters with more than 15 years' experience and 11 common reporters engaged in the field for less than 10 years from national daily newspapers and Internet papers. It was confirmed that the news sources which were used by reporters were moving from the closed sources to the open ones. It revealed that the executive reporters consider their personal connections the most important news sources and gather important news at closed private tables. On the other hand, the very many reporters spend more time gathering open news and realize that they have to possess the expertise and analyzing capacity rather than the closed-door coverage to survive the competitions for coverage.

4. Conclusion

Entering the digital age, news doesn't remain as the information source that is produced and offered by a small number of people any more. As the receivers of the news can emerge as the suppliers, the environment for news production and its offer is changing. Particularly, as the environment for the use of information of reporters, the functions of analysis and interpretation of the open information are becoming much more important than ever before. In the Internet age, papers should work out their strategy to strengthen the use of information and analyzing capacity in order to survive. In the first place, the function of the information specialists in the editorial department must be beefed up. Even though the coverage based on the personal relationships of reporters, i.e., coverage in off-the-record way, has been much appreciated till now, the comprehensive faculty and analyzing capacity of information decide the quality of the articles in the open age. Various information is collected and the articles are written with this information in short time for newspapers. Therefore, it is effective to receive the support from the information specialists in producing the newspaper articles. The information specialists of the newspapers should not be mere information searchers and should have the comprehensive faculty and information capacity regarding social issues. For more effective use of the information specialists, information support must be offered by the information specialists that are to participate in the editorial conferences and then to grasp the direction of the important articles of each day. The information specialists of newspapers must let others know actively of their skills and area of work. They should ensure that the decision makers who own and run newspapers understand accurately what the function is of the information specialists in newspapers. For this, establishing the days like «Information Day» and inviting the members of other departments to introduce their department to them and to let them know how the information support would be possible can be put into practice. And also, the analyzed information support capacity should be improved. All information specialists must be acquainted with not only the Internet but all on-line and off-line information channels to the extent that their capacity could annul the proposition that on the Internet information can be searched out by everyone. And then, all must improve the capacity for supporting the analyzed information for article production. This is the capacity of the information specialists possessing both the know-how and the sources of information, and such knowledge provides a short cut through which information can be recognized to be a good, reliable and trustworthy source for the production of better news.

References

Choi, Jinbong. 2003. *Korean Mass Media and Popular Culture*. Woojin landom Publishing Co.:Seoul.

Chomsky, Noam. 2002. *Media Control*. Steven Stories Press: New York.

Chu, Heting. 2003. Information *Representation and Retrieval in the Digital Age*. Information Today: New Jersey.

ITU. 2005. *WSIS Thematic Meeting on Multi-Stakeholder Partnerships for Bridging the Digital Divide*. ITU.

Jang, Seonhwa. 2005. A Study on Newspaper Reporters' Information-Seeking Patterns. *Journal of the Korean Society for Library and Information Science*. 39(3). 65–182.

Kim, Min-Hwan. 2003. *The History of Korean Press*. Seoul: Nanam Publishing.

Korea Times. «Korea 28th in Human Development». 18 December.

Ministry of Information and Communication. 2005. *Survey on the Computer and Internet Usage 2005' from MIC*. Seoul: MIC.

World Association of Newspapers. 2004. *World Press Trends*. WAN.

DIGITAL NEWS: KEY TO GLOBAL LITERACY AND INFORMATION LITERACY EDUCATION

Lisa Janicke Hinchliffe & Dawn M. Schmitz

University of Illinois at Urbana-Champaign

The advent of digital newspaper databases is a boon to the burgeoning interdisciplinary field of Global Studies in the United States. Students and educators now have greater access than ever to instant information about events happening around the world and issues that are important to people in other countries. Using global news in the classroom is an effective way for students to expand and widen their perspective on global issues by incorporating multiple viewpoints into their own understanding of the forces that are shaping the world in the twenty-first century. Today we will discuss some of the benefits of incorporating news as a source of information in the Global Studies curriculum and how doing so can advance media literacy skills. We will also consider some of the challenges of using news as a pedagogical tool.

News and Global Studies

News has many qualities that make it ideal for use in the Global Studies classroom. First, news is accessible. With the advent of digital library databases and commercial Web search tools, news from around the world is more easily available than ever to university students in the United States. Resources like LexisNexis and Global NewsBank provide instant access to news published in newspapers and broadcast in other countries. Even for institutions that cannot afford these resources, websites like Google News, which indexes news articles from websites published around the world, are of great benefit. Electronic access complements the timeliness of news, which is another of its unique attributes. Students can learn about what happened yesterday, or even find out about today's events happening across the world.

News is intellectually accessible as well. Unlike scholarly communications, there is no specialized vocabulary, and it is often written in an engaging style. Issues and ongoing events are followed, producing a narrative that can be tracked across time.

News is also linguistically accessible. Unfortunately, most United States students are monolingual when they arrive at the university. But that doesn't mean that they have to be cut off from news published in non-English-speaking countries. There are many English-language newspapers and news websites from countries around the world, such as *The Korea Herald* and *The Japan Times*. Library databases like Global NewsBank carry news articles from the BBC monitoring service, which gathers news published and broadcast around the world and translates it into English.

Whether or not the news is translated into English or originally published in a language American students can read, it is critical for Global Studies that students have access to news that is produced in other countries, not just news that is published in the United States about other countries. The little international news that is published in the United States is focused overwhelmingly on natural disasters, war, terrorism, famine, disease, and other devastating events. Taken out of context, such news coverage does not foster identification with other cultures, but rather makes the situation in other countries seem terrible and beyond hope. Relying on the United States alternative media for comprehensive news about other countries is of little help since these news organizations do not have the resources to have reporters on the ground throughout the world.

On the other hand, news articles published in other countries have a unique capacity to foster identification with the problems and issues confronted by people around the world. Many news articles have a human interest component, which can be particularly effective for developing identification with people from other countries. Cultural reporting is another genre of journalism that can foster identification with people throughout the world, since culture – music, dance, literature, film, theatre, and storytelling – is arguably what defines what it is to be human.

Perhaps most importantly, news articles produced in different parts of the world reflect differing perspectives on global issues and problems. Helping students to have a more cosmopolitan sensibility by incorporating divergent perspectives into their understanding of global issues is perhaps the primary goal of Global Studies education in the United States. Drawing on the work of philosopher Martha Nussbaum, Eve Walsh Stoddard and Grant H. Cornwell (2003) articulate how a liberal arts approach to Global Studies can advance the ideal of global citizenship. They not only stress that knowledge is crucial for the ethical global citizen, but they also propose that knowledge is perspectival, stressing the notion that «things look completely different from different locations or different points of view» (Stoddard & Cornwell p.44).

News can allow students to de-center their own ways of seeing the world in order to understand issues and events from different perspectives, including those that have been traditionally marginalized on the global scale. News can expose students to many global perspectives so they can then analyze, synthesize and integrate them into their own understanding of issues and concepts: Stoddard and Cornwall write, «Geocitizens … need to seek points of view globally; hence, critical thinking becomes the project of triangulating the sources, clearly identifying the contradictions and incommensurabilities, building a reconciled narrative to the extent possible» (Stoddard & Cornwell p.50).

The capacity of electronic databases to allow searching news by topic is perhaps what makes them the most valuable for Global Studies, because searching across international papers for articles on particular topics is a way to pull together a more global view of a particular issue related to a Global Studies course. Students can read several articles on a particular issue, compare and contrast them, and put together an account of the issue that is a synthesis of different perspectives on it. For example, a student group who chose to search for articles on urbanization found out that:

1. A Nigerian news source reported that the Nigerian Congress declared that dealing with urbanization was a major priority. According to Nigerian urban planning scholars, cities must be made more liveable in order to deal with growing urban violence and disease.
2. The *Korea Herald* reported that China's rapid urbanization and economic development had contributed to pollution in that country and its neighbors, prompting Asian media officials to meet in Beijing to discuss sustainable development in China and the role of media in economic development and environmental protection.
3. A French news agency reported researchers' warnings that urbanization and transportation have resulted in «biotic homogenization,» meaning that almost all plants and animals will live almost everywhere, but there will be fewer species overall. The worlds'-dominant species will take over in every area of the world, resulting in much less biodiversity.
4. The *Accra Daily Mail*, a Ghanaian newspaper, reported on U.N. Secretary General Kofi Annan's views that lack of public services such as education, health services, water, and sanitation are main reasons why informal settlements occur in cities, and that convic-

tions and demolitions are not the answer to the problems brought on by urbanization.

5. A Chinese news agency reported that the World Bank provided a $180 million loan to build infrastructure in China's rural southwest, where mountainous topography and inadequate water supply have stalled the urbanization process.

In their report, the students noted similar themes that were addressed in the articles: the effects of urbanization on living conditions for the poor and the interplay of environmental problems and urbanization. They also noted some of the different ways in which the problems of urbanization play out in different places around the world.

The fact that the topic «urbanization» is a very broad topic – probably broader than many librarians would like to see in a typical research project – can allow for students to gain a more global understanding of an issue. If the topic is too narrow from the outset, then the students' pre-conceived ideas about the issue, based upon their perspective as United States residents who have only been exposed to issues through the United States media, can steer the research too narrowly in the direction of framing issues or problems in ways with which they are already familiar.

For example, in the United States, urbanization is rightly seen as a phenomenon that occurred largely in the nineteenth and twentieth centuries, with the current stage of migration being from the cities to the suburbs – which results in trends with narrower terms such as «urban blight» or «urban sprawl.» Yet these are not terms that would reflect the massive farm-to-city migrations now happening in many places throughout the world, notably China.

Thus, the librarian's impulse to narrow the topic from the outset of the research project can have the effect of placing what we, as Americans, already know or care about an issue in the forefront and minimizing the potential for the assignment to present a more global perspective on the issue. The goal of the exercise is for students to learn how to synthesize several articles on a global topic from around the world, to come to an understanding of the issue that reflects a more cosmopolitan sensibility than they had before the assignment.

Media Literacy

Using news in the Global Studies course is a way for students to become more media literate. This includes an understanding of how and why the United States media fall short in reporting about other countries and thus why it is important to find news from around the world. It also involves the ability to determine where a newspaper article was published – as examples, to search a website to find out where it originates from and to understand that a dateline reflects where the reporter was when he or she reported on the event but not the city where the news organization that produced the story is actually located.

Media literacy and Global Studies goals are both advanced when students can learn to notice which sources are cited in a news article and, beyond that, to think about how the sources cited usually reflect and help to shape the perspective from which an article is written. Students can also learn to consider how larger economic and political factors in a society can shape the news that is produced in a given country. For example, in countries where the government does not formally control the media, informal mechanisms and the structure of the media industries create an environment where the media still rely very heavily on large, powerful institutions such as the government and large corporations for their information.

Advertising is one of the most profound factors shaping how news is produced. One of the drawbacks of using electronic databases is that it can be difficult to see the influence of advertising on news, because the articles have been extracted from their original context in which they were juxtaposed with, and financed by, advertisements. Still, the idea that most news from around the world tends to reflect the perspectives of powerful institutions like governments and corporations that advertise in the media, although a fairly advanced concept, can be introduced in a Global Studies assignment that uses news as an information source.

But we must consider carefully how to direct students to analyze news from other countries. For educators in the United States, it is important to recognize that American students are already critical readers of news, but the critical tools they have been trained to use may not be the best ones in a Global Studies context. Without any direction, students will draw on the critical tools they have derived from having learned United States news values, such as the detachment on the part of the reporter. Related to the norm of detachment is another common conceptual framework for Americans in analyzing the news: the biased/objective binary. Thus, when they are asked to consider the different perspectives from which different articles are written, students may resort to a term they are more familiar with – bias –and criticize news articles for carrying a biased point of view. This is understandable: the difference between bias and perspective is very subtle – the main difference being the connotations of the two words. Bias is negative; perspective is not.

The result of thinking in terms of bias rather than perspective is significant. Students may gather and read news articles from around the world about a topic and rather than attempting to synthesize the articles into some more cosmopolitan understanding of the issue by noticing how it is considered differently in the news articles gathered from around the world, they may tend to criticize each article in turn, depending upon whether they believe it is biased or unbiased. One student group said the articles they read about the Asian Tsunami of 2004 were biased «since they were printed in or around the disaster area» – The Philippines, Sri Lanka, and Thailand. The suggestion here is that a reporter must be detached from the event in order to be unbiased and to cover it responsibly.

American students' seemingly instinctive approach to news criticism – to limit their analysis to the biased/unbiased binary and the ethos of detachment – is challenging in almost any type of media literacy context. However, it is particularly problematic in a Global Studies context, since these news values tend to themselves be reflections of a particularly American ethos of journalism. While many news values and practices are shared by professional journalists throughout the world, the ethics of detachment and objectivity are not the most central journalistic values in every part of the world. Rather than valuing a dispassionate journalistic voice and representing «both sides» of an issue in every article, many journalists throughout the world place the greatest values on autonomy and advocacy. That is, the journalists' value their ability to act autonomously-free of government control-and they also believe journalists can and should play an advocacy role, relying on the multiplicity of newspapers to make sure all perspectives are aired (Brislin, pp. 134–136). As Tom Brislin of the University of Hawaii at Manoa School of Journalism writes, «Many Western European, Japanese, Taiwanese, and Korean news organizations are comfortable with an advocacy model, in effect 'wearing their politics on their sleeves,' achieving balance in the aggregate rather than within each organization» (Brislin p. 135). Therefore, an assignment that uses international news can fall short of its goal of helping students incorporate various perspectives from around the world unless attention is paid to helping students de-center their own ways of thinking about what constitutes responsible journalism.

Conclusion

Global Studies curricula in the United States benefit greatly from digital access to news resources because immediate access to news from many countries, in a context that is searchable by subject, exposes students to information about global events and issues from perspectives of people from other parts of the world. International news sources are particularly important in helping students to develop a global perspective on an issue instead of relying on a framework of how a particular issue is discussed in United States media. We encourage academic libraries to collaborate with Global Studies faculty to develop approaches to teach students how to use digital resources to find news produced in other countries. Our experience doing so resulted in the creation of an online tutorial (available online at http://www.library.uiuc.edu/village/globalnews/) that instructs students in seeking out and thinking carefully about global news sources. We invite you to contact us with any questions or comments about this topic or the instruction we offer to students.

References

Brislin, T. (2004). Empowerment as a Universal Ethic in Global Journalism. *Journal of Mass Media Ethics* 19(2), 130–137.

Stoddard, E. W. & Cornwell, G. H. (2003). Peripheral Visions: Towards a Geoethics of Citizenship. *Liberal Education* 89(3), 44–51.

IFLA Publications

Edited by Sjoerd Koopman

The *International Federation of Library Associations and Institutions* (IFLA) is the leading international body representing the interests of library and information services and their users. It is the global voice of the information profession.

112-114
World Guide to Library, Archive and Information Science Associations
2nd edition. 2005. 510 pages. Hardbound
€ 168.00 (for IFLA members: € 131.00)
ISBN 3-598-21840-0

115
e-Learning for Management and Marketing in Libraries
e-Formation pour le marketing et le management des bibliothèques
Papers presented at the IFLA Satellite Meeting, Section Management & Marketing / Management & Marketing Section, Geneva, Switzerland, July 28 - 30, 2003
Edited by / Edité par Daisy McAdam
2005. 165 pages. Hardbound
€ 74.00 (for IFLA members: € 55.50)
ISBN 3-598-21843-5

116
Continuing Professional Development – Preparing for New Roles in Libraries: A Voyage of Discovery
Sixth World Conference on Continuing Professional Development and Workplace Learning for the Library and Information Professions
Edited by Paul Genoni and Graham Walton
2005. 307 pages. Hardbound
€ 78.00 (for IFLA members: € 58.00)
ISBN 3-598-21844-3

117

The Virtual Customer: A New Paradigm for Improving Customer Relations in Libraries and Information Services / O cliente virtual: um novo paradigma para melhorar o relacionamento entre clientes e serviços de informação e bibliotecas / Le usager virtuel: un nouveau paradigme pour améliorer le service à la clientèle dans les bibliothèques et services d'information / El cliente virtual: un nuevo paradigma para mejorar el relacionamento entre clientes y servicios de información y biblioteca

Satellite Meeting Sao Paulo, Brazil, August 18-20,2004

Edited by Sueli Mara Soares Pinto Ferreira and Réjean Savard

2005. XVIII, 385 pages. Hardbound

€ 128.00 (for IFLA members: € 96.00)

ISBN 3-598-21845-1

118

International Newspaper Librarianship for the 21st Century

Edited by Hartmut Walravens

2006. 298 pages. Hardbound

€ 78.00 (for IFLA members: € 58.00)

ISBN 3-598-21846-X

119

Networking for Digital Preservation. Current Practice in 15 National Libraries

Ingeborg Verheul

2006. 269 pages. Hardbound

€ 78.00 (for IFLA members: € 58.00)

ISBN 3-598-21847-8

120/121

Management, Marketing and Promotion of Library Services. Based on Statistics, Analyses and Evaluation

Edited by Trine Kolderup Flaten

2006. 462 pages. Hardbound

€ 128.00 (for IFLA members: € 96.00)

ISBN 3-598-21848-6

IFLA Series on Bibliographic Control

Edited by Sjoerd Koopman

IFLA Series on Bibliographic Control publications provide detailed information on bibliographic standards and norms, the cultivation and development of which has become indispensable to the exchange of national bibliographic information on an international level. The IFLA Series on Bibliographic Control publications also give a comprehensive and accurate overview of a wide range of national bibliographic services on offer.

Volume 25
Subject Retrieval in a Networked World
Proceedings of the IFLA Satellite Meeting held in Dublin, OH, 14–16 August 2001 and sponsored by the IFLA Classification and Indexing Section, the IFLA Information Technology Section and OCLC.
Ed. by I.C. McIlwaine 2003. IX, 193 pages. Hardbound
€ 78.00 / sFr 134.00
IFLA members € 58.00 / sFr 100.00
ISBN 3-598-11634-9

Volume 26
IFLA Cataloguing Principles: Steps towards an International Cataloguing Code
Report form the 1st Meeting of Experts on an international Cataloguing Code, Frankfurt, 2003
Ed. by Barbara B. Tillett, Renate Gömpel and Susanne Oehlschläger
2004. IV, 186 pages. Hardbound
€ 78.00 / sFr 134.00
IFLA members € 58.00 / sFr 100.00
ISBN 3-598-24275-1

Volume 27
IFLA Guidelines for Online Public Access Catalogue (OPAC) Displays
Final Report May 2005
2005. 61 pages. Hardbound
€ 34.00 / sFr 59.00
IFLA members € 26.80 / sFr 46.00
ISBN 3-598-24276-X

Volume 28
IFLA Cataloguing Principles: Steps towards an International Cataloguing Code, 2
Report form the 2nd Meeting of Experts on an international Cataloguing Code, Buenos Aires, Argentina, 2004
Ed. by Barbara B. Tillett and Ana Lupe Cristán
2005. 229 pages. Hardbound
€ 78.00 / sFr 134.00
IFLA members € 58.00 / sFr 100.00
ISBN 3-598-24277-8

Volume 29
IFLA Cataloguing Principles: Steps towards an International Cataloguing Code, 3
Report form the 3rd Meeting of Experts on an international Cataloguing Code, Cairo, Egypt, 2005
Ed. by Barbara B. Tillett, Khaled Mohamed Reyad and Ana Lupe Cristán
2006. 199 pages. Hardbound
€ 78.00 / sFr 134.00
IFLA members € 58.00 / sFr 100.00
ISBN 3-598-24278-6